MICHELLE OBAMA
THE REPORT TO THE FIRST LADY

2009

In honor of the First Ladies
who dutifully served their country,
we present this Report

MICHELLE OBAMA
THE REPORT TO THE FIRST LADY
2009

Project Director & Editor
ROBERT P. WATSON

The Report to the First Lady is a not-for-profit, non-partisan project presented to the First Lady and her staff every four years at the time of the Inauguration as a public service by professional historians, scholars, and public officials.

Nova Publishers
New York

NOTICE TO THE READER

The Publisher has taken reasonable care in the preparation of this book, but makes no expressed or implied warranty of any kind and assumes no responsibility for any errors or omissions. No liability is assumed for incidental or consequential damages in connection with or arising out of information contained in this book. The Publisher shall not be liable for any special, consequential, or exemplary damages resulting, in whole or in part, from the readers' use of, or reliance upon, this material.

Independent verification should be sought for any data, advice or recommendations contained in this book. In addition, no responsibility is assumed by the publisher for any injury and/or damage to persons or property arising from any methods, products, instructions, ideas or otherwise contained in this publication.

This publication is designed to provide accurate and authoritative information with regard to the subject matter covered herein. It is sold with the clear understanding that the Publisher is not engaged in rendering legal or any other professional services. If legal or any other expert assistance is required, the services of a competent person should be sought. FROM A DECLARATION OF PARTICIPANTS JOINTLY ADOPTED BY A COMMITTEE OF THE AMERICAN BAR ASSOCIATION AND A COMMITTEE OF PUBLISHERS.

LIBRARY OF CONGRESS CATALOGING-IN-PUBLICATION DATA

Available upon request

ISBN 978-1-60741-081-2

Published by Nova Science Publishers, Inc. ✦ *New York*

CONTENTS

Welcome ix
Rosalynn Carter

Congratulations xi
Frances Hughes Glendening

About the Report xv
Robert P. Watson

History and Development of the Office

Chapter 1   Martha Washington: The Lady Who First Created the Role 3
Patricia Brady

Chapter 2   Listening to Dolley 9
Catherine Allgor

Chapter 3   Living in the White House 17
Robert P. Watson

Chapter 4   "Party Politics": The Social Role of the First Lady
and its Political Influence 23
Edith P. Mayo

Chapter 5   Eleanor Roosevelt: The Yardstick 29
Susan Roth Breitzer

The Modern Office: Challenges and Issues

Chapter 6   The First Lady's Relations with the Mass Media 37
Betty H. Winfield

Chapter 7   Public Discourse and the American First Lady in the 20th Century 45
Myra G. Gutin

Chapter 8   Public Opinion and the First Ladies 51
Barbara C. Burrell

Chapter 9   Special Projects of First Ladies   **57**
                   Carl Sferrazza Anthony

Chapter 10   Life in the White House: Challenges, Burdens, Responsibilities   **63**
                   Tabitha Alissa Warters

Chapter 11   The First Lady as an International Diplomat   **69**
                   Molly Meijer Wertheimer

Chapter 12   Development of the Modern Office of the First Lady   **77**
                   Anthony J. Eksterowicz

Resources for the First Lady

Chapter 13   Advice to the Incoming First Lady on Her Records and
                   Establishing Files that Successfully Reflect Her New Role   **85**
                   Nancy Kegan Smith

Chapter 14   Presidential Wives, The White House, and Washington, D.C.:
                   Recommended Readings and References for the First Lady   **91**
                   Elizabeth Lorelei Thacker-Estrada

Chapter 15   National First Ladies' Library   **101**
                   Pat Krider

Advice to the First Lady

Chapter 16   My Advice to the Next First Lady   **107**
                   Eleanor Roosevelt

Chapter 17   Looking Back: Lessons for the First Lady –
                   and Her Husband – from History   **113**
                   Gil Troy

Chapter 18   20 Tips: Walking in the Footsteps of History   **117**
                   Robert P. Watson

Chapter 19   Women and Political Leadership   **123**
                   Lori Cox Han

Chapter 20   Legal Considerations for a New First Lady   **131**
                   Sindee Kerker

Biographies of Recent First Ladies

Chapter 21   Bess Truman   **139**
                   Raymond Frey

Chapter 22   Mamie Eisenhower   **145**
                   Robert E. Dewhirst

Chapter 23   Jacqueline Kennedy   149
                  Gil Troy

Chapter 24   Lady Bird Johnson   153
                  Claudia Wilson Anderson

Chapter 25   Pat Nixon   159
                  Mary Linehan

Chapter 26   Betty Ford   163
                  Jeffrey S. Ashley

Chapter 27   Rosalynn Carter   169
                  Virginia A. Chanley

Chapter 28   Nancy Reagan   175
                  Mary Linehan

Chapter 29   Barbara Bush   181
                  Jean Becker

Chapter 30   Hillary Rodham Clinton   187
                  Myra G. Gutin

Chapter 31   Laura Bush   193
                  Molly Meijer Wertheimer

Appendix   201

About the Contributors   203

LETTER FROM FIRST LADY ROSALYNN CARTER

Dear Michelle,

Congratulations!

Being First Lady of our great country is a wonderful opportunity. Having been active in political life already, I imagine you have your own ideas about how you would like to use your position to make a positive difference in the lives of others in our nation and abroad. I also know it is not easy juggling these responsibilities with your first priority – caring for your children.

My advice to you is to choose how you will spend your time, select a few key projects, stand by your convictions, and ignore the criticisms. From now on, for the rest of your life, you will have the ability, perhaps even the obligation, to be a force for good in the world. I am looking forward to seeing the efforts you undertake.

Jimmy and I extend best wishes to you for the next four years. Our prayers are with you and your family.

Sincerely,

Rosalynn Carter
First Lady of the United States, 1977-1981

CONGRATULATIONS

Congratulations and best wishes to you! Although it has been a long and arduous road, you have reached the White House! Permit me to add my voice to the millions of Americans who wish you and the President every success.

As America's First Lady, you have embarked on the opportunity of a lifetime. You will affect history in your incomparable way, in the choices you make, the initiatives you undertake, and the style you employ. Without question, the world is watching, and will continue to every step of the way, because contemporary First Ladies undergo intense public scrutiny. And, your contribution is both vital and complex because your journey to the White House has been uniquely historic.

First and foremost, I sincerely hope you have decided to enjoy this new job. Remember, to a certain extent, you can write your own job description; however, it is both interesting and instructive to review how your predecessors have perceived and defined this role. Like every worthwhile endeavor throughout life, this one brings with it important roles and responsibilities.

In so many ways, the status of women has advanced significantly since Martha Washington became the country's initial First Lady in 1789. She faced many challenges and complained of the role's imprisonment. Nevertheless, today the words of Eleanor Roosevelt, perhaps the first "modern" First Lady, echo a similar sentiment: "You must live up to the standards just as any other First Ladies have done and will do... the First Lady is a little like the prisoner of history in the White House." Despite significant progress, certain aspects of the First Lady's role and the challenges she faces have not changed in more than two hundred years.

Fortunately, serving as your husband's most trusted advisor and supporter in the past has prepared you well for this exciting new challenge. Because you will be bombarded with requests more than ever before in public life, I strongly recommend you enlist the help of capable staff to ensure your priorities remain in focus. As you know well by now, you cannot do it all. You still are only one person, but one person with a vast constituency. As Barbara Walters would say, often you will need to trust your gut. In sorting out your multiple priorities and deciding with whom you will work on issues of national and sometimes international importance, relying on your intuition can enhance decision-making.

At the same time, it is vital to your physical and mental health to maintain a reasonable balance when setting both your priorities and schedule. To help accomplish this, I suggest you schedule time regularly with your husband, children, and friends as you would any important event. Even as you set your agenda, create exciting new initiatives, plan public appearances, and manage state dinners and other White House events, it will be necessary to schedule personal and family time first.

As Maryland's two-term First Lady, I found expanding on the interests I began as a private citizen while volunteering time outside my professional career to be a logical and comfortable place from which to begin. Fortunately, I had a clear state of mind as I began this exciting new role. In fact, I viewed it as a great opportunity to provide leadership, as appropriate, in my own style. U.S. Senator Barbara Mikulski's words about leadership are compelling. She said, "Leadership is creating a state of mind in others... A leader first of all, has to have a clear state of mind, which is usually her own vision, which energizes her, motivates others, and then creates that state of mind in others."

For me, leadership as a First Lady meant advocating family issues centered around women and children, especially their health and well-being. It also meant establishing an arts initiative I could employ as a creative tool to broach some difficult social issues, like mental health, hospice, youth violence, and the numerous debilitating diseases many citizens face, including breast cancer and Alzheimer's disease.

You already have your priorities in place. Even if you have not had adequate time to articulate them, they are in your heart as much as your mind. Communicate them clearly to the world from the start. Enjoy the fact you can attract some of America's brightest minds, who are eager to help affect positive change for America's families and communities. Unlimited resources are at your disposal to help achieve your goals. At the same time, however, I urge you to allow some flexibility. Leave room on your agenda to expand a particular priority or to adjust your priorities as time passes, and as you meet your goals or new challenges pique your interest.

As former chair of the National Governors' Association Spouses' Leadership Committee, I encourage you to work with us as we undertake non-partisan projects to strengthen America's families and communities. And, on behalf of the National First Lady's Library (NFLL) Board of Directors, you should know we are working to ensure each First Lady takes her rightful place in history. To this end, I suggest you begin archiving your activities from the onset of the administration, turning your papers over to the NFLL periodically. Because I have been a lifelong women's history advocate, I have been working with the Maryland State Archivist and I am meeting with much success in this endeavor.

I invite you to visit the Library at your earliest convenience. Even before visiting the beautiful library facilities in Canton, Ohio, you can access our virtual library from your computer at www.firstladies.org. In fact, because of today's innovative information technology, the world will know you better than any of your predecessors. To this end, you may wish to be proactive in ensuring historians will characterize you accurately.

My parents were dedicated public servants, and they raised me to believe public service is one of life's highest callings. And so, while I congratulate you, I also commend you for undertaking this new role as First Lady with the same enthusiasm and dedication you have exhibited throughout the years. It will be daunting at times, but I believe your work also will be immensely gratifying.

Please be assured I would be delighted to help or encourage you in any way possible. I wish you much health and happiness in your new capacity and eagerly look forward to working with you.

Frances Hughes Glendening
Former First Lady of Maryland
Vice-President, National First Ladies Library
Former Chair, National Governors' Association Spouses' Leadership Committee

ABOUT THE REPORT

As is the case with the Presidency, the First Ladyship has been held by only a few individuals, with considerable variation among them in terms of their abilities and interests. Some presidential wives like Jane Pierce and Margaret Taylor were reluctant First Ladies, who went to the White House against their wishes and avoided as many public duties and appearances as possible; while others, such as Julia Tyler and Julia Grant, considered their White House years among the happiest and most rewarding of their lives. They happily involved themselves in numerous public affairs during their tenures and won rave reviews for their service.

There have been many different approaches to the office and, not surprisingly, considerable variation in the degree of success enjoyed by First Ladies. Overall, however, it is fair to say that, as a group, they have discharged their duties admirably and the nation has been well served by the presidential wives.

Every so often a presidential spouse has come along who has reshaped the very nature of the office and, in so doing, has become the yardstick by which subsequent First Ladies are measured and viewed. This has been the case with Dolley Madison, Eleanor Roosevelt, and others. It would appear then that the First Ladyship is, like the Presidency, a highly individualistic office, one shaped and molded by each occupant. It would seem that the office assumes the personality and character of each office holder. To an extent this is true. But it is also a position with a history, one rich in traditions and customs. All First Ladies, after all, have not only been compared to Dolley Madison and Eleanor Roosevelt, but have had their roles and responsibilities shaped to a degree by the legacies of Mrs. Madison and Mrs. Roosevelt. This also unites you with those that served before you.

All First Ladies have faced enormous pressures and challenges. This "comes with the job" and this you will also share with your predecessors. In the words of First Lady Pat Nixon: "Being the First Lady is the hardest unpaid job in the world." But, take solace in the fact that all First Ladies have been afforded unparalleled opportunities to serve their country and all have left their mark in one way or another.

In short, each First Lady has forged her role with consideration to the past while embracing her own interests and style. As you join those few so privileged to have served as First Lady, it is my hope that this *Report* might provide you with insights and ideas as you undertake what will assuredly be the most monumental challenge you will face in your public life. This *Report*, printed by Nova Publishers, brings together a group of scholars, public servants, and leading experts on the First Ladies with the purpose of presenting to you information on your predecessors, the history and development of the office you now hold, the resources available to you, and the modern roles and challenges you will address for the next few years.

On behalf of all the contributors, it is an honor to present to you this *Report* and may you find in these pages and in your self the necessary wisdom, charity, and inspiration to serve the President, people, and ideals of this nation. I encourage you to let the uniqueness of your marital relationship work to the benefit your husband's agenda, let your heart's passion inspire your deeds and projects, and let the experiences of your predecessors inform your service. To that latter end, as you develop your new role, I think that you will find history to be a good teacher.

Robert P. Watson, Ph.D.
Director & Editor, *Report to the First Lady*
Director, American Studies Program, Lynn University

HISTORY AND DEVELOPMENT OF THE OFFICE

Chapter 1

MARTHA WASHINGTON: THE LADY WHO FIRST CREATED THE ROLE

Patricia Brady

THE CHALLENGE OF PUBLIC LIFE

The savaging of presidential families by the press, fueled by the general public's obsessive interest in the lives of public figures, makes moving into the White House a frightening proposition for any President's wife and children. Think, for instance, of the cruel jokes and derogatory remarks about the looks of vulnerable young girls – Amy Carter and Chelsea Clinton – made by adult commentators and comedians, men who, one hopes, would be horrified if anyone were so cruel to their own daughters.

Unfortunately this incivility is nothing new. The impulse to observe the first family closely and criticize at will has been part of the American political landscape since George Washington first became President. It is the instant means of communication to millions through the broadcast media and the Internet that are new, not the content. There has never been a truly private life for the presidential family: for them, the social is the political.

Some First Ladies have been committed political partners; others have been reluctant to share the limelight. All of them, willing or not, have been the objects of extravagant attention and world-wide celebrity. As the first in that position, however, Martha Washington had no idea of what to expect. She felt that her husband had sacrificed enough in the long years of leading the Revolutionary army.

A NEW NATION AWAITS

Martha Washington's dream was permanent retirement at Mount Vernon where she and her husband would "grow old in solitude and tranquility together." She wrote to a nephew, "I think it was much too late for him to go in to public life again, but it was not to be avoided, our family will be deranged as I must soon follow him." Never in the long happy years of their marriage were they separated for more than a few months at a time, even during the war.

When the news of his election arrived in 1789, Washington set off immediately for New York City, the nation's interim capital. Mrs. Washington and two grandchildren from her first marriage, whom the Washingtons were bringing up as their own, would follow behind with household belongings. Washington had the burden of setting precedent in every action he took as President, putting meat on the bones of the office created by the Constitution.

But he soon faced a serious social dilemma. Many Americans believed that, as citizens of the republic, they had an inalienable right to communicate in person with their President at will and without appointment. Always hospitable, Washington found this propensity for intruding on him on the smallest excuse (or indeed, none at all) made it almost impossible for him to carry out the work he had been elected to do. When he began to set bounds on access to his office, critics charged that he was aping royalty.

Martha Washington's journey to join her husband in their rented house in New York may be seen as the honeymoon of her sojourn as First Lady. Despite a late start caused by tears and farewells, overflowing trunks and boxes, and coach-sick children, she especially remarked on the acclaim that she received ("the great parade that was made for us all the way we come"), reflecting as it did the nation's respect for her husband. The family was met at Elizabethtown Point, New Jersey, by the President in a fine new barge, originally commissioned for his reception; twenty-six men rowed the party the fifteen miles to the tip of Manhattan Island.

FORGING CUSTOM, FORGING AN OFFICE

Mrs. Washington very soon, however, discovered the tedium of constant public attention. Contrary to her usual habit at home, her hair had to be set and dressed every day, and she attended much more to her clothes, putting on white muslin habits for the summer. As she reported to her niece: "you would I fear think me a good deal in the fashion if you could but see me," clearly conveying her dissatisfaction with the changes in her life.

The boundaries of social life to be observed by the President's lady were just being defined, and often the definition arrived at by her husband was not to her liking. Washington had decided that they would receive callers officially at a weekly evening drawing room. On only the second day after her arrival in New York, she was the hostess at the first of these parties, which continued throughout Washington's Presidency. Seated, she received her guests, who were greeted by the President and then were free to circulate among the other visitors. In addition, they also hosted weekly dinner parties for government officials, members of Congress, and foreign dignitaries, invited in rotation. Limiting their social life to official entertainments, Washington had announced that he and his wife would not accept invitations to private gatherings nor return calls.

Of all the roles expected of the First Lady, that of the nation's hostess has been one of the most challenging for Presidents' wives throughout American history, as they have sought to balance their private preferences and friendships with their duties to the citizenry. As the first to fill the position, however, Martha Washington had not foreseen the formality of the rules that would govern the role, nor had she anticipated that her own private socializing would be so curtailed.

Like many subsequent First Ladies, Mrs. Washington was considerably disgruntled to find herself so fettered by political considerations. She repined and stayed at home, pouting: "I never go to the public place (indeed I think I am more like a state prisoner than anything else, there is certain bounds set for me which I must not depart from) and as I can not doe as I like I am obstinate and stay at home a great deal."

Such a very sociable woman might have settled happily into the routine of presidential entertainments, but the easy habits of Virginia planters in which family and friends dropped in to visit for days, weeks, or even months would not do in the capital. Most of the presidential guests were strangers, men whose wives were still back home, chosen in a fairly rigid rota governed by political considerations, not social desirability or friendship.

And there was, of course, the damned-if-you-do, damned-if-you-don't factor, the hyper-critical attention lavished on every aspect of presidential entertainment (one had to be careful that it was not too lavish, too cheap, too formal, too free). One political opponent recorded details of every entertainment in his diary, criticizing them as "all in the taste of high life" and declined to join Mrs. Washington and the ladies upstairs for after-dinner coffee. He took spiteful note of a dinner where, he even reported, the "large, fine-looking trifle" was spoiled by rancid cream. Nonetheless, he wrote nastily, "Mrs. Washington ate a whole heap of it."

During the first year of the Presidency almost all the First Lady's regular visitors were the wives of government officials. Fortunately, Lucy Knox, the wife of the secretary of war, was an old friend from Revolutionary War days. An unexpected new friend, given the differences in their personal styles, was the wife of the Vice President, the outspoken Abigail Adams, who wrote soon after meeting her that "Mrs. Washington is one of those unassuming characters which create Love & Esteem. A most becoming pleasantness sits upon her countenance & an unaffected deportment which renders her the object of veneration and Respect."

Government ladies and grandchildren were all very well, but Martha Washington was bored and lonely without the accustomed companionship of her women friends. As the eldest of a large family, she had been surrounded all her adult life by younger sisters, numerous nieces from both sides of the family, her daughter-in-law, and the wives of junior military officers and aides. At the presidential mansion, she missed this circle of feminine support, particularly as critics multiplied.

But no one who attended the presidential entertainments would have known of her dissatisfaction. Although Washington was sometimes faulted for stiff ceremoniousness, Martha Washington was always praised for charm and graciousness. Even her husband's political opponents succumbed to the effortless kindness with which she made all her guests feel at ease. After the nation's capital was moved to Philadelphia in 1790, the Washingtons' group of purely social acquaintances grew as the President relaxed some of his earlier strictures against private invitations. For the most part, these friends were well-educated, sophisticated, and wealthy, but Mrs. Washington with her simple dignity, self-confidence, and graceful manners never found herself at a loss socially.

Only about her writing ability did the sketchily educated First Lady suffer from any sense of diffidence. When it was necessary to write to the wives of foreign officials or accomplished correspondents or to respond to tendered gifts, her letters were drafted by Washington or his secretary. She then copied these drafts and signed them as her own. But the formal correspondence with its attention to grammar and literary turns of phrase lacks the charm of her own unselfconscious letters to her intimates (which were sensible, homely, and frequently lightened with self-deprecating humor).

LADY WASHINGTON

After two weary terms in office with their inevitable disappointments and failures, the President and his wife longed for retirement to Mount Vernon. George Washington had set the example for a government that could survive a change of executive, avoiding the cycles of revolution and dictatorship that would plague other, later republics elsewhere. Martha Washington, too, had set a precedent for future First Ladies, maintaining some degree of familial and personal privacy while welcoming the public and politicians of all stripes at official entertainments. The Washingtons both belonged to and represented the nation.

Like many later First Ladies, Mrs. Washington was exhausted by the endless calls on her time and angered by the attacks on her husband. She looked forward to leaving the presidential mansion as though she were departing for the promised land. Although she wished for many more years of peaceful retirement, the short final two and a half years that she and George Washington enjoyed together were filled with solid contentment.

As their successors have also found, their lives were forever changed by having led the nation. Public attention may diminish, but it never goes away completely. All Presidents and First Ladies forever continue to belong to the nation in some sense.

The habit of visiting Mount Vernon as a national shrine did not cease with Washington's death in 1799. Visitors continued to flock there to pay their respects to his widow, who received them graciously even though she was visibly aged by sorrow.

Until her death in 1802, Martha Washington remained the President's lady in the hearts of the American nation. She took seriously her role as representative of her husband and his achievements. In the dark days right after Washington's death, there was a flood of letters of condolence and requests for mementos. The tenor of many of the letters of condolence was not just sympathy for personal loss, but of the loss to the country.

After 1775, George Washington had never again belonged solely to his family. Moreover, although he had relinquished the Presidency, no future holder of that office could achieve the almost mythical status of being the founding and first President, nor could any future First Lady recreate Martha Washington's role.

Martha Washington, every bit as complex and interesting a woman as Abigail Adams, had already lived a very full life before she met George Washington. As a tiny brunette of seventeen with seductive almond eyes, she had attracted and married one of the richest men in Virginia, Daniel Custis, twenty years her senior, despite the objections of an eccentric father who had thwarted all the son's previous attempts to marry. During the next decade, she suffered the grievous losses of a younger brother and sister, her father, two children under the age of four, and her husband. Left with a large fortune, she had a wide choice of second husbands, but had the good judgment to choose a man who shared her views on domestic happiness. And for more than forty years, they lived intimately and harmoniously together.

One of the two surviving letters by Washington in 1775 to his "dearest" avows "I retain an unalterable affection for you, which neither time or distance can change." How much light would have been shed on their loving relationship by the many missing letters. George

Washington was the key to Martha's joy in life, but she was just as essential to his happiness, and the destruction of their letters has long obscured that simple fact.

LESSONS FROM THE FIRST PRESIDENTIAL SPOUSE

What possible lessons can a twenty-first-century First Lady learn from the first of her predecessors, an eighteenth-century woman? There are many: As much as possible, define a zone of family privacy. Maintain your own judgment of what is best for your children – socially, educationally, and morally – regardless of the inevitable critical comments. Realize that you and your future will be changed by this experience. You are now part of the nation's history. Do not burn those private papers. You certainly should not be expected to share every aspect of your family's intimate life with the public as it unfolds, but please feel some responsibility to the future. Restrict present-day access, but make your papers available to future scholars. In other words, please do not make Martha Washington's mistake. At some point, when political rivalries have dulled, let history know the real, at times imperfect, interesting *you* that may be partially hidden at present. Eventually let us know and sympathize with you – a remarkable woman who has struggled with the huge responsibilities of being First Lady while maintaining her family and personal life.

Chapter 2

LISTENING TO DOLLEY

Catherine Allgor

HEEDING THE CALL OF HISTORY

As a historian and teacher, I could not get out of bed in the morning if I did not believe that studying the past helps us make sense of the present and future. The lessons of history, however, are subtle ones, rarely directly applicable to a particular situation. It would be hard to imagine, for instance, that a present or future President, faced with whether or not to colonize Mars, would find much guidance in the Monroe Doctrine. In studying the office of First Lady as a historical phenomenon, however, the actions and experiences from the past can speak almost directly to us.

In many ways, the unelected office of First Lady is a throwback position, with significant elements frozen in time. But make no mistake – that the parameters and configurations of "First Lady" were laid long ago does not render it irrelevant or powerless. On the contrary, this retrograde quality holds its own peculiar power and potential for authority. Few Americans understand the models on which the position was based, but by returning to the founding moments, we can recover the obscure elements that I believe are essential to comprehending the sources of the First Lady's power. The best place to start may be with the woman who almost single-handedly created the position of the "President's Lady," setting a model that would go unchallenged until the twentieth century: Dolley Payne Todd Madison.

INTRODUCING MRS. MADISON

Dolley Madison was *famous*. During and immediately after the War of 1812, she was probably the most well-known person in the United States, and intriguing footprints of her fame come to us from her contemporaries. Upon the widowed Dolley's return to Washington in 1837, Congress granted her a seat on the floor of the House, and famed orator Daniel Webster declared Dolley to be "[t]he only permanent power in Washington, all others are transient." Dolley's work endowed the unofficial position of President's wife with its own title; when Congress adjourned for her funeral in 1848, then-President Zachary Taylor pronounced: "She will never be forgotten because she was truly our First Lady for a half-century."

Dolley's fame continued through the nineteenth and early twentieth centuries. Dolley was associated with many famous firsts: She participated in the first inaugural ball, she instituted state dinners, and she began the custom of rolling Easter eggs on the White House lawn. But all this evidence of her fame puzzles modern historians, who cannot comprehend how she attained such lasting prominence. After all, Dolley Madison achieved renown as *hostess*, an occupation that seems to belong to private life, to the frivolous, to the female, and thus to the powerless. Indeed, her major accomplishments could be reduced to a list of traditionally female endeavors: She decorated the White House, she gave great parties where she wore fabulous clothes, she had a "good heart." The answer lies in a paradox. Dolley Payne Todd Madison *was* powerful *and* she did indeed gain her power by being a hostess and a wife; this seeming contradiction may be resolved with a reevaluation of the meaning of that womanly role in the political culture of the early republic.

WELCOME TO WASHINGTON CITY

In the early 1800s the ruling ideology of the official men and their new government was what their leader Thomas Jefferson called "pure republicanism," a philosophy which had fueled the American Revolution, informed the new Constitution, and would also serve as the blueprint for the capital and federal government. Republicanism was a theory with long roots; at its heart was a fear of the absolute power that an abusive monarch could wield. In fact, republicanism decried everything associated with court politics – titles and kings, hereditary aristocracies, the workings of personal interests, displays of luxury, and the involvement of family members and other "unofficial characters." In short, anything that smacked of exercising political power.

As it turned out, this anti-power, anti-political political theory was not a good basis for a government. The new United States *needed* politics and the centralizing power that republicanism forbade. Royal courts might be as corrupt as republican theory would have us believe, but they do provide order and structure, supplying the machinery of politics. Court settings are also useful in their visible assertion of power and status, providing emerging nations with a patina of legitimacy in the eyes of the world, and, in the best cases, imparting a feeling to the people that they are being properly ruled.

And who needed stability and reassurance more than an upstart people who found themselves with a republican experiment that nobody was sure would last? The new Americans had been western European colonists not too long ago, and the symbols of aristocracy remained the only vocabulary of power and legitimacy they knew. So from the outset, the new government unfolded within a culture that simultaneously rejected monarchical forms, embracing simplicity and republican virtue, all the while longing for the status and stability provided by aristocratic markers.

"THE PRESIDENT'S HOUSE IS A PERFECT PALACE"

In 1809, when James and Dolley Payne Todd Madison took up residence in the President's House, Dolley's list of assignments included legitimizing her husband's administration and the national capital (for both Americans and outsiders), helping James deal with a fractious Congress and a tense relationship with France and Great Britain, and imparting to the citizenry a sense of "Americanness." The couple truly had to "go to housekeeping" in a global way, firming the foundations of the nation's structure while presenting a good face to the neighbors. Being members of the gentry class, they reacted the way they knew how in order to establish their presence on the national landscape – they built a house.

Of course they already had a physical house – the President's House, or President's Palace, as it was sometimes called – but whether from indifference or republican rigor, it had languished under Jefferson. The interior and exterior exuded shabbiness. Its location away from the rest of the official buildings was probably supposed to suggest lofty distance – in 1809, it just suggested isolation. Fearing any appearance of courtliness, Jefferson had instituted a very restricted social schedule and few of the official or unofficial elite of Washington City visited.

Dolley changed all that, and she began with the President's House. We might consider it natural that James Madison turned this project over to Dolley, but in the eighteenth and early nineteenth centuries, house-building among the elite was more than an expression of a private aesthetic, more than a desire for privacy and comfort. In a world that did not yet radically distinguish public from private, elite men and women did the business of the day in their houses, often during social events such as dinners, parties, and afternoon calls. Furthermore, these houses were symbolic, dominating the landscape of an area. Consequently, gentry men (such as George Washington at Mount Vernon) involved themselves in choosing paint colors and silverware to a degree puzzling to us in the twenty-first century, who think of these activities as "girl stuff." But for political families for whom the family business was politics, the house was a manifestation of superior status, a concrete signifier of their right to rule.

So when James entrusted Dolley with the re-creation of the executive mansion, he assigned her a public duty, one crucial to establishing his authority. She did not let him down. Dolley and architect Benjamin Latrobe embarked on a project that was less a redecorating than a *restructuring* of the executive mansion. Their aim was not to construct a habitable home or a haven from public life for the President. Rather, in designing a state dining room, a parlor, and a grand receiving room, they produced a national symbol, a focus for the local Washington communities and the people of the United States, and a space for the day-to-day business of politics.

The choices of decor and function for these rooms reflected the tension in American culture between aristocratic-monarchical impulses and republican-democratic energies. Rather than trying to subdue this tension, Dolley appropriated all the best parts. She and Latrobe created a gorgeous set of rooms, filled with rich fabrics, dazzling mirrors, and silver pieces, as well as nationalistic art and American manufacturers. They included furniture and decorations with a Greek theme, as befitting a government that involved its citizenry.

Dolley's genius lay not in her "taste" but in her ability to combine Republican simplicity with Federalist high style. She invented a public space for the executive that reassured both

Federalists and Republicans alike, while impressing European visitors and officials with the sophistication of the infant nation. In a culture that understood the powerful symbolism of architecture, the new "White House," as it was increasingly called, became a focus for visitors of all nationalities and all classes, the most powerful house in the power center. This period marks the beginning of the American people's identification with "their" house, an identification that would prove critical in 1814, when the British burnt the White House. Galvanized by the atrocity of the act, the American people would rally around their government and their President.

But these sumptuous rooms were not just a symbol of nationality, the capital's stability, and Madison's right to rule. They were a stage setting for Dolley's primary mission – to strengthen a constitutionally-weak Presidency by establishing her White House as a practical place for politics. She adapted a form of the courtly levee, which she and James dubbed with the more democratic appellation "drawing room." There Dolley also blended the pull of aristocracy with the push of what would become known as "democracy," creating what Dolley Madison scholar Holly Cowan Schulman calls "ceremonies suitable for a new republic." Where Martha Custis Washington and Abigail Smith Adams created entertainments that linked formal ceremony and exclusive invitations with simple settings and dress, Dolley's solution to the "aristocratic/republican" paradox combined sumptuous settings and regal sartorial choices with an inclusiveness that was downright democratic.

"Mrs. Madison's Wednesday nights" began on March 30, 1809, and lasted through both administrations. Guests moved freely about the three receiving rooms, much like a modern cocktail party, with groups gathering and regrouping throughout the evening. At some points before and during the War of 1812, the drawing rooms provided the only place where political enemies met and talked civilly. Dolley accomplished and extended many of her goals and projects with these soiree, for they brought Republicans and Federalists, cabinet secretaries and congressional members together, and they integrated official and local elites. Drawing rooms also furnished an event for visitors, distinguished and ordinary, that allowed them to feel a part of the national scene. Above all, Dolley's drawing rooms devised a new kind of political space, one that afforded access to men in power and, like European court events, allowed for the participation of women and other political family members.

This power of possibility did very nicely for a political environment of government officials trying to build a working structure, and everyone politicked at the drawing rooms. Access is the key to politics, and at no time in the history of the executive, before or since, was the President so accessible. Members of all branches of the government also had access to each other, and sources reveal much politicking between and among the diplomatic corps and the cabinet and congressional families at the drawing rooms.

"TIS THE WOMAN ALTOGETHER I WOULD HAVE YOU SEE"

Dolley herself did her share of "meat and potatoes" politicking, including practicing patronage, at which she was particularly adept; the staffing of the early federal government owes much to her efforts. But her work also included a category of meta-politicking, centered around her role as the charismatic figure for her husband's administration. She used her charisma in two ways: First, to personify legitimacy and power to the new nation, especially during the War of 1812; and second, to help her husband deal with what many historians call the worst Congress ever dealt a President.

The secret of Dolley's success as a charismatic figure lay in her creation of what I call "The Republican Queen," a fittingly paradoxical title. Dolley created her reassuring persona by combining regal themes in clothing and jewelry and the bearing of a leader with a caring, accessible personality. While the republican political culture would not allow men to exhibit royal prerogatives, Dolley trailed around her drawing rooms in a pink ermine gowns, sporting suspiciously crown-like headgear, exhibiting manners that, as one diplomat put it, "with equal dignity, blended equal sweetness." And the people openly and lovingly referred to her as "Queen Dolley."

Contemporaries and historians have long lauded Dolley for what they called her "good heart," describing her kindness and charm as personal, womanly qualities. But these categorizations obscure Dolley's objective, which was to bind people to her and to her husband, forging the alliances that would solidify her husband's administration. This was the era of terrible divisions within Congress over the declaration, and the subsequent handling of the War of 1812.

Furthermore, there was no constitutional way for the President to control an unruly legislature, no avenues of control and structure in the government, no political parties. The President's best strategy lay in the use of "statecraft," of which socializing forms an important component, and so at her weekly drawing rooms, Dolley focused her political energies on winning over members of Congress.

Dolley has long been famous as a hostess, a woman who rose above politics to include everyone under her roof. As Representative from Pennsylvania, Jonathan Roberts, commented approvingly, "by her deportment in her own house, you cannot discover who is her husband's friends or foes." This was an era where politicians accused each other of heinous acts and even murdered one another over those words. Yet week after week, Dolley Madison, with a smile and a gracious sally, welcomed men into her home who had publicly pilloried her husband and who had accused her and her beloved younger sister of sleeping with men for votes.

Though her personality may have provided a genuine-looking mask, Dolley disguised her emotions, providing enemies with access to herself, her husband, and other legislators, moving easily in a bipartisan milieu of cooperation – because she was master politician. Many "Dolley stories" show that she foreshadowed a modern attitude toward politics, one that encompassed a two-party system. In an age characterized by "passion," by heated all-or-nothing rhetoric, Dolley's assumption that compromise would be the salvation of the system marks her as one of the most sophisticated politicians of her time. Power sharing and compromise – the requisites for an effective democratic political culture – seemed inconceivable to the men in the power structures, but not to Dolley, who made connections every week at her drawing rooms.

The ideology of republicanism forbade the open assertion of authority and legitimacy, as well as the institution- and coalition-building which the embryonic federal government needed to grow and thrive. Dolley Madison, the "Republican Queen," and other political women translated the abstractions and ideals of republicanism into practical politics, using the techniques they knewBsocial events, benevolence, and networks of kith and kin. Their efforts helped to secure the government, the capital, and the nation. Oddly enough, their willingness to take on the unrepublican tasks of politicking allowed their husbands to retain at least a surface commitment to the revolutionary legacy. But when the democratic surge forced U.S. politics to change in the 1820s and 1830s, the rudimentary machine that Washington political families had built would ease that transition at the federal level.

THE UNOFFICIAL SPHERE

Even in this brief discussion, the lessons Dolley leaves us are obvious – a First Lady can accomplish much as a political actor, as well as providing legitimacy and an image of stability. But *how* she did so require analysis. Dolley and women like her were not feminists; they were the essentially conservative wives, mothers, and daughters of political families, and they saw their work as furthering their families' interest. They succeeded precisely because they were covered by the veil of gender prescriptions. Let me say here that I *am* a feminist, and a committed one at that. Though I am fascinated by the unofficial power that has long been the province of women, I am glad that I live in an era in which women regularly have access to open achievement. I do not advise my women students to aspire to be the wives of powerful businessmen and community leaders; I encourage and train them to run the corporations or to take the bench themselves.

But, as you know better than I do, politics – especially high politics – is different. Modern Americans are as horrified with First Lady activities that smack of the "official" as were the republicans of yore with monarchial pretensions. Female behaviors and aspirations that Americans tolerate and even laud in everyday life, they do not want associated with their First Lady. Without realizing it, the American public asks their First Ladies to step back in time, to occupy a place that is a relic in our modern culture – the "Lady," who rules over the private sphere. But what ordinary people call "private space," we can call "unofficial space," a place generally agreed to be outside the "legitimate" public forum. In the realm of politics, the unofficial sphere is as crucial as the official sphere. One way in which people discuss (however grudgingly and fearfully) the influence of women is to use the metaphor "behind the scenes." But this metaphor does not reflect reality, and I propose we abandon it. Every good political player knows that when it comes to politics, everywhere and anywhere can be centerstage – a board room, a dining table, an airplane, a Rose Garden. What differs is the potentially and tasks offered by different settings.

Part of our refusal to take seriously the role of the "unofficial" space, peopled by "unofficial" actors, lies in sexism. Whether because a patriarchal society considers that women do trivial things or that things become trivial when women do them, women's presence signals unimportance. Another explanation exists, however. Exposed to the same objective study and criteria as official space, the unofficial sphere would cease to function in its useful way.

This place allows more room to maneuver than does "official" space, permitting the flexibility necessary for the successful transactions of business. At a Dolley Madison drawing room, male politicians and their female family members used the atmosphere of sociability to propose, to probe, to negotiate, and to compromise. During a mere "social occasion," one may propose matters that would seem too chancy if made in an office. Food, drink, music, conversation, and dramatic setting comprise the components of the freedom necessary to risk.

The myriad of distractions of the event can be used by both parties to deflect or withdraw if the situation warrants it. The power of the unofficial lies in its unconsidered nature.

I feel a bit a abashed telling you about what it means to be a woman of a political family. No doubt you have recognized much of what you have always done in what I have discussed. But nothing is so practical as a good theory, so I hope that through this framework of understanding, you can conceptualize your work in a way that will further it. In deciding what kind of First Lady you will be, you may find yourself echoing your mother: "Act like a lady," but you should know, too, the potential and possibility that lies in that seemingly restrictive injunction. Welcome to the unofficial sphere. If you listen, there you will hear the voice of Dolley Madison and her sisters welcoming you to their world.

Chapter 3

LIVING IN THE WHITE HOUSE

Robert P. Watson

"But nobody, *nobody*, can prepare you for
what it's like being in the White House."
Nancy Reagan

You now reside in the very building where Thomas Jefferson planned the "Louisiana Purchase," Abraham Lincoln wrestled with his momentous responsibility during the Civil War, and Franklin D. Roosevelt received updates from the battlefields of World War II. As spouse of the President, you inherit the home where Abigail Adams advised her husband on political matters, Dolley Madison hosted her famous socials, and Lucy Hayes decided for personal reasons to limit the serving of alcohol; and it was on the second floor of what is now your living quarters where Eleanor Roosevelt had her historic meeting with the new President, Harry Truman. After word of FDR's death, Truman called on Mrs. Roosevelt to offer her his condolences, asking "Is there anything I can do for you?" In a prelude to briefing the new Commander-in-Chief on the status of the War and Presidency, Mrs. Roosevelt responded, "Is there anything *we* can do for *you*? For *you* are the one in trouble now."

Welcome to the White House, your new home. It is a home with a history like no other. Indeed, it is less accurate to suggest that this is your home, than to state that you now belong to the White House. Former First Lady, Lady Bird Johnson, admitted that, on entering the White House, she "tiptoed" through the building, filled with a sense of history. This is a home with a history, a home that comes with great responsibilities and enormous challenges; but it is also a home that promises an unparalleled opportunity to serve your country. But you should also know that it was in the White House where many of your predecessors, including Julia Tyler, Sarah Polk, Julia Grant, and others, spent the happiest days of their lives.

THE STORY OF THE WHITE HOUSE

Writing to the daughter who shared her name, Abigail Adams described her new home in unflattering terms: "The house is made habitable, but there is not a single apartment furnished." The first presidential spouse to reside in the "President's House," as it was then known, Abigail minded the cold and dampness during her short four months in residence. She found a building still incomplete and designed with little thought for livability – so much so that she resorted to hanging her wash in the East Room. In a letter to her sister, Mary Cranch, she complained, "Not one room or chamber is finished of the whole. It is habitable by fires in every room, thirteen of which we are obliged to keep daily, or sleep in wet & damp places."

The White House was not the building it is today. Frances Cleveland recalled the upstairs of the White House having "the smell of an old house by the sea, a musty scent..." Abigail Adams also endured a lack of running water. Servants carried water from hundreds of yards away until President Thomas Jefferson built a cistern system of wooden pipes. Later, in 1833, President Andrew Jackson had iron pipes installed to carry spring water to the White House; President Martin Van Buren built a reservoir in the basement.

Modernizations continued throughout the nineteenth century, with mixed success. In 1848 the Polks installed gas lamps to replace the old oil lamps. But shortly afterward during a social event, the new lamps malfunctioned, leaving the guests in the dark. Fortunately a chandelier of wax candles in the East Room had not yet been replaced and saved the occasion. Abigail Fillmore purchased a new kitchen stove, which was put into use next to the old open fireplace. First Lady Caroline Harrison introduced electric lighting to the White House, even though her staff was too nervous about the new technology to use it.

So too has the 18-acre estate surrounding the White House undergone change. Thomas Jefferson was the first to erect a fence on the property, which he later replaced with a stone wall. With the help of architect Benjamin Latrobe, Jefferson landscaped the estate's lawns. A gardening enthusiast, John Quincy Adams planted gardens and expanded nurseries on the property. Later, Harriet Lane, niece of and hostess for bachelor James Buchanan, had a greenhouse full of flowers built to provide fresh flowers for occasions throughout the year. Some of the modernizations and changes still exist. One of those is the magnolia tree Andrew Jackson planted in honor of his recently deceased wife, Rachel, which still stands near the South Portico. Jackson also had new stables built for his favorite horses.

The White House has been and remains the centerpiece of American democracy. Even its founding embodied the concept of popular governance when proposals for the design of the mansion were submitted in an open contest won by Irish architect James Hoban. George Washington selected the site in the city that bears his name for the location of "The President's House," the name he preferred for the building. The site commanded a view of the Potomac River and rested on a small hill carved out of wilderness and swampland.

The White House has survived threats to the system of government it has served and threats to the building itself. Near the end of the War of 1812, British troops laid seize to the federal city and burnt the building on August 24, 1814. Only the courage and quick thinking of Dolley Madison saved some of the priceless pieces from the Mansion, as the First Lady, almost single-handedly, gathered a wagon full of objects as the British marched into the city. Perhaps the most famous item in the White House – the Gilbert Stuart portrait of George Washington – owes its existence to Mrs. Madison's heroics. Only a timely thundershower saved the building. Later, during the Civil War, President Abraham Lincoln had Company K of the 150th Regiment of the Pennsylvania Volunteers stand guard on the grounds of the White House. The "Bucktail Brigade," as they were known, was pledged to protecting both the President and the President's House.

THE FIRST LADY'S HOUSE

Today the National Park Service oversees the Executive Mansion and its grounds. However, the First Lady remains as the White House's manager, preservationist, and homemaker-in-chief. Mamie Eisenhower, for instance, ran the White House like her own house, personally checking the kitchen's food stocks and worrying about its cleaning. In her words, the White House "takes quite a bit of housekeeping."

Until the latter part of the twentieth century, the annual salary for the President was $25,000. However, much as if the White House was their own residence, the first family had to pay for their household help, political staff, and the costs of entertaining as well as the maintenance of the Mansion. This was in addition to all family expenses. Congress did appropriate funds for furnishing the building, but these funds were minimal and were subject to the political whims of the members of Congress. In fact, both Thomas Jefferson and James Monroe were so short of finances after two terms in office that they resorted to selling land to pay their debts. The expense of providing wine and champagne for thirsty guests was particularly burdensome for early Presidents.

It was not until the Tafts lived in the White House that Congress finally covered the wages of the domestic staff and servants. And the Hardings were the first White House residents to have funds from Congress to cover the costs of entertaining. Today the first family is expected to pay for their personal expenses (food, phone bill, dry cleaning, etc.) and the costs of private affairs such as birthdays and parties for family and friends.

To assist her in running the White House the First Lady has an extensive staff with expertise in all facets of social hosting and protocol, including chefs, stewards, ushers, and even painters. All White House furnishings and wares, such as tables, silverware, glasses, drapery, and other items necessary for official functions are provided for the first family. Yet, by custom it is the First Lady who oversees the selection of furnishings, menus, entertainment, and any redecoration in the private living quarters upstairs. While she also manages the public rooms and events of the Mansion, any proposed changes to the official rooms must be approved by the Committee for the Preservation of the White House. Foreseeing the need to preserve the White House as a living museum, Jacqueline Kennedy began a process which later resulted in the establishment of this Committee in 1964.

The most visible of the First Lady's White House duties is serving as hostess. In this capacity First Ladies have hosted kings, queens, and heads of state. Presidential spouses preside over meals – from state dinners to summer gatherings on the rooftop terrace (first started by the Tafts) – and other forms of entertainment such as artistic performances. Many First Ladies have featured American artists and performances and Americana in their cultural entertaining. In 1970 the Nixons even celebrated George Washington's birthday by having a Broadway musical about the signing of the Declaration of Independence performed in the White House.

Overseeing renovations of the White House is another prominent "duty" of First Ladies. The first overhaul occurred after the close of the War of 1812 when the burned-out Mansion had to be renovated. This included having the exterior painted a brilliant white. But not all renovations were so dramatic and most were the work of First Ladies. One of the common contributions of First Ladies has been restoring the historical integrity of the Mansion. The most famous instance of this was Mrs. Kennedy's historic restoration, which featured the collection of original pieces and historic period furniture, all of which was highlighted in her famous televised tour of the White House. Such efforts have been especially important because so much of the building's past has been lost. For instance, after Abraham Lincoln's assassination, opportunistic collectors carried off many White House pieces. After President James Garfield's assassination, Chester Arthur was so shocked at the shoddy condition of the White House that he sold most of the building's interior items loaded in many full wagons at a public auction, and then completely and lavishly redecorated the Mansion to his own tastes.

The need to renovate the White House also arose from the need for additional space. Originally the living quarters and official offices shared space, leaving no privacy for the first family. Visiting dignitaries and guests came into the building at all times and in all areas of the White House. To remedy this, First Lady Caroline Harrison had several different plans for renovation drawn up, including one to reorganize the living space and provide more space for entertaining and another that proposed adding wings for offices and guest quarters to the existing structure. But she also pushed to construct a completely new Mansion. The First Lady ended up securing funds from Congress only for cleaning and repairs, but Mrs. Harrison's vision would eventually lead to the new expansion of the East and West Wings.

Some redecorating has been personal. Examples include the Hoovers, who brought furnishings from their travels around the world into the White House. The Trumans brought pianos with them and Mamie Eisenhower installed drapes and decorations in her favorite color, pink. The most extensive work on the White House occurred from 1948-1952, when the interior and foundation were replaced after the President noticed the chandeliers swaying for no reason. The building was in jeopardy of collapsing or, as was said at the time, the "White House was standing up purely from habit." Harry and Bess Truman moved out of the building to nearby Blair House. Many items have become a permanent part of the White House collection, such as the President's desk; the oak desk was presented to President Rutherford Hayes by Queen Victoria and made from the wreck of *H.M.S. Resolution*, after it was recovered from being abandoned in the Arctic.

Most personal redecorating occurs in the private living quarters. It is also in these quarters that the first family attempts to attain some degree of a normal, family life in the public Mansion. Many have retreated to the privacy of these quarters to enjoy music or quiet time reading. Abigail Fillmore, Jane Pierce, and other First Ladies spent a lot of time here, away from the public eye. Others have had relatives living with them at the White House. A widower, Andrew Jackson enjoyed the company of nieces and nephews, Bess Truman's mother lived at the White House, and Mary Lincoln dealt with the stress of the Civil War by having family members come for extended visits. In an effort to personalize the White House, Eleanor Roosevelt had swings and slides put on the lawn for all the visiting grandchildren and Jackie Kennedy established a kindergarten in the building.

Other attempts at recreating a sense of family life include the croquet court built by Rutherford and Lucy Hayes, horseshoe pits installed by Harry Truman and George Bush, and a swimming pool helped Gerald Ford stay fit during his Presidency. Warren Harding hit golf balls off the White House lawn, while Dwight Eisenhower practiced on his personal golf green. Bill Clinton used a jogging path around the lawn and, since Theodore Roosevelt's Presidency, a tennis court has served the recreation needs of first families.

The White House is a public house where first families have struggled to forge private lives. All First Ladies have dealt with the challenge of being on "display" in the White House and have tried to find that elusive balance between retaining some degree of privacy and avoiding being cut off from the public, and between being accessible and being held captive. Such recent First Ladies as Betty Ford and Hillary Rodham Clinton expressed frustration with the notion that they were constantly on display while trying to achieve a satisfactory balance between the public and private facets of life in the White House.

HISTORY, CUSTOMS, SERVICE

In spite of threats to American democracy and changes to the building, the White House remains as "The People's House." Future first families will find some customs, furnishings, and events much as their predecessors found them. The First Lady is charged by custom as the keeper of customs. These traditions could be as informal as making Christmas in the White House special and decorating the building or could involve something as tangible as maintaining the White House china collection. The public expects this of First Ladies. Another custom is the White House Easter Egg Roll, which takes place on the South grounds of the estate. An annual custom begun by Lucy Hayes (although earlier First Ladies infrequently participated in similar events), crowds of children gather on Easter Mondays for the event which, in recent years, has often included such festivities for the participants as balloons, bands, clowns, and of course Peter Cottontail. Other traditions are more official, including state affairs and dinners, such as the annual picnic for all members of Congress held on the South lawn.

First Ladies are assisted in hosting official affairs of state by a staff, as such functions involve an array of customs and protocol. For instance, many first couples have traditionally greeted distinguished guests at the North Entrance, amid the stately white columns, and made informal conversation with them in the Yellow Oval Room located on the second floor. When the social list is large, guests were usually instructed to arrive by the East Entrance, then ascend the marble stairway to the State Floor. The East Room has been used as a place for guests to congregate, where they have been attended to by social aides, typically officers in the armed forces. The practice of announcing VIPs as they pass through the Entrance Foyer is another common custom. Perhaps the most famous tradition involving official state functions is playing the fife and drum rendition of "Ruffles and Flourishes" as the President and First Lady descend the stairway from the family quarters to meet their assembled guests, followed by the President's triumphant tune, "Hail to the Chief." After meeting their guests, custom required the President to adjourn to the State Dining Room in the company of the ranking woman in the audience, while the First Lady took the arm of the ranking gentleman.

The President's House remains open and accessible to the public and for social functions, and this accessibility has been curtailed only during war or times of severe economic recession. For reasons of practicality, the custom of opening the White House for a public reception on New Year's Day was ended by the Hoovers in 1933, after thousands of visitors showed up for the event year after year. The First Lady has been charged by custom with the duty of keeping the Executive Mansion as "The People's House." As a group they have succeeded in impressive fashion and the White House stands unique among the residences of the heads of government from around the world for its openness. Pat Nixon paid attention to the needs of the disabled in extending the accessibility of the building, Florence Harding even ordered the drapes be opened so that the people might be able to see into their house, and all recent first families have accommodated the extensive public tours that are conducted in the White House.

The charge before you is a formidable one and the home in which you now reside is a formidable one. History and custom accompany your service and I wish you well. As guidance, many of your predecessors have looked to the words of President John Adams, the first to reside in the White House. On his second night in the Mansion he composed a letter, the words from which were inscribed on the mantel of the State Dining Room years later by FDR. The words of Adams might be taken as a prayer and the eternal hope for both democracy and those following in his footsteps:

"I Pray Heaven to Bestow
The Best of Blessings on
This House
and on All that shall hereafter
Inhabit it. May none but Honest
and Wise Men ever rule under This Roof."

Chapter 4

"PARTY POLITICS": THE SOCIAL ROLE OF THE FIRST LADY AND ITS POLITICAL INFLUENCE

Edith P. Mayo

OVERVIEW

Welcome to the White House and to your exciting role as First Lady of the Land! I want to acquaint you with the social role played by the First Lady, an aspect of the position which has been much disparaged of late – but one which is of paramount political importance in our system of government. As our nation began, there were no rules for a new democracy to follow, only the well-established social customs of the courts and royalty of Europe. George and Martha Washington, as well as their advisers and the people of the new nation, were acutely aware that we had just fought a revolution to throw off royalty, so the Chief Executive and his wife did not want to appear to be re-creating regal trappings. The Founders thought it important to create a distinct American style that reflected the values of the republic they had fought so hard to establish. They also wanted to establish an appropriate social style in civic and public life that reflected these values in dress, comportment, and entertaining – elegance without excess, power without pomp, and dignity without disdain for the common man.

The Washingtons and their contemporaries debated how to comport themselves in public so as to convey dignity, command respect, and project authority without regal behavior. The Washingtons chose a dignified and formal style but, mindful of creating an administration and a government of the people, they welcomed ordinary citizens to mingle with the President and Mrs. Washington every week. The emphasis on public access to the Chief Executive marked a critical difference between American style and the styles set by European courts. In addition, George and Martha Washington's precedent-setting decision to host state events and public entertaining jointly established the role of the President's wife (or the presidential hostess, often in the nineteenth century another female family member) as the social and ceremonial partner to the President and hostess for the nation. That role has been the basic one played by every First Lady from Martha Washington's time to the present day. Far from being mere "cultural fluff," the First Lady's social role has enabled her to wield great political power as well.

Establishing Social Affairs as Political Affairs

As the seasoned wife of a politician, I am sure you have already done your full share of entertaining to promote your husband's career and help secure his political position. But now you have the opportunity to do it on a grand national and international scale. Formal dinners, and those of state, held at the White House represent the epitome of the President's social entertaining – a potent and heady mixture of food, culture, power, and politics. As the hub of social life in the nation's capital, the Executive Mansion has given previous First Ladies the opportunity to structure this space as a national and international stage for the conduct of politics and diplomacy. Nowhere else in American life do political power, cultural achievement, and historic setting combine to produce the festive elegance and atmosphere of a White House social function. Structuring and overseeing state dinners and White House entertainments have historically been a primary way for First Ladies to establish their visibility and influence within the presidential administration and, by extension, over the powerful social and diplomatic networks of the nation's capital. A woman who is socially adept and politically savvy can promote her husband's political agenda, and structure the style and image of her husband's presidential administration.

John and Abigail Adams, the first couple to actually live in the new city of Washington and to inhabit the "President's House," followed the Washingtons in their style of hosting events, but were not in residence long enough to establish precedents in the nation's capital before Adams' term in office ended. John and Abigail had always had a political marriage, and Abigail continued to voice her political opinions publicly, so much so that Adams' enemies referred to her as "Mrs. President" – not a term of endearment! But in remaining her politically outspoken self, Abigail established the other side of the First Lady's role, that of political partner.

Our nation was particularly fortunate that, at its beginning, we had two strong women who interpreted the role of First Lady in very different ways, setting wide boundaries for those women who would follow. Subsequent First Ladies could choose to follow Martha or Abigail, depending upon their personality and interests – or they could combine, extend, or re-define these roles.

It remained for the gracious Dolley Madison to establish the crucial importance of the First Lady's leadership in the nation's capital. Mrs. Madison frequently served as hostess for Thomas Jefferson, a widower, during his Presidency, but came into her own as First Lady during her husband's terms of office. It was Dolley Madison who organized the first Inaugural Ball in the nation's capital.

James and Dolley Madison were experienced hosts before they arrived in the President's House, and had the financial means to entertain elegantly. Dolley, a hostess extraordinaire, merged her political knowledge with her role as hostess, skillfully camouflaging her politics under the guise of entertaining to advance her husband's political agenda. Having served as hostess for Jefferson as well as for her husband, Dolley was the acknowledged social leader and most important woman in the nation's capital for sixteen years. She, more than anyone else, established a true American style in entertaining by filtering European influences, particularly the decorative arts and cuisine of France, through the lens of American popular culture and democratic sensibilities. Dolley, with famed architect Benjamin Latrobe, was the first to design and decorate the interior of the President's House, deliberately creating it as a stage for her husband's political and diplomatic initiatives. Through her careful "creation" of the President's House, she played a crucial role in defining the public social space of the chief executive and his wife – the home which will be your new residence.

Dolley Madison, as the wife of the president, was aware that she stood at the juncture where public and private life meet. Through her skills as a hostess, she was the one who defined a sphere of extraordinary influence between the private and public – that of society – where women wielded enormous power through the social and ceremonial forms of dinners, receptions, and entertainment. As First Lady, she presided over this sphere, establishing a true American style in social entertaining and creating public ceremonies appropriate for a new republic. Dolley's style was less formal than the Washingtons' or that of John and Abigail Adams, but more formal than Thomas Jefferson's, who had abolished all distinction of "rank" among his guests and done away with protocol. Dolley did not "receive" as Washington and Adams had, but mingled freely with her guests. Her Wednesday night "drawing rooms" (receptions) were so well attended they were known as "Mrs. Madison's crush." Mrs. Madison's understanding that entertainment was a venue for political lobbying, her creation of the President's House as a stage for politics and diplomacy, and her shaping of the hostess's role as a powerful position for women, set precedents for the women who would follow.

INSTITUTIONALIZING THE SOCIAL ROLE

First Ladies of the nineteenth century followed those precedents, including Mrs. Lincoln. But her reign as hostess of the Executive Mansion is a story of well-meant intentions versus negative public perceptions. While Mary Lincoln followed in the footsteps of her predecessors in viewing social entertaining as a display of political power – believing that her elaborate entertaining was upholding the power and prestige of the Presidency at a turning point in history – she seriously misjudged the mood of the public. Many perceived her well-intentioned efforts as self-aggrandizing; or worse, that she displayed a callous disregard for the fighting and dying on the battlefield. She ordered lavish and expensive new china while many of her countrymen went hungry. She redecorated the Executive Mansion while the homes of others were being torched. While she wanted desperately to contribute to the effectiveness of her husband's Presidency and to support the Union cause, her intentions were seriously misread. The lesson of Mary Lincoln is clear: The role of public perception in your new position is all important.

At the dawn of the twentieth century, the United States emerged as a world power following the Spanish American War. Appropriate to this new stature and to the new century, the core of the nation's capital was redesigned in neo-classical symmetry through a design called the McMillan Plan. Theodore and Edith Roosevelt entered the White House as the nation entered the new century. The President believed the mansion needed a new image to reflect the nation's international stature as a world power. The Executive Mansion was enlarged and restored as part of this larger vision, and officially renamed the "White House." Teddy deliberately employed the White House as his stage and used drama and ceremony to symbolize what was readily emerging as the imperial Presidency. Teddy Roosevelt envisioned entertaining as a means of promoting the United States as a world power. Edith was thoroughly in accord with his vision. The couple initiated a series of dramatic changes that physically restructured the mansion, moving the presidential offices and those of his staff to the newly-constructed West Wing; they codified and formalized rules for social style, protocol, etiquette, and entertaining; purchased a new state china service that objectified the restrained elegance they sought; and initiated a series of musicales that were the talk of the capital city's social crowd. At the start of its second century, White House style appeared as an institutional expression, rather than personal expression of style that it had previously been.

Institutionalizing the First Ladyship as well, Edith Roosevelt hired the first social secretary to a First Lady, Isabelle "Belle" Hagner, to assist with the increased demands of entertaining and state occasions, and to help generate and manage the First Family's "image" – lest someone else do it for her! Initiating control, Edith screened photographers, oversaw the selection of photographs, chose the journals in which articles and photographs would appear, and selected authors to write the stories she thought would place her husband and family in the best light. Those were the "good old days," when a First Lady could exercise that much control of the press!

The Roosevelts' renovation of the mansion, their formulas for entertaining, their rules of etiquette, and the institutionalization of the First Lady's position reflected the new position of international power of the United States, and established the social forms of the imperial Presidency that dominated the political and social scene for the twentieth century.

A "PARADE OF CULTURE"

Within that established formula, more recent First Ladies have injected innovations to stamp their personal style on the position. Within these formal traditions there gradually emerged an assertion of artistic expression that emphasized American culture as the equal of any in the world. With the Kennedy years as the watershed, this pattern has continued to the present under the influence of Hillary Rodham Clinton.

Jacqueline Kennedy's historic restoration of the White House brought fine period antiques and portraits back to the mansion, emphasizing this country's important cultural heritage. She established the White House as a brilliant international stage for the finest in cultural achievement, presenting Shakespearean theater, American and international composers, the American Ballet Theater, the National Symphony Orchestra, the American Music Festival, and the opera. Some of America's most prominent conductors and composers were also among the invited guests. Through her legendary entertaining, Mrs. Kennedy staged brilliant cultural events which were part of her vision to demonstrate that American culture was the equal of any in the world, and to emphasize that this nation could now assert its rightful place as a cultural world power as well. Mrs. Kennedy launched an American cultural dominance that matched the nation's economic and military might, projecting world leadership through cultural prowess.

While not as well publicized, Lady Bird Johnson continued with verve in the Kennedy style, bringing what she called a "parade of culture" to the White House stage. But, she introduced a series of innovative settings: events on the White House lawn; state dinners in the Rose Garden; outdoor suppers on the south lawn featuring popular music, opera, Broadway show tunes, dance, jazz, and contemporary sculpture. The Johnsons also used their Texas ranch to entertain world leaders, presenting the best of food and culture in a regional setting. They were also the first to hold a "cook out" at the White House!

Rosalynn Carter extended this legacy of cultural artists at the White House, arranging for PBS to telecast the elegant entertainment to the public. Appreciating the impact of the White House cultural performances staged by her predecessors, Nancy Reagan continued the tradition with a series entitled, "In Performance at the White House." These televised events featured acclaimed performers – some of whom were old Hollywood friends – but also showcased the talents of promising young performers.

YOUR PERSONAL SOCIAL STYLE

As you enter your new home on this national stage, I hope that understanding some of the history of the First Lady's social role – and the wide variety of ways in which it has been played – will assist you in deciding how to play your part in the national drama. I am sure you and your staff have many wonderful ideas of your own regarding style and substance, tradition and innovation. The experience of previous First Ladies provides both wonderful models to build upon, as well as cautionary tales to be mindful of. First, you will fare best, I think, if you ground yourself in the experience and history of the First Lady's social role. Follow tradition, then innovate your own style. Do not purchase new state china during a Depression, a War, or some other national catastrophe! If you do purchase new china, make sure the press and the nation know it was paid for by a wealthy private donor (the tradition for some time now) and not with taxpayers' dollars. Reflect even your innovations in terms of following in the footsteps of your predecessors – you are mindful of tradition, but are adding a new twist, something to personalize the tradition and make it your own.

Follow the personal style with which you are comfortable – in dress, food, hosting, and entertaining. Find a great "rationale" with which to justify it, and you will weather any crisis. Ignore the criticism. This is one job where you will be "damned if you do, and damned if you don't." So my most important piece of advice is to be your own person and do what "makes your heart sing," as Lady Bird Johnson phrased it.

As the former curator of the First Ladies collection and exhibition at the Smithsonian's National Museum of American History, may I offer to take you on a tour of the exhibition, which now presents not only the famous gowns but explores the contributions of First Ladies while in the White House. Perhaps you might even want a "behind the scenes" tour, which we would be honored to provide!

May I extend my very best wishes for health, happiness, and success to you and your family as you enter you this historic new home.

Chapter 5

ELEANOR ROOSEVELT: THE YARDSTICK

Susan Roth Breitzer

CASTING A LONG SHADOW

The legacy of Eleanor Roosevelt, as a yardstick by which all subsequent First Ladies have been measured, has taken on a life of its own. Yet, the reality is somewhat more complex, both in terms of the barriers she broke, and the boundaries her tenure as First Lady helped to define. Eleanor Roosevelt was not the only First Lady in history to become the standard against which others were measured. For much of America's history, Dolley Madison, hostess to two presidents (she occasionally hosted for the widowed Thomas Jefferson) was the often-idealized role model for the President's spouse. In the early twentieth century, Eleanor's own aunt, Edith Kermit Roosevelt, had achieved a certain role model status as the "ideal" First Lady who, it was said, "never made a mistake." When Franklin D. Roosevelt was first elected in 1932, Eleanor Roosevelt feared that, among other things, she would not live up to the expectations created by Aunt Edith. Whether she finally did is debatable, but what is more important is that she reshaped those expectations.

When examining the legacy of Eleanor Roosevelt, it can be too easy to oversimplify or even exaggerate her accomplishments, especially when they are taken out of context. For example, contrary to popular belief, Eleanor Roosevelt was not the first First Lady to speak on the radio, publish under her own name, or even go down into a coal mine. And there have been a number of First Ladies preceding Eleanor Roosevelt, beginning with Abigail Adams, who wielded political influence over their husbands. Likewise, Eleanor Roosevelt was not the earliest First Lady in history to be criticized for either stepping out of her "proper" role or "meddling" in official government business. Finally, by giving equal weight to every little "first" that she accomplished, without distinction between the truly pioneering and the mere historical curiosities, it becomes too easy to trivialize the legacy of Eleanor Roosevelt as simply about trying new things.

While ER is now too often simply regarded as "St. Eleanor the Good," in her own day she was criticized and reviled, much as was Hillary Rodham Clinton more recently. For instance, she was accused of profiting from her position through her speaking and writing fees (which all went to charity), of meddling in public affairs, and of gadding about at the taxpayers' expense. Some considered her a Communist, while others called her a traitor to her race. The FBI kept a file on her that grew to the size of a telephone book. Such were the hazards of creating a role for the President's wife, which went well beyond giving teas and cutting ribbons.

EXPANDING THE ROLE BEYOND THAT OF SIMPLY HOSTESS

It should be noted that, contrary to the expectations for the First Ladies who followed her, Eleanor Roosevelt had no "project" per se. Rather, she took on issues as they arose, most of them growing out of her pre-White House career as a social and political activist, and many coinciding with New Deal programs. For example, her reputation for being "everywhere," inspecting and reporting as FDR's "Eyes and Ears" (and legs), grew out of her experience as First Lady of New York, in which she learned to see and report the smallest details concerning conditions of New York's public institutions.

It should also be remembered that her reputation as "Eleanor Everywhere" did not mean that she was never home fulfilling the traditional hostess role of the First Lady. Although at first she expressed little interest in the "First Hostess" role, after living in the White House for a while she began to grasp its significance to the American people and of the role she played in welcoming guests to it. She was not, however, merely satisfied to expertly fill the hostess role. Rather, she expanded White House hospitality beyond the activities of the traditional aristocratic social season to bring Americans from nearly all walks of life to the White House. Even when she supervised official entertaining she was not afraid to court controversy, such as when she engaged the celebrated African-American contralto Marian Anderson to perform for the King and Queen of England.

In the hostess role alone, therefore, Eleanor Roosevelt transformed what could have been a confining role into one that was not only genuinely satisfying, but one that could be used to make the White House a more welcoming and inclusive space, and in so doing indirectly advancing the New Deal. But Eleanor Roosevelt would not have long been satisfied even to simply expand the hostess role. In her life before the White House, she had been a writer, teacher, businesswoman, Democratic Party activist, and social reformer. And slowly but surely, she would incorporate at least some of these roles into her position as First Lady.

What then is the lasting legacy of Eleanor Roosevelt that has made her (for better or worse) the standard against which all subsequent First Ladies have been measured? Her greatest impact can be found in two major areas: political activism and social activism – the former once almost completely off-limits to presidential spouses and the latter largely limited to traditional charitable activities. And in many cases, her greatest accomplishment was not so much doing new things as helping to make them acceptable activities for a First Lady.

POLITICAL ACTIVISM

Her legacy in the area of political activism can be divided into two areas: campaigning and speaking out on political issues. In campaigning Eleanor Roosevelt helped transform the expected role of the candidate's spouse from silent prop to active participant in the campaign. Speaking out on issues (and disagreeing with the President), long practiced behind the scenes, was brought into the open by Eleanor Roosevelt, who also managed to establish a boundary (sometimes with difficulty) between the right to express a differing opinion as a citizen, and the need to visibly support the President as First Lady. There are numerous examples of Eleanor Roosevelt's efforts in both of these areas, but there are a few significant cases, some predating her tenure as First Lady of the United States, worth examining.

Eleanor Roosevelt was no stranger to the political process. From her days as the wife of a New York State Assemblyman from 1910 to 1913, politics and campaigns more often than not were part of her daily life. At first her participation was limited to the traditional role of hostess. By the 1920's, however, Eleanor Roosevelt had emerged as a political presence in her own right, speaking, writing, organizing, and campaigning. As First Lady of New York, she realized that it was politically prudent to curtail her public partisan activism (which did not stop her, however, from continuing her political activities covertly). And while her teaching job in New York City prevented her from having a more significant advisory role in FDR's gubernatorial administration, as First Lady of New York, she began many of the practices she would continue in the White House; these ranged from her inspections of public institutions to offering advice on official appointments. And when she began speaking on the campaign trail during the 1932 election season, her active and visible presence prompted more coverage than conventionally assigned to candidates' wives.

Eleanor Roosevelt continued to campaign for her husband in 1936, but it was in 1940 when FDR sought an unprecedented third term that Eleanor Roosevelt achieved her finest hour as a campaign speaker. The Democratic National Convention, having made the historic choice to nominate Roosevelt for a third term as President, was threatening to divide over the selection of his running mate, Henry Wallace. With the United States teetering on the brink of entering World War II, FDR chose not to attend the convention (or campaign, for that matter). When the Democratic National Convention appeared to be disintegrating, however, Eleanor was summoned. Although the idea of a First Lady or candidate's wife speaking at a national party convention is now fully accepted, even commonplace, Eleanor's presence on the podium in 1940 was enough to get the warring delegates to at least sit up and listen. And without a prepared speech she was able to bring the delegates behind Roosevelt and Wallace by urging them to "rise above considerations that are narrow and partisan" in order to enable the President to lead the nation through what she called "no ordinary time." The return to "ordinary times" of stability and prosperity has not diminished Eleanor Roosevelt's accomplishment of giving the First Lady an accepted place on the American political stage.

SOCIAL ACTIVISM

In terms of social activism, Eleanor Roosevelt's greatest legacy was (taking a page from her uncle, Theodore Roosevelt), making the First Ladyship a "bully pulpit" for social change. Although her activism took her into numerous areas of American society, many of her causes were similar in that they grew out of her previous interests as a social activist. If there was a particular unifying theme to her activism, it was serving as a voice for the voiceless, something she accomplished in many ways and areas during her years in the White House.

Eleanor Roosevelt's White House activism was also a product of her impressive, if somewhat uneven, career prior to the White House. Prior to her marriage, she taught dance at the Rivington Street Settlement House and volunteered with the National Consumers' League. Although she spent much of her early married life focused on her prescribed roles as wife, mother, and hostess, by World War I, she resumed and began to expand her volunteer activism. During the War, she was an active Red Cross volunteer, working in a canteen for soldiers, organizing knitting projects, and visiting soldiers in the military hospitals. Near the end of the War, she persuaded the Secretary of Interior to increase congressional funding for St. Elizabeth's Hospital (the federal mental hospital), after viewing the terrible conditions there. As her children grew older, and her marriage was affected both by FDR's extramarital affair and his paralysis, Eleanor increased her social as well as political activism. During the 1920s she became active in progressive organizations such as the Women's Trade Union League and the Women's International League for Peace and Freedom. In the latter, she helped organize a controversial contest to develop a plan for world peace.

After a brief period of adjustment, Eleanor – far from restricting herself as First Lady – found new and unique outlets for her activism on behalf of social justice. Some of these coincided with New Deal programs, others went beyond them. Among her most famous efforts was her role in the creation of the Arthurdale Housing project which, despite its shortcomings, greatly improved its residents' lives. Her efforts on behalf of African Americans are also well-know and significant, although her resignation from the Daughters of the American Revolution over the Marian Anderson incident is only the most famous example. In some cases, her social activism coincided with her professional interests, especially in journalism. Examples include her support of other women journalists through her women-only press conferences and demonstration of solidarity with organized labor by her membership with the Newspaper Guild as the only First Lady in history to belong to a union. Finally, during World II, she was one of the few prominent public figures in the United States to speak out on behalf of either European Jewish refugees or interned Japanese Americans.

ELEANOR ROOSEVELT'S LEGACY

When she departed from the White House in April 1945, Eleanor let inquiring reporters know that, as far as she was concerned, "the story is over." Yet the story has continued beyond her own death in the form of reshaped expectations concerning the President's spouse. And whether each subsequent First Lady chose to follow Eleanor Roosevelt's approach, modify it, or reject it, all have been affected by it. The response has also shifted along with expectations concerning women's roles in general over the last half-century. For example, immediately following Eleanor Roosevelt, Bess Truman explicitly rejected her public activism, though she maintained an important role advising her husband behind the scenes. Mamie Eisenhower appeared to retreat even further into the traditional roles of hostess and companion, though she belatedly began charitable work on behalf of the American Heart Association following Ike's heart attack.

By the 1960s and early 1970s, Jacqueline Kennedy, Lady Bird Johnson, and Pat Nixon more visibly reintroduced the idea of the First Lady having a public "project," although they confined theirs to politically and socially "safe" issues such as promotion of the arts, public outdoor beautification, and volunteerism. It was not until the Ford Administration that there was a First Lady as willing to speak her mind and even risk controversy in her public interests, as Betty Ford did with her support of the Equal Rights Amendment and her lead in pioneering the discussion of personal health problems in the name of public service, when she brought a previously unmentionable condition like breast cancer into the public consciousness. Rosalynn Carter took the scope of the First Lady's activities even closer to Eleanor Roosevelt's model, attending Cabinet meetings, visiting several Latin American countries as an unofficial presidential envoy, and making her primary project mental health reform, the last of which helped to give voice to another group of Americans who had largely been voiceless.

More recently, the special projects of Nancy Reagan and Barbara Bush – anti-drug education and literacy, respectively – have been visibly on the "safe" side of public concerns, yet each has managed to influence the public consciousness on these issues. Finally, the most recent First Lady, Hillary Rodham Clinton, taking inspiration perhaps more directly than ever before from Eleanor Roosevelt, once again attempted to expand the bounds of the First Lady's role and encountered controversy in the process.

The nature of future First Ladies' roles will ultimately be up to them, but the legacy of Eleanor Roosevelt – both as a role-breaker and role-creator – will remain a viable force, continuing to cast a shadow over the Office of the First Lady.

THE MODERN OFFICE: CHALLENGES AND ISSUES

Chapter 6

THE FIRST LADY'S RELATIONS WITH THE MASS MEDIA

Betty H. Winfield

CHALLENGES

Congratulations on becoming the country's 39th First Lady! You are about to embark on the adventure of a lifetime, with the news media as your constant companion. So I offer you condolences as well, for the stress you will no doubt endure. With careful planning of your mass media relations, you can indeed make a difference, not just by your position and image, but by your very public actions in the East Wing. How you use this "velvet pulpit" will convey to America who you are as an individual, and your attitude toward power.

If it is not already, your personal privacy will soon be a distant memory. Prepare to be complimented and condemned, sometimes all in a single day, for what you do, as well as what you fail to do. The criticism will sting and, inadvertently, will most likely be what you remember. But take comfort from the fact that you are not alone; even the most popular First Ladies – Dolly Madison, Eleanor Roosevelt, Jacqueline Kennedy, and Barbara Bush – were at one point or another criticized by the press. Never forget that, for the mass media, you are newsworthy even if you say or do nothing. This is a system, after all, that thrives on conflict and reporters have an incentive to find and emphasize discord, even in your un-elected, unpaid office. It does not help that the First Ladyship as a position is a paradox and, by being so ill-defined, is predisposed to critical coverage. Your detractors will find a sympathetic ear and will be quoted regardless of their motives. You must prepare yourself for them, whether they are opposition members of Congress, public figures outside the beltway, or scholars. On top of all that, as one of the most public female figures in the United States, you must now negotiate an image that is expected to embody American womanhood, a troubling concept that begs for an impossible ideal.

WHAT TO DO?

How do you respond? One bit of advice remains constant: be yourself in public. Any attempt to imitate some previous First Lady from another time in history will surely fail. This new century is a different kind of world and you cannot be a princess of Camelot, like Jacqueline Kennedy. Your age, life experiences, and education prevent you from assuming the matronly posture of Barbara Bush. You are not a steel magnolia, like Rosalynn Carter, who rode in on "second wave" feminism and enjoyed a very open partnership in the White House. Nor are you a slick western fashion trophy, as was Nancy Reagan in the 1980s. Each previous First Lady has been a distinct personality, drawing on varied experiences and role models to guide her tenure in the White House. This new century offers considerable potential for women in the private and public spheres. Define yourself in a way that feels most comfortable to you. If you are sincere, the American public and the mass media will generally accept you for being true to yourself. And remember to laugh about who you are in this new position; with a sense of humor, you will be admired all the more.

MEDIA STAFF

To manage your new relationship with the mass media, you must first choose a strong staff and then, together, map out a strategy for news coverage that reflects your vision of the office. Your staff should consist of the best possible people you can find, not necessarily loyal friends from the campaign, but energetic and trustworthy people who understand the mass media, public opinion, and image making. Just as the most recent First Ladies had a White House staff for overall news coordination, you need such a director and a staff to convey your image and intentions. Your staff's principal task is to promote you and your accomplishments while you are in the White House. Your causes, travels, and public appearances should all be planned for media consumption and give an appearance of how active and dedicated you are as the wife of the President of the United States. In doing so, you define yourself and the position of First Lady. Your staff should assist in articulating to the public how you fit the era, this new century when women enjoy family and career.

COMMUNICATIONS STAFF

One major hiring suggestion is to appoint a Communications Director to your staff who will oversee the media strategy. She will work with your press secretary, who arranges for regular news meetings and schedules interviews. She should also oversee and work with your media aide: an image person responsible for the video, still photography, and textual images as well as with your "cyber director," who is responsible for web-based information, and their assistants.

The communications director should coordinate the First Lady's messages with her staff and also with the President's communications staff. Key components to successful media relations are to coordinate how your activities are covered and presented and to have a unified media message. In order to do this your staff – scheduler, advance person, appointments secretary, speechwriter and coach, and general secretary – should work with the communications director. Together with the media aides, the First Lady's staff should do long-range planning for news, images, and public opinion. The coordination of the two groups – the "media unit" and the personal staff – might be achieved by calling weekly or daily meetings to promote a message and image of the day that fit an overall focus. If the press secretary will meet with reporters daily, there will be an expectation for regular news and subsequently continual news coverage.

E-COMMUNICATIONS STAFF

Because of the demands for access as well as the new media dictates, the media office needs a Cyber Director, a type of overall web master to ensure Internet-based information is updated and useful. One web site should be for the general public with information conveyed in a visually attractive manner and linked to and from the official White House site. The site should also link to other existing First Lady sites. It is recommended that the general public site include a biography, information on such topics as "Life in the White House," White House recipes, Christmas decorations, Christmas cards from each year, the Easter egg roll, and an e-mail address for communication. In the First Lady's office, there should be someone, perhaps a volunteer staff, to answer the First Lady's e-mail queries. So much research indicates a more positive reaction to our government if there is two-way communication. This is but one approach to achieving that end.

Another web site should provide the media with access to information that journalists would need. Such a "news web site" would help you to take pro-active news initiatives, not only for the beltway journalists, but also for local, regional, and specialized media. Journalists should be able to logon to this web site and follow links to the First Lady's daily and weekly schedule, the most recent briefs, answers to the most frequently-asked or anticipated questions, her latest remarks, updated photos, her speeches by topic and date, her biography, her family, and so on. This site should also have clips of previous favorable news coverage, snippets of previous stories, and recent photos of the day – all agenda setters which, in the journalists' rush to meet their deadlines, would probably be used. There should also be links to other White House news, such as the President and First Lady joint appearances, White House entertaining, official dinners, and the First Lady's charitable activities.

PRESS AND COMMUNICATIONS STRATEGY

The press or media office should have a strategic news plan that not only reflects the First Lady's vision of the position, but also one that emphasizes openness. Such an effort has to be justified not only to gain the respect of journalists no matter how painful the story (Betty Ford's breast cancer or alcoholism), but also because there can be no secrecy concerning the First Lady. All information about her will eventually become public.

Your communications strategy must take into account three steadfast expectations that both the media and the public have about the First Lady. As such, the images made public as well as the stories should reflect what has traditionally been associated with the First Lady throughout the past century: (1) the supportive wife; (2) a style leader of White House social events; and (3) a doer of good works. When the messages about the First Lady in these areas are unclear or mixed, the coverage also becomes unclear or mixed, leaving the public unsure about who you are and what you represent as a First Lady. This happened in the early Clinton years when Hillary Rodham Clinton ignored the expectations of the traditional First Lady roles and then took a strong political and advisory role as head of the Clinton administration's health task force. Yet, even with her leadership role, she kept the actions of the task force secret for many months. But the secrecy did not end press scrutiny or interest. The attempt to explain Mrs. Clinton was imprecise and fell back on her hairstyles as metaphor. She conveyed confusing images, which were reflected in news stories and web sites. The fact that Hillary Rodham Clinton made so many mass media decisions herself and often in a reactive manner, resulted in a lack of a strong, strategic, overall news plan.

Such planning should provide for pro-active First Lady news coverage. It should take into account the varied types of media as well as different kinds of general and special news access to the First Lady. For instance, the plan should include such media entities as the daily news media, lifestyle sections of print and visual media, national news sections, women's magazines, broadcast evening news, such vehicles as "Larry King Live" and daily talk-show television, and cable programs. This planning should begin right away; there must be no hesitation during those crucial, first months when the press and public are most inquisitive, "honeymoon" or not. An immediate plan with an overall vision for the First Lady's image will produce more positive, expected news coverage and immediate responses to news queries.

A coherent media plan should include both the news setting agenda as well as a discussion about timing. Through agenda setting, the story is broken by the White House, rather than other sources. In politics, timing is everything. Experience shows that early weekday news results in the most prominent coverage of a White House story, unless there is strong competition from breaking news. Friday is the best day for negative stories because most media units already have their weekend stories planned. If covered at all, depending on other story "hits," controversial stories are less likely to be noticed on the weekend. Saturday is generally an unread, unwatched news day.

Repetition of a particular message is a necessity for public perception and memory. The press or media office can devise numerous creative ways to repeat a message, visually or otherwise, whether by press briefings from the press secretary, a First Lady's remarks or press conference, a public appearance, and so on. Staying on the message is important for all kinds of media. The television and web-based media require images; you must plan for them daily or the media unit will rely on its own file for what might become an unflattering or incongruent image. How the First Lady communicates requires careful attention as well. A mix of vehicles can be employed: briefings by the press secretary; press conferences; statements on the record or off-the-record; and the use of cameras or video or recording devices. Regardless of the means by which it is communicated, consideration must be given to the "where, when, and about what" of the story. The news planning strategy should include ways of utilizing the lifestyle coverage, magazine and women's reporters, and editors. The gender-related functions of a First Lady must be communicated. Remember that for the most part, these lifestyle stories are not only covered in a positive light, but are seen and read by American women. In other words, the First Lady news will have a lot of women watchers and readers. Her gender-related audience must therefore be considered in media planning for coverage, especially of female-related events. Journalists have an expectation for various kinds of access. If such access is neglected, it is greatly noticed not just by journalists, but by all women.

TRADITIONAL AREAS OF MEDIA COVERAGE OF THE FIRST LADY

There have been five particular areas in which the news media have historically covered First Ladies. The First Lady's strategic media plan should consider these areas, no matter how stifling they may seem. The goal should be to impact the storyline, the image, and the public response, based upon media consumption.

The first type of mass media story about the First Lady is the oldest: the gender-specific roles of being an *escort* – as the wife of the President, a mother of his children, and as a woman. This type of news coverage relates to anything in which the First Lady is strongly connected with the President. These types of stories were presented throughout the 2000 campaign. Now, as First Lady, this role will be manifested in, for instance, coverage of your travel with the President on official trips and informally on vacations and related travels. First Ladies of the past thirty years have been surrogates for the President, representing him with other nations, for example. In this capacity Pat Nixon went to Peru, Rosalynn Carter traveled through Latin America, and Hillary Clinton went to the Olympics. In other words, the news coverage dwells on her by the mere fact that she is the President's wife and, as such, is carrying out the President's wishes. This kind of news coverage also extends to other gender-based functions, such as the First Lady being the mother of the President's children.

News coverage of this type is usually positive if the First Lady is supportive, available, and nurturing. If she is looking adoringly at the President when he speaks, as did Nancy Reagan, the press takes notice. If she is glaring and distant when she walks with the President to the helicopter, as Hillary Clinton was seen doing in1998, the news media observe that too. If she appears to be a nurturing mother, as did Jackie Kennedy, stories lauding her efforts appear in women's magazines. The news media covered all First Ladies through this "wife role" since the days of Martha Washington.

The mass media have also covered the First Lady's *protocol* role since the country's earliest days. This particular pattern of coverage focuses on the First Lady as the chief of White House cultural events and as a style setter, whether in her own personal dress and decorum or whether in decorating the nation's house and entertaining there. This news coverage includes the First Lady's particular personal style in dress and manner. For example, journalists notice if the First Lady has extravagant clothing tastes, as happened in the coverage of Jacqueline Kennedy and Nancy Reagan.

The mass media are also curious about the First Lady's White House *hostess* role. The public needs to know not just about state dinners, but wants to know about private dinners. The Franklin Roosevelt family had friends and White House staff in for those Sunday scrambled egg suppers, and shrewdly enough, included journalists. Reporters loved those off-the-record informal sessions; and they paid off in positive news coverage of the President and the First Lady. Barbara Bush successfully stressed the hostess role by talking to journalists on a regular basis about her many private dinners and by photographing the dinners and guests. While the Clintons frequently entertained informally during their early

White House years, they were however secret about these private events and did not allow for recorded images. One bit of advice about public perception is to entertain in a manner which is tastefully done, but not so extravagant as to appear wasteful, especially if the country is in the middle of a recession.

The President's formal State Dinners should be widely covered and the First Lady's Office would be wise to release the information, rather than the State Department, as has happened the past eight years. Regarding the First Lady's protocol role, as with any social function, if she is relaxed and has a good time – even dances, for instance, as did the Reagans, the Johnsons, and the Fords – then the guests also relax and enjoy themselves. If the First Family attends White House formal functions, even if reading at the table as did little Amy Carter, then such events become part of the family's social image in the mass media.

Remember that the White House is the people's house. It belongs to the American public. Presidents as far back as Thomas Jefferson and Andrew Jackson, and more recently as with the Clintons, knew that. They all received positive coverage from the images of ordinary people coming through and being greeted by the President and the First Lady. For the past 70 years, First Ladies have publicly shown the White House rooms and explained how they are decorated; this act is deemed newsworthy and such coverage is usually positive.

Another area of expected, yet traditional, news coverage concerns the First Lady's noblesse oblige, her *good works* role. As a remnant of the country's progressive era, this kind of charitable or volunteer project should make some meaningful contribution to the betterment of society and has often resulted in positive coverage. If efforts are clearly focused on one area or a single project, that cause is given legitimacy by such a public emphasis. Such a cause also garners national and local support because of the First Lady's affiliation with it. If the First Lady takes on too many of these activities, then such social work runs the risk of having no "imprint." The other side of such good deeds work is that negative news coverage would result if the First Lady is superficial about her support and if she does not put in the depth that it takes to make a difference in the issue.

Such projects can become concerted White House policy, such as Lady Bird Johnson's "beautification" project, which became part of the Highway Act, or Rosalynn Carter's mental health initiative, which eventually became law. The only twentieth century First Lady to avoid this expected role and get away with it was Jacqueline Kennedy, who was raising young children. Mrs. Kennedy publicly made a point of saying that, if she did that (parenting) badly, nothing else really mattered. She also put her energies into decorating the White House and had public attention drawn to those who donated furnishings and art to the nation's first home.

Your choice of a charitable work project must be your own. In your media planning, you must focus on how to make this project "your" own and put your own stamp on it, rather than giving the impression you are repeating a former First Lady's project. In other words, in a public manner, you should explain how you will differ, add to, and expand a project that is similar to another First Lady's undertaking. For your strategic plan, you also need to consider how you will integrate your work with the President's goals. If your good works choice is to set public policy, I suggest that you plan the media coverage mighty carefully. Explain what you will do, why this is an issue or problem, and justify your actions. If you are open about your political interest in a particular policy area, know that the public has been used to politically active First Ladies since the days of Abigail Adams and Dolley Madison.

In areas relating to policy as well as political power, previous First Ladies have run into negative reactions from the public and press. The story risks becoming, "who elected her anyhow" and the media will quote congressional critics of the First Lady's policy initiatives. Political actions raise the issue of the First Lady's unelected political power. Yet, those First Ladies who have dared to express their opinions may have become controversial in their own time, but have ranked among the strongest and most admired First Ladies for their attempts to make a difference. Abigail Adams and Eleanor Roosevelt are examples.

Every First Lady is in one sense a *political advisor*. The public knows this but those First Ladies who did not make an issue out of this role have had more positive media coverage. Most modern First Ladies have been the President's most trusted confidante, as the First Lady is uniquely positioned to be the President's sounding board. Unlike many aides, she can tell him when he is right and when he is wrong and the President does not need worry about the First Lady leaking information or writing a tell-all book, as might his aides. How does this relate to the mass media? The media will seek to learn what type of advisory role the First Lady plays and what advice she offers. They will ask if she has too much power. Issues concerning the First Lady's political activities and advice must be included in the overall strategic plan for news coverage.

All public figures must consider the media and are dependent on staff support. Remembering this and prioritizing the efforts of the media staff will assist you as you embark on these challenging and exciting new endeavors. Good Luck!

Chapter 7

PUBLIC DISCOURSE AND THE AMERICAN FIRST LADY IN THE 20TH CENTURY

Myra G. Gutin

OVERVIEW

Since 1920, the year that women were granted the right to vote, First Ladies have assumed one of three distinct roles as public communicators: 1) ceremonial presences; 2) emerging spokeswomen; and 3) political surrogates and independent advocates. Relative to these three approaches to communicating with the public has been the development, consciously or unconsciously, of three corresponding communication philosophies. Consideration of the nature of the First Ladies' public discourse from the perspective of these three conceptual approaches sheds light on this important function of the office, a source of power for presidential spouses, and the First Lady's relationship with the press and American public.

Those First Ladies that can be classified as *ceremonial presences* – Florence Harding, Grace Coolidge, Bess Truman, and Mamie Eisenhower – devoted little, if any, thought to the idea of communicating with the public. They gave few or no speeches, advocated no causes, and did little to no campaigning for political candidates. Despite the enormous potential of the First Lady's position, these women either sought or were cast into the role of inactive communicators. Still, they served numerous functions outside of the public communicator role, such as hosting White House social affairs and serving as their husband's supporter or confidante. Because such roles are beyond the focus of this paper, and tell us less about the public discourse of, for instance, recent First Ladies, attention will be paid to the second and third communication approaches. In them, there are lessons to be learned about a First Lady's discourse with the American public.

The "Emerging Spokeswomen"

The *emerging spokeswomen* – Lou Hoover, Jacqueline Kennedy, Pat Nixon, Barbara Bush, and Laura Bush – were more aware of the need to share their ideas or projects with a national audience, and made limited use of the press and other media.

Lou Hoover embodies this transitional communicator role. She was an efficient, if somewhat less than enthusiastic, public communicator. She had honed her skills speaking to audiences about women and athletics and about a variety of issues such as the Girls Scouts, with whom she served as National President. Mrs. Hoover achieved two significant communication milestones as First Lady. Shortly after her husband's inauguration in March 1929, Mrs. Hoover became the first First Lady to give formal speeches. During her time in the White House she gave a total of 15 speeches on topics ranging from her husband's Depression relief programs to the Girl Scouts to other youth organizations. Though authorship of her speeches has never been firmly established, Mrs. Hoover's speeches were most likely written by Lou herself and her secretary, Mildred Hall.

In April 1929, Mrs. Hoover also became the first First Lady to speak over the radio. (Grace Coolidge had been offered the opportunity to speak over the radio, but she had declined because of her husband's "No quote, no interview" policy.) Mrs. Hoover's utilization of radio lent the new medium greater legitimacy as an instrument of communication.

Jacqueline Kennedy lent the same legitimacy to television when she took viewers on "A Tour of the White House with Mrs. John F. Kennedy" on February 14, 1962. Outside of her nationally-televised tour, Mrs. Kennedy never addressed the American public about any issue and gave only a small number of speeches while traveling outside the United States.

A prolific speaker, Barbara Bush probably delivered a few hundred speeches; a majority of her public discourse dealt with her White House project, literacy. One particular exception was her speech at Wellesley College's graduation ceremony in June 1990. Widely acknowledged as one of the finest examples of First Lady rhetoric, Mrs. Bush gently lectured an initially ambivalent graduating class by exhorting them to believe in something greater than themselves, find joy in life, and cherish human connections. She concluded her speech to the students that had protested her selection as speaker by saying, "Who knows? Somewhere out in this audience may even be someone who one day will follow in my footsteps and preside over the White House as the President's spouse. And I wish *him* well." The response was enthusiastic and supportive.

Though she was not initially enthusiastic about addressing audiences, Laura Bush has developed her podium skills and become a capable speaker. From January 2001-July 2004, Mrs. Bush gave remarks on over 200 occasions. Many of these were ceremonial in nature, but some of the remarks were related to education, reading, and literacy, Mrs. Bush's White House projects. She became the first First Lady to deliver an entire Presidential Radio Address on November 17, 2001 when she spoke to Radio Free Afghanistan. During May of 2002, the First Lady traveled to France, Hungary, and the Czech Republic by herself and spoke at the Organization of Economic Cooperation and Development Forum (OECD); she gave additional speeches on the trip. In 2004, Mrs. Bush took an active role in efforts to reelect her husband. Her warmth and gentle manner drew enthusiastic responses from many audiences.

THE POLITICAL SURROGATES AND INDEPENDENT ADVOCATES

The *political surrogates and independent advocates* – Eleanor Roosevelt, Lady Bird Johnson, Betty Ford, Rosalynn Carter, and Hillary Rodham Clinton – utilized all the available means of persuasion to encourage national conversation of certain issues and dramatize their own commitments to certain endeavors.

ELEANOR ROOSEVELT

Eleanor Roosevelt believed that, in a democratic society, "the channels of communication... should be open, lively and sympathetic." Mrs. Roosevelt took her own advice and used all the available communication outlets for reaching the public. She also followed advice given to her about speaking by her friend, Louis Howe, who counseled, "Never make a speech unless you feel you have something really worthwhile to say; then say it, and having said it, stop talking..."

The volume of Mrs. Roosevelt's spoken discourse is astonishing. From 1933-1945, she gave in excess of fourteen hundred speeches, lectures, and radio broadcasts. Though she had occasional assistance with research, she usually worked alone, turning out outlines and full texts for presentation. Unparalleled as a public speaker, Mrs. Roosevelt was adept at audience analysis and adaptation; she could adjust to any group with ease. The author estimates that almost half of her speeches were delivered extemporaneously. The First Lady prepared detailed outlines for her comments, but faced audiences without a fully developed text. There were times when she spoke from a prepared manuscript, but these manuscripts were subject to extensive revision at the podium. The range of topics Mrs. Roosevelt addressed included controversial issues such as civil rights, the nation's youth, Depression programs, preparation for war, and women's issues. She also gave dozens of ceremonial speeches.

From 1934-1942, Mrs. Roosevelt spoke over the radio in several commercially-sponsored broadcast series. Her topics, which were fairly innocuous, included "Rest and Relaxation," "Shall a Woman Be Herself?" "When Will a Woman Become President of the United States?" and other topics. These scripts were prepared for her by a team of writers, but she chose the subjects. As the years passed, the topics became more substantive to the point where, in her final broadcasts she was discussing anti-Semitism, national morale, and German propaganda.

Concurrent with her radio broadcasts, Mrs. Roosevelt traveled the country as a lecturer for the W. Colton Leigh Bureau of Lectures and Entertainments. Mrs. Roosevelt believed that lectures presented her with another avenue for reaching her fellow Americans. Twice a year, for two-week periods, she traveled around the country speaking about such topics as "The Mail of a President's Spouse," "Peace, and "Problems of Youth." Mrs. Roosevelt's secretary, Malvina Thompson, would write down lines that seemed to generate positive audience response. The author estimates that the First Lady gave 600 lectures during her tenure on the lecture circuit while living in the White House.

More than any other First Lady in the 20th century, Mrs. Roosevelt understood the value of frequent and effective spoken and written discourse. In addition to her speeches, radio broadcasts, and lectures, the First Lady wrote a daily column, "My Day," participated in 353 press conferences, wrote nine books, and many magazine articles. Her communication achievements are among the most extraordinary of any First Lady or any public official, for that matter.

LADY BIRD JOHNSON

Lady Bird Johnson gave 164 speeches during her years as First Lady. Like several other First Ladies, many of Mrs. Johnson's speeches focused on her White House project: "beautification" and conservation. Other speeches highlighted her husband's War on Poverty and Operation Headstart. Also like her predecessors, Lady Bird Johnson was initially uncomfortable behind the podium. Prior to the 1960 presidential campaign, she took a public speaking course and then studied privately with a speech professor from the University of Maryland. Mrs. Johnson worked diligently to craft her comments and present them in the most effective manner, a valuable lesson in that she became a highly effective and popular speaker.

Frequently, Mrs. Johnson's speeches were a collaboration between the First Lady and her Staff Director and Press Secretary, "Liz" Carpenter. When planning a speech, Mrs. Johnson would ask the question: "Who am I looking at?" Carpenter would then provide the First Lady with details and an audience analysis, where upon the two would discuss possible approaches. In planning the speeches, Mrs. Johnson spoke and Carpenter wrote down phrases and points she had made. Then Carpenter would "marry the phrases" and present her employer with a draft of her comments. The First Lady typically marked up the draft, adding, deleting, and changing thoughts and sentences. When she was satisfied with the result, she began a period of intense rehearsal. Mrs. Johnson made few changes to her manuscript once she ascended the podium; she was a verbatim speaker who felt more secure with polished remarks and left little to chance.

One of Mrs. Johnson's important communication achievements was the 47 speeches she gave from October 6-9, 1964, when she campaigned for her husband during a whistlestop train trip through several southern states. Mrs. Johnson made the trip because there was an intense distrust of Lyndon Johnson by white southerners because of his support of the Civil Rights Act of 1964 and it was necessary for her to reassure her fellow southerners that their President had not forgotten them. She believed she was up to the task. Though she encountered hostile and sometimes jeering audiences, Mrs. Johnson persisted.

BETTY FORD

Betty Ford told the author that she had taken a public speaking course in high school and that she and other young congressional wives had hired a public speaking teacher to help them with the fundamentals of oral communication. As to her formal training, "That was the limit, mine was on-the-job training," according to Mrs. Ford. But, Mrs. Ford was more comfortable facing audiences than many other First Ladies. Her discourse was not stylistically complex, but listeners found her warmth, informality, and folksiness quite apparent and reassuring.

Mrs. Ford's 100 speeches as First Lady were penned by her speechwriter, Frances "Kay" Pullen. The First Lady expressed a preference for having a fully developed manuscript when she spoke, but she made numerous changes at the podium. She was sensitive to the mood of her listeners and could effectively adapt her comments to make them feel more comfortable.

ROSALYNN CARTER

Rosalynn Carter once admitted, "I do pray before I stand up in front of an audience..." Early in her public career, Mrs. Carter was so apprehensive about facing audiences that she became physically ill. Her husband suggested that she jot down a few key words or phrases to remind her of what she wanted to say and then "... just get up and talk about them." Over time, Rosalynn's experience at the podium helped her to relax and become adept at delivery.

In fact, she was a polished speaker by the time she arrived in the White House. Mary Finch Hoyt, Mrs. Carter's Press Secretary, also served as her main speechwriter. Her speeches were a combination of the First Lady's ideas and phrasing with background material prepared for her by her staff and contributions from Hoyt and other speechwriters. Occasionally, but not often, entire speeches were drafted for Mrs. Carter and she made a few changes prior to presentation. One critic observed that she spoke more effectively when her comments were extemporaneous and that she was at her best when speaking about her husband and the goals of his presidency.

The First Lady's speeches lacked humor, quotes, and anecdotes. Yet, Mrs. Carter had good instincts as a speaker. According to Hoyt, "She has a great ability to simplify and to speak in a way that she is comfortable with and does seek to reach her audience." Mrs. Carter gave approximately five hundred speeches. Many presentations were simply brief remarks or comments that were ceremonial in nature, but the sheer volume is nonetheless impressive. A majority of her longer speeches dealt with her White House project, mental health.

HILLARY RODHAM CLINTON

Mrs. Clinton comes closest to rivaling Eleanor Roosevelt as a speaker and communicator. When the future Clinton Library compiles Mrs. Clinton's speeches, they are likely to number from 900-1200, independent of her Senate campaign and election discourse. Like Mrs. Roosevelt, Mrs. Clinton was able to keep her discourse open, lively, and sympathetic.

Mrs. Clinton was comfortable at the podium. She occasionally relied on a speech text for a particularly important occasion (her speech to the International Women's Conference in Beijing, China is one example), but she excelled at extemporaneous speaking. Observers noted that she invariably tailored the opening remarks of her speeches to fit her audience and then artfully moved into her prepared message. Levity was rarely evident in her discourse, but Mrs. Clinton periodically utilized self-depreciating humor. Unlike some of her predecessors, she used language precisely and often spoke about policy and political matters with an ability to think rapidly and construct arguments supported by statistics.

In addition to her speeches, Mrs. Clinton wrote a weekly newspaper column "Talking it Over," which commenced publication in March 1995. She also authored two books while serving in the White House. *It Takes a Village* (1996) presented a serious discussion of ways in which to raise responsible and caring children, and *An Invitation to the White House: At Home with History* (2000) looked at the cultural and political importance of the Executive Mansion as it celebrated its 200th anniversary.

LESSONS LEARNED

It is possible to combine all three approaches to public discourse and communication philosophies. No one approach is best and no one approach is worst. Although today, the public and press demand an accessible and public First Lady. Nancy Reagan's tenure as First Lady is interesting in that it spanned all three communication styles presented in this essay. At the beginning of her husband's Presidency, her approach could be classified as a ceremonial presence. After the attempt on President Reagan's life and criticism of her, she developed an interest in anti-drug use initiatives and began speaking to groups about her concern. Later, she entered a period of great rhetorical activity when she traveled across the country supporting her "Just Say No" project. Mrs. Reagan's speeches numbered in the hundreds and she was reticent, yet enthusiastic, when appealing to listeners. She also seemed to feel more confident with a prepared manuscript, her preferred approach to speaking.

The First Lady of the United States has one of the most influential podiums in the world at her disposal. Some have chosen to ignore it or make only limited use of it. Future First Ladies are likely to feel greater media and public pressure to assume a more visible and committed communication presence. The pressure will translate into more speeches and remarks, as the American public will want to know even more about their First Lady. Although many First Ladies were apprehensive about public speaking at first, most became quite proficient and wisely used the services of speechwriters along with investing hard work and practice into honing their technique. Most also focused considerable discourse on special projects, which provide a vehicle for addressing a wide audience, gaining political support for not only the project, but the First Couple as well, and approaching a variety of other issues. The trends in discourse set by the First Ladies of the twentieth century will continue and their experiences should still guide future First Ladies.

Chapter 8

PUBLIC OPINION AND THE FIRST LADIES

Barbara C. Burrell

OVERVIEW

Polling about the public's impressions of presidential candidates' wives and the First Lady has both an historical record and a contemporary emphasis. For instance, prior to 1992 when Hillary Rodham Clinton created a stir for campaigning on behalf of her husband's presidential bid, wives of presidential contenders were seldom the focus of public opinion surveys. Only one previous poll was taken: In October 1988, an NBC News poll asked a sample of likely voters about their opinions of Barbara Bush and Kitty Dukakis. In that poll, 48 percent had a favorable opinion of Barbara Bush, 11 percent of responses were unfavorable, and 41 percent were unsure. Kitty Dukakis was viewed favorably by 42 percent, unfavorably by 11 percent, and 47 percent were unsure of their opinion of her.

More recently, in the presidential election of 2000, national polling organizations surveyed the American public a total of ten times regarding their favorable and unfavorable impressions of Tipper Gore. Seven times they asked the public about their impressions of Laura Bush. On one occasion pollsters asked a national sample: if they were allowed to cast a separate ballot for First Lady, for whom would they vote. Thirty-two percent said Tipper Gore and 30 percent said Laura Bush. So too were prospective First Ladies' popularity measured.

Over the course of the campaign, Tipper Gore's favorable ratings varied across the polls from 39 percent to 63 percent (the latter at the time of the Democratic national convention). Laura Bush's favorable ratings varied from 14 percent to 49 percent (at the time of the Republican national convention). Only a very small percent – less than ten percent – viewed Laura Bush unfavorably and less then 20 percent viewed Tipper Gore unfavorably. But large percentages of the voters did not have an opinion of either of these potential First Ladies during the campaign.

First Ladies have tended to be popular during their tenure. To the extent that we have had public opinion polls to measure how much Americans like their First Lady, they show a public supportive of these women, even those who have been outspoken and actively engaged in their spouse's administration. Overall, the public has been much more likely to be favorably impressed than not with the individuals who have held this position and to approve of the job they were doing.

POPULAR SPOUSES

"Mrs. Roosevelt More Popular Than President, Survey Finds" ran the headline in *The Washington Post*. In what was probably the first national survey of public opinion of a First Lady, the Gallup Poll in 1939 asked a national sample *"Do you approve of the way Mrs. Roosevelt has conducted herself as "First Lady"?* Sixty-seven percent said "yes," and 33 percent responded "no." Eighty-one percent of Democrats and 43 percent of Republicans approved of Mrs. Roosevelt and women were more supportive than men – 73 percent to 62 percent approving. In the same survey, Franklin Roosevelt received a 58 percent approval rating as President.

After this 1939 inquiry, Gallup did not again ask the public about their opinions of the First Lady in a national poll until Jacqueline Kennedy entered the White House in 1961. In a Gallup Poll in June 1961, 59 percent of the public expressed a favorable opinion of Jacqueline Kennedy, while 13 percent had an unfavorable impression, 6 percent said they had a mixed impression, and 22 percent had no opinion. These surveys are the only national polls available regarding First Ladies prior to the Nixon administration. In 1969, after she had been in the White House for six months, Gallup asked a national sample *"Do you approve or disapprove of the way Mrs. Richard (Pat) Nixon is handling her role as "First Lady?"* Fifty-four percent of the people said they approved of the job she was doing as First Lady, only 6 percent disapproved, and 40 percent said they had no opinion. Responding to a Harris Poll in 1971, 55 percent said they had a "great deal" of respect for Mrs. Nixon, 34 percent said they respected her "somewhat," 9 percent said "not at all," and 2 percent said they were not sure.

Given a card with boxes going from the highest position of + 5 for a person "liked very much" to the lowest position of – 5 for a person "disliked very much," 28 percent rated Mrs. Nixon at +5. Fourteen percent rated her at -1 or lower. In the same rating scheme in 1976, Betty Ford received a +5 from 13 percent of the population, and -1 or lower by 20 percent of the national sample. She was viewed positively by 71 percent of the people, while 24 percent had a negative opinion in the only national poll available from the Ford administration. No early readings are available on the public's impression of Rosalynn Carter. But in 1979 she obtained a 55 percent favorable and 33 percent unfavorable response from the public, and during the 1980 campaign she received a 46 percent favorable, and a 9 percent unfavorable rating, while 37 percent said they did not know enough to respond, and eight percent were undecided.

Nancy Reagan began her service in the White House with a 28 percent favorable rating and 10 percent unfavorable rating, with 57 percent stating they did not know enough about her to have an opinion, and five percent had no opinion, according to a CBS/*New York Times* poll. However, she became quite popular during her time in the White House, beginning only months into her First Ladyship. In November 1981, 51 percent responding to an ABC/*Washington Post* poll said they had a favorable impression of Nancy Reagan, 23 percent were unfavorable, and 26 percent either did not know or had no opinion. Yet, sixty-two percent agreed with a Gallup Poll question in December 1981, that she *"puts too much emphasis on style and elegance during a time of federal budget cuts and economic hardships,"* while 30 percent said they were *"pleased with Nancy Reagan because they feel she has brought more style and elegance to the White House."* In the same poll, 61 percent thought she was less sympathetic to the problems of the poor and underprivileged when compared to other First Ladies, 16 percent thought she was more sympathetic, 9 percent selected "the same," and 14 percent said that they did not know. Throughout most of the remainder of the Reagan administration, Nancy Reagan was viewed favorably by over 60 percent of the public, and occasionally the polls reached a 70 percent positive rating. But her popularity declined by the end of her husband's second term with a bare majority expressing approval of the First Lady and about three in ten saying they disapproved.

When Barbara Bush entered the White House in January 1989, 34 percent of the public had a favorable opinion of her, only 3 percent were unfavorable, while the remainder were undecided or had not heard enough to give an opinion. After being in the White House for six months, she received an "excellent" or "pretty good" job rating from 66 percent of the public, while 28 percent rated her as doing an only fair or poor job. By the 1992 campaign, Barbara Bush was considered a great asset, obtaining an 85 percent favorable rating in an August 1992 poll, while only 9 percent were unfavorable. She remained popular with unfavorable ratings staying consistently below 20 percent.

While there were public opinion polls conducted on Barbara Bush at the beginning of the Bush administration and during the campaign of 1992, during the interim, however, she was not a subject of national polls. Presumably her approval was not considered newsworthy because of the noncontroversial nature of her First Ladyship. There was little to dislike about Barbara Bush or to disagree with in her role as First Lady. The people's views of her were a poll item throughout the 1992 campaign, however. It appears that these poll questions were a reaction to the Hillary Clinton phenomenon, because polls employed a comparative perspective. Barbara Bush, based on poll ratings, was the most popular First Lady in recent times while Nancy Reagan became the least popular up until Hillary Rodham Clinton's tenure in the White House.

Hillary Rodham Clinton, too, began her tenure as a popular First Lady, 67 percent had a favorable opinion of her in a January 1993 Gallup Poll, which was at the time of the first Clinton inauguration, and 20 percent expressed an unfavorable opinion. A number of public opinion surveys in the states during the first year of the Clinton administration highlighted her high approval ratings. The low points in Hillary Rodham Clinton's connection with the American public came in mid 1994 and early 1996, both periods in which she was called to account for any role she might have played in the Whitewater affair. During this time there was a near equal split between positive and negative ratings. By the end of 1998, Hillary Rodham Clinton had achieved the same high level of favorability that she enjoyed during the 1993 inauguration. Polls taken toward the end of her tenure indicated a level of popularity, with a Gallup Poll in December 1998 giving her a 67 percent favorable rating.

EXPECTATIONS OF THE FIRST LADY

Public opinion polls have shown that the American public has one set of expectations for a First Lady in the abstract – a set that stresses more traditional activities – but at the same time, has been favorably impressed with more activist First Ladies. Accordingly, the public has accepted a public policy advisory role in general, as long as the person performing that role appears to be successful. Historically, the one systematic public opinion poll taken during the Roosevelt administration (described above) showed Eleanor Roosevelt to be a very popular First Lady. Other examples included Rosalynn Carter's controversial trip to confer with Latin American heads of state in 1977, which was generally met with approval upon her return, and overall the public applauded Betty Ford's outspokenness on issues and contemporary concerns.

There is much we do not know about public opinion on the First Ladies. Prior to Hillary Rodham Clinton's tenure in the White House, there were only a few systematic measures of what role or roles Americans prefer their First Ladies perform. Nor has the public ever been asked whether we should even have a First Lady. However, a few surveys in the late 1980s did explore aspects of this issue. In 1987, *USA TODAY* commissioned a national poll that asked *"In the past, some First Ladies have been more active than others in their husband's administration. Generally speaking, which do you think is the most important for a presidential spouse? Should the spouse: be involved in important administration decisions, support a national program, serve as a hostess of social events, stay in the background?"* Following are the responses: 15% – active in important administration decisions; 32% – support a national program; 29% – be a hostess for social events; 18% – stay in the background.

At the time Hillary Rodham Clinton was about to become First Lady, 37 percent of a national sample queried by *U.S. News & World Report* favored her sitting in on cabinet meetings; 34 percent thought she should be a major adviser on appointments and policy; 70 percent favored her being a traditional First Lady; 90 percent thought she should be an advocate for policies and programs to benefit children; and 71 percent favored her testifying before Congress on issues that concern her.

Although they may have opted for a traditional First Lady when asked about that role in the abstract, the little polling evidence available indicates that Americans have actually tended to approve when First Ladies have taken on a task as a public policy assistant to the President. The popularity of Eleanor Roosevelt supports this idea (but we should not forget that she was also a very controversial figure and had her enemies), and reactions to activities of Rosalynn Carter and Hillary Rodham Clinton further illustrate this point.

In 1977, President Jimmy Carter sent his wife Rosalynn as his representative on a tour of Latin American countries to meet with their heads of state. This presidential action created a great deal of controversy in its planning stages. After her return from Latin American, the Roper Organization asked a national sample of American adults two questions about their views on her trip. First, Roper asked the public how they would evaluate the job she had done: *"Regardless of how you feel about what the role of a First Lady should be, is it your impression that on her tour of Latin America, Rosalynn Carter did an excellent job as a representative of the Untied States, a good job, not too good a job or a poor job?"* Seventeen percent gave her an excellent rating and 51 percent said she had done a good job, while 9 percent said it was not too good of a job and 3 percent said she had done a poor job. Second, Roper wanted to know if this is a role the First Lady should play. Fifty-five percent responded that she should undertake such a role and 33 percent said she should not. Thus, although she did not again travel in such a capacity during her husband's administration, Rosalynn Carter won much more approval than disapproval from the public for her venture.

When Hillary Rodham Clinton was first appointed as head of the Health Care Task Force, six out of ten Americans either approved, supported, or thought it was appropriate for the President to appoint her to this position. Support for her leadership on this issue fell in 1994, however, as the Clintons' faltered in trying to win approval for their health care initiative. Had they been at all successful in creating some aspect of a health care reform program, perceptions of the presidential spouse being involved in the presidential advisory system would be very different today.

Another aspect of the First Lady's role is the issue of a spouse having her own career outside of the White House. The option was first presented to the public in a 1988 *Ladies Home Journal* poll. Respondents were asked *"Suppose we were to elect a President whose wife has an independent career. Do you think she should continue to work at her full-time job, or give up her career and devote full time to her duties as First Lady?"* A plurality opted for being a full-time First Lady (49 percent), while 41 percent thought she should continue to work at a career. In 1996, the *Washington Post* asked a national sample *"Do you think it is a good idea or a bad idea for the wife of the President of the Untied States to hold a full-time job in addition to her duties as First Lady?"* Forty-five percent believed it was a good idea and 38 percent thought it was a bad idea. When asked in the 1996 election campaign whether Elizabeth Dole should resume her job as president of the American Red Cross should Bob Dole be elected president, 75 percent of a national sample said Ayes," while only 20 percent said "no." Thus, we have an ambivalent public concerning their perspectives on what the role of the First Lady should be, how active she should be in her husband's administration, and whether she should pursue her own career; but overall Americans are supportive of their First Lady.

Chapter 9

SPECIAL PROJECTS OF FIRST LADIES

Carl Sferrazza Anthony

OVERVIEW

The notion that a First Lady has had a "special project" only since Jacqueline Kennedy's restoration of the White House is an error often repeated. In fact, going as far back as Martha Washington's tenure one finds evidence of First Ladies being identified with a specific cause, whether national or local in scope, whether a full-fledged policy-related agenda or simply a charitable effort.

Consideration of past special projects highlights several important points about the special projects of a First Lady: the project will almost always rapidly become political in nature, despite efforts to keep it from being so; the project will often be the most defining aspect of a First Lady's agenda and period of service; projects need not require the machinery of federal government to be successful; and the project can be enormously beneficial to the intended constituency, but it can also benefit both the First Lady and President.

A HISTORY OF SPECIAL PROJECTS

Martha Washington, as the wife of the General of the American troops during the Revolution, was well known and beloved by those who fought for independence. When she became First Lady, it was to her, personally, that many veterans hard on their luck came for financial assistance. And she responded by aiding them in an entirely informal way, becoming well known for her support of veterans. Dolley Madison, when approached by her friend Marcia Van Ness, agreed to lend her prestige as First Lady to fundraising efforts for the first all-girl's orphanage in Washington, D.C. Again, it was an informal appeal and an informal effort from a First Lady, and not part of any larger "agenda." In this respect, the social "projects" of early First Ladies resembled the sort of charity effort often organized by society women. Likewise, Mary Lincoln's support of a local Washington branch of the "Contraband Relief Society," a relief agency for education, housing, and employment for former slaves, most certainly came through the influence of her seamstress and friend, Elizabeth Keckley, a former slave herself. Mrs. Lincoln was an avid abolitionist as First Lady and, along with her association with Keckley, she was publicly ridiculed on occasion for supporting such a controversial and public cause.

In the post-Civil War era, more upper-middle-class women took a public role in community and civic affairs and this was reflected in the charity efforts of, for example, Lucy Hayes on behalf of Native Americans, orphans, and Civil War veterans. However, despite Mrs. Hayes's personal commitment to alcohol abstinence and the banning of spirits being served in the White House, and the fact that she was the first college graduate to become First Lady, she steadfastly refused to align herself with invitations to involve herself in larger public efforts pertaining to banning alcohol and promoting women's education. For instance, she turned down the Women's Christian Temperance Union as well as many individual pleas for her to use her position to encourage women to seek higher education. What is interesting and ironic is that she is almost exclusively thought of today as a pioneer leader for temperance and women's education. Her refusal stemmed not from her disinterest – on the contrary, she felt strongly about the issues – but rather she feared that she would be used for political purposes.

A similar example can be seen with Caroline Harrison, who is remembered as a First Lady who assumed a special projects-type focus on women because she accepted the presidency-generalship of the newly-formed Daughters of the American Revolution in 1889 and pushed for the enrollment of women students at Johns Hopkins Medical School. In fact, her role in both endeavors was limited. She did help the DAR form as a politically-cohesive organization of largely working women (who were excluded from the original Sons of the American Revolution) by giving a remarkable speech to the founders, and she lent her name to Hopkins fundraisers. Yet in neither case, however, were the "projects" part of a conscious agenda that occupied much of her time. Nevertheless, in both situations, Lucy Hayes is associated with temperance and Caroline Harrison with the DAR.

Helen Taft's effort to create West Potomac Park was the first First Lady project to involve the federal government, in this case the Army Corps of Engineers. Mrs. Taft managed to carry out her vision of a park with bandstand, thousands of Japanese cherry blossom trees, and a tidal basin in what had been a swamp through the intercession and cooperation of government officials thanks to the First Lady. The project dovetailed with a larger project to improve and landscape the national capital area. Mrs. Taft's immediate successor, Ellen Wilson, undertook a specific project which became the first to involve direct federal legislation. The Alley Dwellings Act of 1914 was prompted by the First Lady's determination to rid the city of its unsanitary and unsightly housing in alleys around the U.S. Capitol Building. Although well-intended, there was a considerable resentment of it within the African-American community. It was well and good to determine to keep the poor from living in such deplorable conditions, but no provisions had been made for the resulting displacement. Mrs. Wilson's efforts were made more difficult because of negative feelings from her corresponding efforts to improve working conditions in the federal departments (more lighting, lunchrooms, and sanitary facilities) for the racially-mixed government workers. Moreover "Jim Crow" segregation of federal workers occurred simultaneously and Ellen Wilson's "project" has often been incorrectly blamed for its instigation. Curiously, however, there was an utter lack of criticism in the press of the First Lady for such public lobbying on behalf of "my bill" as she called the pending legislation.

Florence Harding embraced a national constituency in her announced plan to look after the concerns of wounded and disabled veterans of World War I. Her efforts were considerable, practical in nature, and broadly based, ranging from personally maintaining case files on individuals in federal veterans hospitals to meeting regularly with officials including the chief of the newly created U.S. Veteran's Bureau – whose appointment she was known to have played a part in. Such efforts, conducted in private, resulted in improved medical care for the thousands of often woefully neglected veterans. Government agencies began to follow through on complaints about the poorly functioning bureau. Publicly, however, the First Lady's activities were played out quite differently. In her "adoption" of local veterans wards, Harding was photographed and reported on as she hosted thousands of the disabled veterans at large White House garden parties. The press covered her when she went to distribute candy, flowers, and cigarettes in the wards, when she bought occupational therapy wares, and when she promoted awareness of the issue, largely through non-controversial and apolitical acts. Mrs. Harding was successful in her effort to spur similar "adoptions" around the country by women and civic organizations. Thus, a First Lady's project was simultaneously propelled on two levels: public and private; non-political and political. Florence Harding became identified as a positive national "spokesperson" for the cause. This helped her in other ways; interestingly, even though she was involved in some of the machinations of the Veteran's Bureau she was never associated in the public mind with the terrible scandals later engulfing it.

Mrs. Harding's two immediate successors are also interesting examples of the gap between reality and perception regarding a First Lady's actions. Grace Coolidge, a teacher of the deaf and board member of the Clarke School for the Deaf, created no project or public effort around such issues as deaf education, mainstreaming the deaf, or audio-training of the deaf (the particular method taught at Clarke) – other than to meet and be photographed with Helen Keller and raise funds for Clarke. Nevertheless, the constant mention of her former profession in press profiles closely associated the deaf as a "cause" for her, resulting in increased public awareness of deaf issues. Another example can be seen in Lou Hoover's First Ladyship, although with the opposite effect. Mrs. Hoover, as president of the Girl Scouts, used the group as well as other organizations to support voluntary relief efforts during the Great Depression. Aiding the needy was one of her passions and something she practiced by personal example. Despite this – and her regular radio broadcasts to various groups on the Depression – she could not shake the image of being a sort of national scout leader and little more. However, given the period in history, neither woman made any public relations effort to define their activities.

RESHAPING THE MODERN FIRST LADY PROJECT

Eleanor Roosevelt shattered and then reshaped the entire concept of a First Lady's project by assuming many projects during her twelve-year tenure, and highly political ones at that. Another difference was the constant press coverage those projects and the issues behind them generated. Reporters followed her every move, she wrote newspaper and magazine columns, and gave a weekly radio show. It was under the rather vaguely defined concept of "the disadvantaged" that she undertook numerous projects. These projects, particularly those that involved official programs of the New Deal (such as the experimental West Virginia community development project "Arthurdale," the Civilian Conversation Corps, and the WPA), were intended to benefit men as well as women, adults as well as children, whites as well as blacks. Yet while adult male farmers, union workers, and coal miners were as much the constituency she sought to help, it was with women and African-Americans that she was most closely associated with in the public mind. Undoubtedly, this was because she pushed for more equitable standards and promoted public welfare, considered radical notions coming from a First Lady. Eleanor Roosevelt's individual "projects" however, were never the specific focus of her First Ladyship. Her priorities shifted as those of the nation did. While she always kept the long-term goals of equal rights in mind, her particular efforts to change or initiate legislation as a way of achieving those goals was constantly evolving.

The direct political content and the breadth of Eleanor Roosevelt's work was intimidating to her two immediate successors, Bess Truman and Mamie Eisenhower. Their own experiences and ambitions were entirely different from Mrs. Roosevelt's, and consequently neither assumed particular special projects on behalf of controversial or political issues. In the traditional context of wife and hostess, Bess Truman did lead the public relations effort to save the four original walls of the White House when plans proposed destroying and rebuilding it rather than renovating it. After President Eisenhower's 1955 heart attack, his wife did become national honorary char and local Washington chair of the American Heart Association and its annual fundraising drives. Still, she was not associated with the effort – she was well into her first term before she worked with the organization and her identity had already become fixed as a "housewife" with no real interest in public or civic affairs. Like First Ladies Roosevelt, Hoover, Coolidge, and wives going back to Cleveland, however, Bess Truman and Mamie Eisenhower did lend their names as honorary chairs to numerous charity chairmanships and causes.

Jackie Kennedy cut back on charity work but, during the transition period, she determined to target the arts and humanities as her "cause," prompted by her personal interests and training. Developing a network of expert antiquarians, as well as leading contemporary arts figures, she continually sought causes and projects related to these issues – while rejecting other worthy causes that were errant from her agenda. She celebrated American history, art, and talent, and was privately influential in the creation of the post of the first Arts Advisor and Advisory Council to the President, as well as the National Endowment of Arts and Humanities, as arm of the government to fund both established and experimental arts and humanities projects. For the jewel of her projects – her planned White House historical restoration – she helped create a federal law permitting the mansion to accept public gifts as federal property and then established an historical association to oversee such efforts and gifts. She successfully sought bi-partisan support for her work, which helped mitigate real political attacks. In the end, however, it was her televised tour of some of the restored White House rooms which captured the public imagination and associated her with the restoration. Not until two decades later did she reveal her role in arts policy and her own administering of her projects.

Mrs. Kennedy's decision to focus her public efforts on local Washington projects was successfully copied by her successor, Lady Bird Johnson. Mrs. Johnson helped in the creation of Head Start and gently but persistently espoused the good of the 1964 Civil Rights Act. But it was a form of urban, suburban, and rural environmental protection and nature restoration, dubbed "beautification" by her astute public relations director and press secretary, Liz

Carpenter, with which this First Lady became permanently associated. Making a conscious decision to first create a "Committee for a More Beautiful National Capital," Mrs. Johnson followed the successful model of starting in her own "neighborhood," thus setting a national example to spur regional beautification groups. Tremendous and careful effort went into publicizing each of her beautification activities and building a wide spectrum of support, from garden clubs to utility companies. Her efforts were also dovetailed with other popular national campaigns such as "Don't Be a Litterbug and Keep America Beautiful. Finally, there was a federal component. Whenever the Johnson administration sought passage of environmental legislation, the First Lady became its public advocate and spokesperson. Her "own legislation," the 1965 Highways Beautification Act, passed through Congress only by enormous pressure from the administration in her name.

Pat Nixon announced that she would have no particular "project" and although she collected more antiquities for the White House and also led efforts to promote volunteerism – which fit into the Nixon administration's efforts to call upon the private sector to support social programs – her identity was not tied to a particular project. When she became First Lady, Betty Ford supported dance and the arts. Later she supported "women's issues," which evolved from her personal trial of a breast cancer mastectomy and her willingness to publicly discuss it. She immediately became a point person on this and other women's issues. Her advocacy of the Equal Rights Amendment intensified her association with women's issues, and she lobbied aggressively for its passage. Mrs. Ford's support for ERA produced attacks from those in her husband's own party who opposed the legislation. Although ERA did not pass, her "projects" are considered successful in that she brought forward unprecedented attention to breast cancer awareness and a new type of honest and political voice for a First Lady in a modern world dealing with real modern problems. Her tenure is a watershed in this regard. All her successors would feel the need to accomplish more than public relations with their projects.

Rosalynn Carter pledged during the 1976 campaign that she would see to it that the federal government reviewed and changed its mental health policy. Once in office, she made good on her pledge when she was made honorary chair of the President's Commission on Mental Health. She headed numerous fact-finding sub-committees, testified before Congress, and presented a national report with recommendations for change within the federal system. Indeed, the Mental Health Systems Act of 1980 was passed largely because of her influence and persistence. Not surprisingly, the First Lady was criticized for her political advocacy, yet there were few critics of the actual achievement. As was the case with other First Ladies, although she worked with a similar intensity for ERA passage, senior citizens rights, human rights, and global relief, Mrs. Carter remained indelibly identified with mental health legislation and awareness.

"Awareness" was the byword for both Nancy Reagan's drug prevention program and Barbara Bush's literacy projects. Neither woman wanted to be thrust into an overtly political situation because of their projects. Neither sought passage of federal law or funding and both resisted having their projects associated with pending legislation on those issues. Yet, they were extraordinarily successful not only in raising public awareness of their issues, but also in creating positive public images of themselves. Barbara Bush, for example, was able to gently address such controversial issues as teenage pregnancy, unwed motherhood, homelessness, AIDS, and crime with the statistical evidence that illiteracy played some part in all those ills. Mrs. Bush's project also had teeth: while First Lady she formed her own private foundation as a fundraising vehicle for regional and local literacy projects. It may not have mitigated the criticism of those who called for more direct federal action, but it helped symbolize a presidency that was not inattentive to those issues. Nancy Reagan's project also presents interesting lessons: begun as a way of preventing young children from first experimenting with drugs, by the middle of her tenure she was publicly advocating the administration's Anti-drug Abuse Act of 1986 and by the end of her tenure she was addressing the United Nations General Assembly on international drug trafficking and interdiction law. The project also helped minimize criticism of her. Perhaps as a result, she willingly accepted the debate and criticism which increasingly came with her role in such a controversial project and ultimately managed a highly political issue from backfiring on her.

Hillary Clinton was more overtly involved in projects that involved legislation and policy advocacy than all of her predecessors combined. Whether it was new FDA guidelines for labeling children's medicine, international enterprise loans for women, proposing the creation of a Justice Department Bureau for Domestic Abuse, hearings on the Gulf War Syndrome, increased research funding for prostate and breast cancer, epilepsy, and asthma, championing the Children's Health Insurance Program, or the drafting and passage of the 1997 Safe Families and Adoption Act, her role was extensive and political. Mrs. Clinton's "project" was the broad-based support of women's and children's issues, but her political involvement extended to all facets of her husband's administration as his political advisor. It is too soon to tell whether the public will absorb the fact that, for example, many of her efforts relied largely on the private sector rather than the federal government, even though her public image would seem to suggest otherwise. That she headed the administration's "failed" Health Care Reform Act effort still looms large in the public memory. Part of the dilemma was that she and her staff consciously decided to focus their limited resources on accomplishing her numerous and growing plate of projects and problems rather than seeking to promote information on what had already been accomplished or to highlight a single issue.

LESSONS LEARNED

Regardless of the specifics of the project, lessons are apparent from the experiences of previous First Ladies: (1) the First Lady will have less public skepticism about her genuine interest in her project if it is something she has already been working on; (2) projects will inevitably have some political aspect or will be vulnerable to some form of political manipulation from either within or outside the administration; (3) there will be some network of smaller advocacy groups around the country eager and willing to support the First Lady's project; (4) the First Lady must define the goals, parameters, and boundaries of her "projects," not only for public relations but as a guide for herself in choosing what to support and not support; (5) dovetailing her project into the larger agenda of the administration will prove wise, considering the support she will receive from the President, and to some extent, Congress; (6) such a linkage to the President's agenda might also serve to promote the President's agenda and popularity; (7) no matter the nature of a First Lady's project, she will inevitably be criticized for some aspect of it.

Chapter 10

LIFE IN THE WHITE HOUSE: CHALLENGES, BURDENS, RESPONSIBILITIES

Tabitha Alissa Warters

INTRODUCTION

For most first families residing in the White House is both a privilege and a burden. Susan Ford once referred to her life in the executive mansion as a "fairy tale," and it can be. Yet, as Susan Ford also learned, life under the constant glare of the public eye carries its own responsibilities — ones that can challenge everyday activities and place stress upon family life. In addition to the public burdens and responsibilities, First Ladies also have the added accountability of maintaining the White House and planning all social functions, such as State dinners. The following is an essay in three parts, which elaborates upon these challenges and responsibilities. The purpose of the first section is to alert first family members, including First Ladies and presidential children, to the changes that will take place in their lives upon entering the White House. It examines public expectations, media scrutiny, and ways of upholding family life. Second is a discussion on the responsibilities First Ladies have toward maintaining and preserving the President's House. Finally, there is a brief analysis of the role of First Lady as the nation's hostess.

CHALLENGES TO BEING THE PRESIDENT'S FAMILY

Upon entering the White House, whether they live in the Executive Mansion or not, presidential families continue to struggle with the initial strains of maintaining a sense of privacy and family with the ever-present media and public attention. This pressure is neither new, nor uncommon. From the inception of the presidency, Americans have been drawn to the presidents' families. Many scholars, such as Betty Boyd Caroli, have speculated that Americans initially reached out to the first family as a substitute for the void as a result of the loss of the royal family after the fought independence from Great Britain.

Early scholars suggested that there is a need for some type of royal family to be present within any form of government. In his 1867 book, *The English Constitution*, Walter Bagehot asserts that all governments have two parts: dignified and efficient. The *dignified* parts of government electrify the population and "preserve" their "reverence." The *efficient* parts of government are the executive and ruling parts. Bagehot points out that in a Constitutional Monarchy, a family on the throne, or the dignified part of government, helps facilitate the efficient parts. Indeed, the royal family forces the leadership to become involved in the "petty life" of the population.

In a similar manner, the American public looks toward the presidential family for the same "dignified" activities. Presidential families in American democracy tend to humanize the Presidents and garner the public's attention as such. For a country without a royal family, it is understandable that the American public seeks out the presidential family as a substitute and this manifests in an intrigue over the everyday life of the American President and his family.

The openness of the American democratic system, especially in terms of its free and open exchange of information through the media, has made it easier to have access to the personal lives of America's chief executive and his family. As Betty Boyd Caroli highlights in her book, *America's First Ladies*, the television age of the 20th and 21st Centuries has created "an illusion of intimacy" between the American public and the president's family.

The constant attention paid to even the minutest details of a president's family life, is the primary challenge to being the spouse, child, or relative of the president. Those who have lived it have labeled the experience in a variety of ways. For instance, Margaret Truman recalled that she felt like public property and lived "under glass" for all to see. Lynda Johnson Robb called the White House a "gilded cage" and President Truman labeled it a "jail." Indeed, the constant clicking of tourist cameras from behind the iron gates of the White House led Jackie Kennedy to declare: "I may abdicate." It is no secret that Jackie Kennedy was averse to the inevitable publicity, especially relating to her two young children. The American public was hungry for even a minor glimpse of the first young children to reside in the White House in over a half century. Not since President Theodore Roosevelt and his rambunctious brood resided in the executive residence had the American public had the benefit of a young family in the White House. The Kennedys filled this void.

However, not all residents of the White House are younger families. Most presidents and First Ladies, upon entering the White House, have already reared their children and have been left them with an "empty nest." Some of the adult offspring of presidents choose to reside in the White House for the experience, with others try to carry on their own family life, careers, and education outside their father's political world. This is not always easy to accomplish. Once a president is inaugurated, and often before, presidential family members become instant celebrities. Even though family members of presidents have always drawn attention, especially after the colorful antics of Alice Roosevelt Longworth, they now face more varied media outlets that did not exist in the early 20th Century. More specifically, family members are now targets of "entertainment" programs, masked as "news." They are also susceptible to the weekly grocery store tabloids whose bottom line is to make money from the images and stories of "celebrities," including presidential family members. These types of "media" are especially interested in the lives of presidential children, as the Clintons and Bushes have clearly learned over the past ten years.

With all of this constant attention, presidential family members need to be very cautious. Susan Ford issued a warning to presidential children at the 1984 National Conference on First Ladies at the Ford Presidential Museum in Grand Rapids, Michigan. She stated that upon entering the White House presidential family members need to be very careful whom they have as friends. She cautioned that old friends have the potential to pull away, while others try to take advantage and only want to be friends because of the connection the presidential child has to the president. With the expansion of tabloid journalism, and their monetary offerings to classmates and friends for information on presidential family members, Susan Ford's warning is even more foreboding today.

What this all implies is that the challenges of being related to the president vary by the age of the family member. This is especially true for the children of presidents. For many presidential children their only complaint was that their Secret Service detail followed too closely or they had to go through a White House operator to talk to their parents. However, for others, such as Chelsea Clinton, they have to deal with photographers following their every move. Thus, for some, their lives do not change much, but for others, (typically children and young adults), the burdens of being related to the president are profoundly felt.

Even though some "friends" and acquaintances may try to take advantage of their connection to a presidential family member, those related to the president must not take advantage either. Many family members in the past have garnered more media and public attention because of actions they took using the name of the president. For instance, Billy Carter's relationship with the Libyan government using his brother's name; Michael Reagan's attempts at retaining military contracts for his company employing his father's name; or Patti Davis' attempts at selling more books by detailing Reagan family secrets. Some may call the media attention irresponsible, but so are actions such as these. The actions of the three above family members attracted notice by the media, but the media does not care about the intricate details or if these actions truly took place with malice. Even the impression of impropriety is enough for a "feeding frenzy" to begin. Therefore, presidential family members need to be extra careful with their friends and business dealings.

Another challenge for first families, and in particular, First Ladies, is the fact that they "live above the store." Unlike many spouses who bring their work home, presidents work at home. This circumstance has actually changed the role of the First Lady because her private home is also the working quarters of the executive branch of the United States government. Therefore, the official duties of First Ladies have increased. Although this arrangement is attractive, difficulties arise for First Ladies because the American public places a series of expectations upon the presidents' spouse, which may be impossible to meet. As historian Lewis Gould elucidates, First Ladies are expected to fill numerous roles with precision and any deviation from the expectations of these roles garners criticism. Gould also highlights that the roles First Ladies are expected to perform change and modify as the expectations of American women as a whole change. Certain activist First Ladies such as Eleanor Roosevelt, were criticized because in the 1930s and 40s, her activism was not an acceptable norm for women in society. Even Betty Ford, Rosalynn Carter and Hillary Clinton were criticized for their activism in the late 20th Century when it had become more acceptable in American society to see more activist women participating in the American political system.

What all of this implies for in-coming First Ladies is that there are actually no defined roles or instruction manual to proceed from. One of the primary reasons for this is that, just as there is for presidents, First Ladies suffer from an "expectations gap." Public expectations are hard to gauge and even harder to meet because of their inconsistencies. For instance, even though it is acceptable in American society to have two career families, many were uncomfortable with Hillary Clinton assuming so much responsibility in her husband's administration in order to execute the promised "co-presidency." Theoretically, the American public is comfortable with working mothers, but because the First Lady is not in an elected position, they feel uncomfortable with her taking on what they consider is too much power. The questions remain: Should a First Lady be more traditional? Should she be more of a career woman? Or, should she be a combination of both? There is no set answer. In fact, circumstances may dictate the behavior of First Ladies. For instance, after the terrorist attacks on September 11, 2001, First Lady Laura Bush took on the role of "comforter-in-chief," a very traditional role, but very welcome during such uncertainty. Therefore, the best advice, because circumstances will dictate behavior, is for First Ladies to just be themselves. As Laura Bush stated when asked which First Lady she would like to emulate, she stated: "I'll just be Laura Bush." This is the healthiest attitude a First Lady can possess. She will never make all critics happy, so she might as well be happy with herself.

In the age of television and the "filming of the presidency," First Ladies also have to live their own lives which includes nurturing a marriage and, at times, raising children. For many American women, maintaining a marriage and raising children are difficult enough tasks, even without the constant attention and public expectations. Therefore, one of the key challenges for First Ladies is how to sustain a healthy family life while still maintaining a demanding public role. Also, as a point of interest, sustaining a healthy family while in the White House is actually important to the public approval of presidents and First Ladies. Beyond the public policy decisions presidents make, the American public is also observing how the president and his family get along. Consequently, as Betty Boyd Caroli, explicates, a "smart" First Lady is one who continues to nurture her family while in the White House.

Many former first family members and First Ladies have made suggestions for how to handle these challenges. Betty Ford suggested that maintaining as normal a home life as possible helps. For the Fords this included having scheduled evening meals with family and friends. The George H.W. Bush family held horseshoe tournaments on the White House lawn, while other first families have used the movie theater and bowling alley within the White House to try and add normalcy to living in such a restricted facility. Even the George W. Bush family began holding tee-ball tournaments on the White House lawn for local Washington, D.C. tee-ball teams. These types of activities are necessary to maintain a "normal" family life. As Harry Truman once said, the best way to survive living in the White House is to "keep your balance." These activities contribute to that challenge.

Even though there are inherent challenges and hardships to being a first family member, as Jack Ford suggests, all of the burdens that are inherent with being a member of the first family are easy to bear when the first family remembers they are helping their husband, father, brother, or uncle lead the country. For many, the first reaction may be to close themselves off from the pressures and many have tried. For instance, Tricia Nixon was reluctant to participate in public events while living at the White House because she wanted to protect her privacy, but realized, as do other presidential family members, that she was given a very limited opportunity to help her father and she must take advantage. The support the first family offers provides the president the strength to fulfill his responsibilities of the highest elected office in the United States. It is also a way to give back to the American public. When examined from this perspective, the burdens and challenges do not seem so hard to bear.

PRESERVING THE WHITE HOUSE

First Ladies not only "live above the store," they also reside in a home that is a national museum. The White House was designated a museum by the American Association of Museums in 1988. Although the original name of the residence was "the President's House," the first family must never forget that it is also the "people's house" and belongs to the American public. This knowledge also brings great responsibility, for every first lady undertakes the role of preservationist of the White House. Indeed, part of the "legacy" of each First Lady is the continued maintenance and upkeep of the White House. As political scientist Robert Watson points out, First Ladies must be amateur architect, interior designer, landscaper, and museum curator. There is no rulebook for this. Instead, each First Lady brings her own unique talents and tastes to bear.

Some First Ladies displayed more interest and dedication to this task than others. In the modern era Eleanor Roosevelt stands out as one First Lady who displayed an almost total lack of concern with the renovation and upkeep of the White House. In contrast, Jackie Kennedy was determined to deliver the White House back to its past grandeur after years of neglect. Structurally, the White House underwent a major overhaul during the Truman administration, but the internal décor had not been restored. Jackie Kennedy took up the mantel to update the appearance of the White House. Along with Lorraine Pearce, a curator at the Smithsonian Institute, Jackie Kennedy collected furnishings and artwork from storerooms, cataloguing all holdings and collecting selections to display in the White House.

Knowing that there would be complaints over cost, Jackie Kennedy raised the money for the restoration by selling White House guidebooks published by the newly founded White House Historical Association. Jackie Kennedy's restoration was the last major renovation, but First Ladies since have made smaller modifications. For instance, Pat Nixon continued Jackie Kennedy's effort to acquire antiques for the White House and Rosalynn Carter was successful in accumulating American paintings. Nancy Reagan undertook a million dollar restoration project, paid for with private donations, which included modernizing the bathrooms, putting in new wall treatments, and replacing the china (for which she garnered criticism). Hillary Clinton also retained private funds to restore the Lincoln Sitting Room and Treaty Room. Therefore, First Ladies do not have to undertake a major restoration project, as did Jackie Kennedy, but are expected to undertake smaller "maintenance" projects, which hold just as much import.

First Ladies need to be warned that no matter what changes are made they will be criticized. This is just part of the territory and another challenge to being First Lady. As historian Betty Boyd Caroli highlights, in the past, if a First Lady restored the White House in a more elegant style, she would be criticized for trying to be royalty. On the other hand, if a First Lady restored the White House more economically, she would be criticized for being cheap and embarrassing the country in front of the world. The idea is to make changes to the "people's house" which reflect the entire nation based on the evolution of American culture.

Therefore, even though there is an expectation for First Ladies to be preservationists, they must be prepared to be criticized for the choices they make.

THE NATION'S HOSTESS

In addition to the preservation of the White House, First Ladies also serve as the nation's hostess and as historian Betty Boyd Caroli elucidates, First Ladies choices in fashion, food, art, and entertainment at White House functions reflect on the entire nation. Early First Ladies quickly realized how politically advantageous mere entertaining can be. As political scientist Robert Watson points out in his book, *The Presidents' Wives*, White House entertaining is as essential to foreign diplomacy and domestic relations as formal talks. The president and First Lady welcome visitors from across the world. Therefore, even in the most private "occasions," entertaining at the White House takes on a political component because these events can be used to build political support for the president. This is accomplished by designing guest lists strategically by inviting "important" guests, entertaining allies, and keeping enemies close.

Entertaining at the White House, whether casual or formal, can help the president influence foreign leaders as well as Congresspersons and the political elite here in the United States. Often, a president's popularity with the American public is tied to the number and variety of people invited and entertained at the White House. As a result, the amount and type of entertainment can affect public perception and approval of presidents, which can in turn influence the level of political capital a president has at his disposal to compromise with Congress or work with foreign leaders. Consequently, entertaining is a personal power available to presidents to use in addition to the formal powers of the office.

Many First Ladies have also used these hostessing opportunities to highlight America. Frequently, through their choices in food, beverage, art, and music, First Ladies have highlighted American culture through entertaining at the White House. Again, this is dependent upon the personal tastes of individual First Ladies.

CONCLUSION

Ever since John Adams and his family moved into the White House in 1800, all first families have faced the same conundrum; how to "live above the store," with the world watching and still have a normal family life? As the above essay highlights, it is not an easy task. Public expectations are high and cameras follow ever movement closely. However, these challenges are overshadowed by the strength and support presidents gain by having their family near. First Ladies have the added responsibility of preserving the White House, as well as entertaining, but these too can be a privilege. Providing the upkeep to the "people's house" is a service to the American public and organizing social events displays the splendor of the executive mansion for the world and helps the president foster friendships.

Chapter 11

THE FIRST LADY AS AN INTERNATIONAL DIPLOMAT

Molly Meijer Wertheimer

One of the most important lessons I learned during my years as First Lady was how dependent the affairs of state and the policies of nations are on the personal relationships among leaders. Even ideologically opposed countries can reach agreements and forge alliances if the leaders know and trust one another.

Hillary Clinton

OVERVIEW

On the day her husband is sworn in as president of the United States, his wife becomes the First Lady, a position with no formal job description yet plenty of precedents set by her predecessors. Nationally, First Ladies play a number of roles, including hostess, social and political partner, surrogate, and advocate. Increasingly, First Ladies are extending these roles into a worldwide arena, where they receive wide coverage in the foreign press. Their celebrity provides them with an international podium by which they can exercise influence beyond our national borders. As the world grows smaller and its people become more interdependent, more and more will First Ladies see the opportunities available to their husbands and themselves of stepping onto this global stage.

From the inception of the nation, First Ladies or their surrogates have influenced foreign relations in different ways. They have entertained at the White House, helping their husbands develop valuable rapport with foreign leaders. Scholars have written about the political dimensions of such social/ceremonial occasions, describing how moments of informal conversation can be interspersed with protocol-governed behavior to build trust in subtle ways. Dolley Madison showed her sensitivity to the English and French ministers when she resolved a protocol conundrum by choosing to sit between them during an inaugural dinner when their countries were at war. Her warmth and kindness must have earned her and her husband the ministers' admiration. In a different way, Pat Nixon built rapport with Premier Chou en Lai when she spoke with him at dinner during the Nixon's historic trip to China.

Reaching for a cigarette case wrapped in tissue paper decorated with panda bears, she told the Premier how much she had always loved them. "I will give you some," he replied. "Cigarettes?" "Pandas." Today, the Chinese pandas are one of the most popular attractions at the National Zoo. They attest to the power of a First Lady to find ways through conversation to build positive diplomatic rapport.

As the presidents' social partner, First Ladies have traveled abroad with their husbands, visiting foreign heads of state. Opportunities for developing friendships with international leaders and their families are an essential part of the trips. Sometimes, first ladies have separate itineraries, spending part of their day visiting venues important to their hosts or pursuing their own agendas. They also travel abroad solo as their husbands' surrogates, performing ceremonial duties such as attending weddings and funerals. At times their solo missions are more substantial. For example, Laura Bush traveled to France 2003, as her husband's surrogate. One of the purposes of her mission was to present a speech recommitting the United States to the United Nations Educational, Scientific and Cultural Organization (UNESCO). Other First Ladies have traveled abroad to promote their own agendas. Hillary Clinton, for example, made many solo trips to promote the rights of women and children worldwide.

First Ladies have also extended the role they play as their husbands' political partners to the international scene. They assume diplomatic support services such as researching newspaper coverage of events, translating foreign manuscripts, decoding confidential documents, and more. When their husbands are required to make tough decisions, they act as sounding boards and provide input on far-reaching foreign policy. Little of this support is documented, but scholars can infer some of it from records kept for other purposes and from biographies and autobiographies.

SOCIAL CEREMONY AND DIPLOMATIC TRUST-BUILDING AT HOME

As the nation's hostess, First Ladies and their surrogates have provided opportunities for developing friendships with diplomatic visitors. Martha Washington's Friday evening levees allowed President Washington and other leaders from the young nation an opportunity to interact with foreign officials. Raised as an aristocrat, she modeled her levees on the customs of English and French drawing rooms, thereby providing foreign leaders with familiar patterns of interaction.

The nation's first great hostess was Dolley Madison, who was as savvy with her foreign visitors as she was with her husband's political colleagues. Well aware of the political importance of social occasions, she created ceremonial forms such as state dinners to impress both foreign leaders and Washington contemporaries with the sophistication of the young nation.

Making the White House a comfortable and fitting place to conduct diplomacy became a natural extension of the First Ladies' duties as hostess. Julia Grant, for example, enjoyed inviting foreign diplomats and Washingtonians to receptions at a redecorated White House. Edith and Teddy Roosevelt also sought to improve the White House by making it suitable for receiving kings, queens, and foreign heads of state. Edith restructured the White House, formalized protocol for social comportment, and began the White House china collection.

Many first ladies have instituted practices to foster witty and meaningful conversation. Lou Hoover gave her guests ample opportunity to talk during dinner by using hand signals to regulate the pace at which waiters served the courses. Jackie Kennedy redesigned how state dinners were staged to maximize social exchange among her guests. Mrs. Kennedy changed the lighting, wall colors, and furnishings. She used round tables that seated eight to ten people and gave great thought when assigning guests to tables. She followed protocol to seat about one-third of the guests; the other two-thirds she seated to promote lively conversation. She kept centerpieces low so they would not interfere with sight lines among her guests.

A recent and notorious attempt to dignify the White House as a place to receive foreign leaders was Nancy Reagan's. She made needed repairs to the White House, for which her successor Barbara Bush praised her highly. What caused controversy, however, was the purchase of new china at a time of economic recession. Mrs. Reagan did not think the White House had enough matched china to make the right impression on foreign guests during state dinners. To accommodate large numbers of guests, place settings from different sets of china had to be mixed and matched. Even though she raised the money privately to pay for the new china, she was criticized in the media for extravagance. In contrast, she regarded the new china as essential to designing a fitting and elegant social environment for building international respect and trust.

Other members of the First Ladies' sorority have expended considerable energy moving the diplomatic venue to different locations, including their homes. Ladybird Johnson, for example, entertained world leaders at the Johnson's ranch in Texas. Using a regional setting, the Johnsons introduced their guests to local customs and served the best of home town foods. Barbara and George Bush entertained similarly at their home in Kennebunkport, Maine. In her autobiography, *A Memoir*, Mrs. Bush recounts many of the foreign guests who were entertained with barbecues, boat rides, and horseshoe games. Writing about her earlier experience as the wife of a U.N. ambassador, she reveals the importance of informal social occasions to diplomats: "At the ambassador's level," she writes, "much of the real work…[was] conducted at these social functions….Your guest list was often composed of people who wanted to meet but couldn't on an official level." Daughter-in-law Laura and son George W. Bush have followed the elder Bushes' lead, bringing world leaders to their ranch in Crawford, Texas, for a taste of Tex-Mex cuisine in a relaxed environment. Visits with the Blairs, for example, gave the British prime minister and U.S. president an appropriate setting in which to get to know each other on a personal level, to build trust, and to launch a joint venture—removing Saddam Hussein, former head of Iraq, from power. These visits also gave Laura Bush and Cherie Blair time to discover a common interest in finding a cure for breast cancer.

Independent relationships between the wives of presidents and foreign heads of state have led to other trust-building outcomes. When Barbara Bush took Raisa Gorbachev to Wellesley College to talk to the graduating seniors, newspapers reported their joint venture as a symbolic summit. Media footage of these two women forging a friendship showed U.S. and international audiences how much women leaders can do to foster global cooperation.

INFLUENCE ON FOREIGN POLICY

As their husband's political partners, first ladies have served as sounding boards, trusted advisors, and sources of ideas for diplomatic decision-making. Martha Washington early set the precedent as her husband's helpmate when he entrusted her with military secrets during the Revolutionary War. She copied important correspondence, scavenged newspapers for articles of use to him, and discussed issues with statesmen and military leaders from home and abroad.

Although temperamentally different from Lady Washington, Abigail Adams was every bit as involved in foreign affairs. Even before her husband was elected president, he had sent her his private journal, containing classified observations made during his tenure as an ambassador. Her son John Quincy, when minister to Holland, also sent her private correspondence that she leaked to the press, carefully underlining passages she wanted emphasized. When her husband was president, Abigail supported the Alien and Sedition Act, making comments that sound apropos to the Patriot Act: "In times like the present," she writes, "a more careful and attentive watch ought to be kept over the foreigners. This will be done if the Alien Bill passes without being curtailed and clipt until it is made useless."

Woodrow Wilson's first wife, Ellen, and his second wife, Edith, both exemplify the close political partnership presidents and first ladies can have. Early in her husband's career, Ellen Wilson acted as her husband's research assistant, translating thick tomes from German. She continued to help her husband after his election; for example, when the United States almost went to war with Mexico in 1914, Ellen read articles and books on Mexican history to provide background material on key issues. Woodrow sent her letters containing confidential information, and they reveal the candid nature of their collaboration. When Ellen Wilson died after seventeen months as First Lady, President Wilson lost a close confidante. After meeting and falling in love with Edith Bolling Galt, he solicited her help even before they were married. After listening to the draft of a speech in response to the Germans who had just sunk the Lusitania, Edith advised the president to change the tone of the speech. Once they were married, she became his cryptographer, decoding secret war messages between her husband and high ranking U.S. officials stationed in Europe. When the war was over, she accompanied him to Europe where he negotiated a peace treaty. Years later, because of Franklin Roosevelt's physical condition, another First Lady, Eleanor Roosevelt, served as her husband's eyes and ears in Europe.

First Ladies have acted as sounding boards on foreign policy, helping their husbands make tough decisions. Elizabeth Monroe, for example, influenced her husband's Monroe Doctrine, a document warning Europeans against further colonization in the Americas; she also played a part during her husband's negotiations with Spain for the purchase of Florida. Similarly, Sarah Polk influenced her husband's policy of Manifest Destiny, encouraging him to go to war to secure territory in the Southwest and West. During the war with Mexico, she helped by studying issues and serving as an advisor. Even invalid Ida McKinley influenced her husband's policy in the Philippines. Her contacts in the Presbyterian Church encouraged him to educate and Christianize the native islanders, before allowing them to govern themselves. Years later, Florence Harding assisted her husband in editing a speech to say unequivocally that he would not support the League of Nations.

First Ladies have helped their husbands by contributing candid opinions during times of war. Bess Truman, for example, was her husband Harry's full political partner, albeit behind-the-scenes. He told Marianne Means that he consulted Bess about every decision he had ever made, including the United States' involvement in Korea, the use of the atomic bomb, and the initiation of the Marshall Plan: "I discussed all of them with her," he said, "Why not?...Her judgment was always good." Similarly, John Kennedy must have respected First Lady Jackie Kennedy's opinion, for she was part of his inner circle of advisors during the Cuban Missile Crises.

Key diplomatic meetings have occurred because of suggestions made by First Ladies. Rosalynn Carter, for example, told interviewer Margaret Truman that the idea for a meeting between Israel's Prime Minister Menachim Begin and Egypt's President Anwar Sadat was hers. Her husband agreed with the idea, and when it came time to write a prayer calling for a successful meeting, she helped him and his press secretary, Jody Powell, draft a prayer that would appeal to the Christian, Jewish, and Muslim attendees. During the peace talks, she took over 200 typed pages of notes. As a symbol of her contribution to the peace process, Prime Minister Begin, President Sadat, and her husband invited her to join them when they signed the treaty before a special joint session of Congress.

Nancy Reagan also encouraged President Reagan to meet with Soviet Mikhail Gorbachev to negotiate an end to the Cold War. In *My Turn*, her autobiography, she writes: "With the world so dangerous, I felt it was ridiculous for these two heavily armed superpowers to be sitting there and not talking to each other. I encouraged Ronnie to meet with Gorbachev as soon as possible, especially when I realized that some people in the administration did not favor any real talks. So, yes, I did push Ronnie a little. But he would never have met Gorbachev if he hadn't wanted to."

DIPLOMATIC ACTIVITIES ABROAD

Many First Ladies have been well-suited for international diplomacy because of their education and experience. Some spoke foreign languages fluently such as Frances Cleveland, who used her language skills to speak to foreign diplomats. Others studied abroad such as Eleanor Roosevelt (England) and Jackie Kennedy (France). Some lived overseas with their husbands; for example, Louisa Adams lived with John Quincy Adams when he served as an ambassador in Russia and Berlin; she, too, has the distinction of being the only First Lady to have been born abroad — in England, although her father was an American merchant.

Some first-ladies-to-be have performed diplomatic duties while abroad. Elizabeth Monroe helped free Madame de Lafayette from jail, and Helen Taft served as first lady of the Philippines. When World Ware I broke out, Lou Hoover helped her husband raise money to evacuate Americans from Europe and to organize food shipments for the people of Belgium.

Barbara Bush, probably more so than most other First-Ladies-to-be, traveled abroad extensively as her husband's career advanced. As Second Lady, she visited sixty-five foreign countries, returning to some of them more then once. Her white hair must have made quite an impression on the dark-haired Chinese as she pedaled her bicycle along the streets Beijing. Of course, no one made quite the same impression on her foreign hosts as did Mamie Eisenhower. She turned down an invitation to live at Villa Trianon, once home of Marie

Antoinette. Instead, she decorated another villa in her favorite colors of pink and green. To remind her of home, she had a plot of corn planted outside her window.

Some First Ladies have dazzled their foreign hosts by virtue of their elegance and fashionable style. Edith and Woodrow Wilson were the first couple to travel abroad while serving as First Lady and president. They traveled to Europe to negotiate a peace treaty at the close of World War I. Edith attended official ceremonies with royalty, some of whom were impressed by her lineage — a descendant of Princess Pocahontas. Her outfits, hairstyle, and manners were described in superlatives by the international press. She was so adored in Paris that the mayor of the city presented her with a diamond brooch of peace doves. She was revered as well in London because of the way she represented a democratic nation while conforming to the customs of royalty. She was present when her husband signed the Treaty of Versailles, though she was seated behind a heavy curtain.

Similarly, during the Kennedy's 1961 trip to Paris, Jackie Kennedy's beauty and exquisite style made a deep impression on Charles DeGaulle, president of France. She served as a translator between the two presidents, a rare diplomatic activity for any First Lady. Recognizing her popularity with the French people, her husband said during a luncheon for the press: "I do not think it altogether inappropriate to introduce myself to this audience. I am the man who accompanied Jacqueline Kennedy to Paris, and I have enjoyed it."

Autobiographies and other sources indicate how well-prepared many First Ladies have been for their diplomatic trips. When Jackie Kennedy traveled abroad, an aide carried her briefcase, filled with background information about the people she would meet. Pat Nixon spent weeks, if not months, learning all she could about the cultures, customs, politics, and people she would visit. Nancy Reagan wrote about the motivation First Ladies can have to do the hard preliminary work: "I was terrified that I might say or do the wrong thing, and find myself accidentally starting World War III. It's so easy to make a mistake when practically every word you utter is taken down by the press, especially when you are operating in an entirely different culture, with its own rules and customs, not to mention the language problem." Knowing what was at stake, Rosalynn Carter prepared well for her solo trip to Latin America; she sat through twenty-six hours of briefings, reading official reports, studying her husband's foreign policy speeches, brushing up on Spanish, and reading literature from the countries she would visit.

First Ladies have traveled solo outside the nation's boundaries for different purposes. They serve as surrogates, representing their husbands and the American people at weddings, funerals, and other ceremonial occasions. They visit U.S. troops abroad, as did Eleanor Roosevelt during World War II. Pat Nixon became the first First Lady to visit a live combat zone when she traveled to Southeast Asia during the Viet Nam War. To reach the soldiers at an evacuation hospital eighteen miles in the jungle from Saigon, she flew in a helicopter while her secret service agents and army sharpshooters readied themselves to return enemy fire.

Furthering their husbands' agendas and promoting their own initiatives are other reasons why first ladies have made solo trips abroad. Jackie Kennedy traveled to India in 1962, to bolter diplomatic ties between her husband and Prime Minister Nehru. Pat Nixon brought humanitarian aid to Peru after a devastating earthquake in 1970. She also visited the Ivory Coast of Africa on a symbolic mission in 1972, receiving praise for accomplishing what her husband's administration had not been able to do — project the compassion and warmth of the American people. Working with the State Department, Hillary Clinton visited five countries in Southeast Asia in 1995. Her presence served as a symbol of her husband's commitment to the region.

Rosalynn Carter's trip to Latin America in 1977 was similar to trips Eleanor Roosevelt had made abroad as her husband's eyes and ears. However, Carter was also asked to explain her husband's views on human rights and nuclear nonproliferation to the heads of state in seven countries. She was instructed to listen to their concerns and take them back to her husband. Her meetings with top officials included formal diplomatic sessions as well as informal social ones such as dinners. She also toured schools and hospitals in her role as First Lady, leading her to quip: "As it turned out, my duties throughout the trip were heavier than the President's on his own official visits: I assumed the official responsibilities plus the chores of a First Lady."

Some First Ladies have addressed international audiences to promote initiatives close to their hearts. Nancy Reagan became the first First Lady to speak at the U.N. General Assembly when she asked the delegates for help in controlling the flow of illegal drugs into the United States. On numerous occasions, Hillary Clinton spoke to audiences abroad about the universal rights of women and children. In 1997, for instance, she spoke in Vienna to 1000 women leaders at a forum on "Women and Democracy." The meeting was supported in part by the U.S. government's Vital Voices initiative to educate and train women to be political leaders in their own countries.

First Lady Laura Bush has traveled abroad on behalf of her husband's administration as well as to promote education and literacy. Her speech to the United Nations in honor of International Women's Day (2002) and her address to the people of Afghanistan on Radio Free Europe/Radio Liberty (2002) demonstrate her commitment to the education of women and children globally. A speech she gave in France (2003) announced U.S. recommitment to UNESCO. She presented startling statistics about the number of men and women world-wide who cannot read, including numbers from Iraq: "One tragic legacy of Saddam Hussein's rule," she said, "is an overall adult illiteracy rate of 61 percent — and a staggering 77 percent — or three in four women in Iraq — cannot read."

Laura Bush and other First Ladies before her have been given an international platform, and some have used it to further the goals of their husbands' administrations as well as their own initiatives. They have served as hostesses for foreign leaders in the White House and at other venues. They have served as social partners, traveling with their husbands abroad, and as political partners, serving as surrogates on ceremonial and more substantive occasions. Future First Ladies would be wise to study the precedents for international diplomacy set by their predecessors, hiring at least some staff members with international experience and competence. Keeping good records and perhaps a dairy of their experiences would be important, too, for the contributions of First Ladies to global diplomacy remain largely unrecognized.

Chapter 12

DEVELOPMENT OF THE MODERN OFFICE OF THE FIRST LADY

Anthony J. Eksterowicz

OVERVIEW

The Office of the First Lady has evolved in the direction of greater professionalization and integration with the Executive Office of the President and other White House offices. This has both allowed modern First Ladies to have active policy agendas and professional relationships with their presidential spouses, and has itself been a response to these policy agendas and relationships. These developments have contributed to increasing professionalization in the staffing, organization, and payment of personnel in the First Lady's office. In addition, Public Law 95-750 passed in 1978, tied the funding of the Office of the First Lady directly to the duties of the President. Many high level appointees in the Office of the First Lady now hold presidential advisor status. This has also facilitated integration of the offices.

The following recommendations for future First Ladies are based upon the above trends:

1. First Ladies should consider hiring personnel well versed in the ways of Washington and balance these appointments with those people whom they know and trust.
2. First Ladies should make appointments to their office quickly to avoid the appearance of indecision or delay.
3. First Ladies should strive to attain presidential advisor status for all high-level personnel in the Office of the First Lady.
4. The Office of the First Lady should be located in geographical proximity to the White House Office. This will facilitate integration and a team oriented approach.
5. First Ladies should consider creating a new position of deputy assistant for legislative affairs, especially if they intend to link special projects with the President's agenda, involve themselves in politics and policy, or lobby for the President's programs.

6. If the First Lady plans to be active in international affairs she should seriously consider creating a deputy assistant for foreign affairs in her office.

7. First Ladies should strive to leave their office stronger than their predecessors left theirs.

NATURE OF THE OFFICE

The Office of the First Lady has undergone significant development during the past fifty years. During this time strong, activist First Ladies like Eleanor Roosevelt, Lady Bird Johnson, Betty Ford, Rosalyn Carter, and Hillary Clinton have contributed to the increasing professionalization of the office and to its increasing integration with the White House Office. The increasing professionalization and integration of the Office of the First Lady have been, in part, dependent upon the type of relationship that First Ladies have had with their presidential spouses. In this century we have witnessed a movement from First Ladies acting as partners in marriage (Bess Truman, Mamie Eisenhower), to a behind-the-scenes role as advisor (Lou Hoover, Barbara Bush), to a partial partner in politics and decision making (Lady Bird Johnson, Nancy Reagan), to a full partner in the presidency (Eleanor Roosevelt, Hillary Clinton). A First Lady characterized as a full partner is a top presidential advisor, very active in public and private politics and active in social affairs. This aforementioned typology emphasizes the professional and personal relationship between the First Lady and the President.

A second element contributing to increasing professionalization and integration is the changing roles and status of women in this century. Relevant to their husbands, women have moved from "satellite status," to "sponsored status," to "autonomous status" during this century. Satellite status implies that women were mere appendages of their husbands with no independent recognition or ideas. Sponsored status implies that women can achieve attention, but it is owed to their relationship with a prominent man. Autonomous status implies that women have their own prominence and ideas and can act independently from their spouses, especially concerning issues important to them. Such models of status are linked with the different types of partnerships noted above.

The implication for modern First Ladies and their office is that they will inherit an office that has been largely shaped by First Ladies who have achieved autonomous status and full partnership with their presidential spouses. Thus the two typologies work together and this leads to increasing professionalization and integration with the White House Office. These characteristics have worked to the advantage of First Ladies as they perform their official social and unofficial public policy duties.

Thus the development of a new model effecting the evolution of the Office of the First Lady is necessary to understand the nature of the Office, one I call the "independent/integrative model." This model assumes that a First Lady can develop a public policy agenda independent of the President's (if she so desires) and still rely on a partnership, either professional or personal, to help in the implementation of such an agenda. Furthermore, such a relationship is highly professionalized by the integration of the First Lady's office with the various offices within the White House Office. In other words, the interests of the First Lady and the President are tempered by their professional and personal relationships (which includes mutual respect and trust concerning professional advice) and furthered by the professional integration of their offices. This integration facilitates the passage of either a public policy or private (charitable causes, social causes) agenda that can be in the interest of both the President and the First Lady or perhaps solely in the interest of the First Lady, although it should serve the large goals of aiding the President's popularity and agenda. In this model a First Lady draws influence from her professional reputation, her work, and knowledge of the issues independent of the President, her political influence upon her husband due to the nature of their relationship, her complimentary public or private policy agenda, or from her influence as confidante, lover, and partner.

Such a model exists along a continuum from a strong manifestation (Hillary Clinton) to a weaker manifestation (Lady Bird Johnson). Partnerships are not perfect and exist in degrees. Public and private policy variables, along with the various interests of Presidents and First Ladies and the inner workings of their offices, will affect the strength of the model. It is now possible to gauge the impact of this type of model upon the Office of the First Lady concerning the professionalization of the office and then its integration with the White House Office.

PROFESSIONALIZATION

Various First Ladies have contributed to the professionalization of the Office of the First Lady through their bold actions, most notable among them Eleanor Roosevelt. Mrs. Roosevelt spoke at a national party convention, wrote a newspaper column, served as a radio commentator, testified before Congress, served as an informal presidential advisor, and held regular press conferences. Because of her activism she hired a personal and a social secretary who was housed on the second floor of the White House and later the East Wing of the White House. The plethora of issues in which Mrs. Roosevelt was involved required her to organize her office formally. Her full partnership with FDR also contributed to this effort.

Bess Truman, while not an activist, expanded the job of her social secretary. Mrs. Eisenhower expanded her staff to six secretaries and a staff director to meet the increasing social demands confronting her. The Office of the First Lady grew tremendously under Mrs. Kennedy. She hired a social secretary and an assistant social secretary responsible for press relations. Her staff approached forty people, many of whom were responsible for social causes.

Lady Bird Johnson had experience in the world of business and ran her husband's congressional office during LBJ's naval reserve duties. Her main issue was "beautification," or environmental protection. She achieved a partnership with her husband and it was apparent in these issues. Her activism led to the appointment of a press secretary for her office and she hired a program director and borrowed people from other bureaucratic agencies, all to help with her project. She was also the first to institutionalize the role of a staff director. Besides the press secretary she also had a social secretary, a special projects assistant, and a Correspondence Office under the direction of her personal secretary. By the end of her tenure, she employed a staff of thirty professionally trained specialists and she organized her office to mirror her husband's West Wing. All of this contributed greatly to the increasing professionalization of the Office of the First Lady.

Mrs. Ford was outspoken on a number of issues, foremost among them equal rights. In order to pursue her social responsibilities and many issues, she based her headquarters on the second floor of the East Wing of the White House and employed twenty-eight staffers. She was the first occupant to have her own speechwriter, a deputy press secretary, and appointments secretary. Thus, Mrs. Ford upgraded the organizational structure of the office.

Another to improve upon the organizational structure of the office was Rosalynn Carter. Mrs. Carter was active in both domestic and international politics, served as a presidential advisor, sat in on cabinet meetings, testified before Congress, and lobbied the Congress. While her staff numbers were smaller, she approached her duties professionally and was the first to hire a management consultant to streamline her staff. In addition, the passage of Public Law 95-750 in 1978 provided for upgrading the pay of the staffers in the Office of the First Lady to more professional standards. The linkage between the funding for the Office of the First Lady and the duties of the President further integrated the two offices. Mrs. Carter also divided her staff into: projects and community liaison; press and research; schedule and advance; and social and personal divisions. She also created a new position of chief of staff to the First Lady.

There were less developments under Nancy Reagan and Barbara Bush. However, Mrs. Reagan added more positions to her staff and both her chief of staff and deputy chief of staff held presidential commissions. Mrs. Bush continued this tradition of securing a presidential commission for her chief of staff.

Hillary Clinton was the most active First Lady since Eleanor Roosevelt and was involved in a plethora of issues from children's issues to heath care to international women's issues. Not surprisingly, this type of activism had an effect on the structure of her office. Mrs. Clinton moved her office to the West Wing of the White House and occupied another office in the Old Executive Office Building near the White House offices. Mrs. Clinton's staff was well paid at a professional level and she attracted professional and experienced staffers to her office in addition to surrounding herself with staffers whom she knew before her White House tenure. Many of these staffers held presidential advisor status.

INTEGRATION WITH THE WHITE HOUSE OFFICE

Professionalization and integration with the White House Office appear to go hand in hand. As the Office of the First Lady evolves into a more bureaucratic, professional organization it becomes increasingly integrated with the White House Office. Much of this is due to the close relationships First Ladies have developed with their spouses and their own, increasingly independent activism.

The first movement in the direction of integration came with Mrs. Kennedy working closely with West Wing aide Richard Godwin to convince Congressman Rooney to fund an effort to save the tombs at Abu Simbel from destruction caused by building the Aswan Dam. Further efforts occurred in the Johnson Administration when Mrs. Johnson worked closely with the Interior Department to pass her beautification programs, borrowing Interior personnel as well as staff from other agencies. In doing so, she fostered a team approach for her agenda.

The effect of Public Law 95-750 (1978) upon integration of the two offices was significant. It tied the President's duties to those of the First Lady. This facilitated integration of the offices and cooperation over joint financing of staff and projects. The use of presidential advisor status for senior appointees to the Office of the First Lady is yet another indication of integration. This has occurred in all administrations since President Carter.

An interrelationship composed of a First Lady's activism and independence on the issues, her relationship with her presidential spouse, public law governing the funding of her office, and her previous work and educational background has resulted in the greater professionalization of her office and increased integration with the White House Office. What does this imply for future First Ladies? What recommendations flow from this analysis?

RECOMMENDATIONS FOR FUTURE FIRST LADIES

To the extent that the Office of the First Lady is integrated with the White House Office it will face similar problems of staffing and bureaucratic management. There are a number of recommendations or suggestions that future First Ladies should take under consideration.

First, all future occupants of the Office of the First Lady should decide exactly what kind of issues they will be involved in and how active they plan to be. An activist First Lady with either a public or private issue agenda must staff the office quickly with highly regarded, Washington-experienced personnel. First Ladies should avoid the temptation to bring in only people who were close to them but lack any significant Washington experience. Balance should be the key here.

Second, First Ladies need to make appointments quickly so that the Office of the First Lady can hit the ground running. Delay can cause confusion for the agenda of any First Lady and miss out on opportunities to define oneself and initiate projects during the "honeymoon period." Confusion can result in negative press and ultimately challenge the effectiveness of the office. First Ladies should make good use of the transition time (election to inauguration) to secure their appointments and plan their agendas and should consider adding advisers to the transition effort for these purposes.

Third, First Ladies should continue the practice of securing the joint designation of presidential advisor for the most important personnel in their office. Such an effort will facilitate integration with the White House Office and provide immeasurable resources for the First Lady.

Fourth, to the extent that geographical proximity aids office integration, future First Ladies should locate their formal working office near those of the White House Office. Previous administrations have found that such integration can aid in the conception and passage of policy initiatives for both the President and the First Lady. Geographical proximity also fosters a team approach in working toward passage of agenda issues and lessens the tensions between the two offices. Face-to-face contacts between these offices can pay real dividends.

Fifth, even if future First Ladies prefer less active and more private (charitable and social causes) issue agendas, they will inevitably realize that the public/private divide is collapsing. Many social and charitable causes now emphasize public/private partnerships. Thus there will be a role, although limited, for government in many of these areas as well as a highly publicized and politicized component to such endeavors. There is also the possibility that First Ladies will be testifying before Congress more frequently and engaging in other political activities. It would thus be wise to hire expert personnel well versed in legislative affairs. Therefore, future First Ladies should seriously consider appointing a deputy chief for legislative affairs whose responsibility would be congressional liaison and integration of First Lady projects with the President's agenda. The occupant of this position could work closely with both the White House Legislative Liaison Office and the White House Office for Public Affairs.

Sixth, if a First Lady is considering activism in international affairs or foreign policy, she should also hire an assistant well versed in foreign affairs. The occupant of this position could work with the relevant personnel in the White House Offices on foreign affairs. Increasingly, the division between domestic and foreign policy is eroding. Domestic decisions have foreign policy ramifications and vice versa. Increasing professionalization in this area of the Office of the First Lady is long overdue.

Finally, First Ladies should realize that they have multifaceted influence. The amount and scope of influence depend on a number of factors including their relationship with the President, the resources they can secure for their offices, their professional personnel, the relationships developed with the White House Office, and so on. Even if unintended, her actions in one area have consequences on many other areas. Good luck in your endeavors and, just as many of your predecessors have done, every First Lady should strive to leave the office stronger and better positioned to serve the President and the country.

RESOURCES FOR THE FIRST LADY

ADVICE TO THE INCOMING FIRST LADY ON HER RECORDS AND ESTABLISHING FILES THAT SUCCESSFULLY REFLECT HER NEW ROLE

Nancy Kegan Smith

OVERVIEW

As the First Lady embarks upon her new role there are many things she needs to consider. What policies or causes does she wish to champion? How much will she be involved in the formulation of her husband's policies, and how much will she assist in implementing those policies? Will she be personally involved in planning the entertainment at the White House? What will her role be in preserving the White House? These are just a few of the many questions that will require the attention of an incoming First Lady, questions that were addressed by many of her predecessors. It is also extremely important that the First Lady and her staff, upon entering office, give careful consideration to the types of records they create, how these files are set up, and how they will best document the role of the new First Lady for posterity. It is on this last question – the types of records the First Lady establishes and preserves and the assistance that the National Archives and Records Administration can provide on this issue – that is the focus of this writing.

THE HISTORICAL TRADITION OF THE FILES OF FIRST LADIES

Historically, the First Ladies have received much less attention and scrutiny than their husbands have, and therefore, their papers have been considered of less significance. At the dawning of the twenty-first century, we have come a long way from the time when our second First Lady, Abigail Adams, felt it necessary to advise her husband John to "remember the ladies, and be more generous and favorable to them than your ancestors." It has only been in recent years that scholars and the public have begun to give due credit and attention to the

First Ladies for their very unique insights, contributions, and personal work on behalf of our citizens and country.

The twentieth – and now the twenty-first – century First Lady, her influence on her husband and his policies, and her own style of management of an office that has no legally prescribed function, have all become topics of great interest, study, and scrutiny for both scholars and the general public. Coinciding with this recent and increased interest and importance of the First Lady is the legal requirement that most of her official records (those records that the First Lady generates as an adviser to the President, or in any official and ceremonial role) are now covered by the Presidential Records Act, passed in 1978.

Before the passage of the Presidential Records Act, the papers of the First Ladies were always treated differently from those of the Presidents because the First Lady is not an elected official and has no statutory role. Therefore, the papers of the First Ladies serving before the twentieth century are largely in private hands, if they have been preserved at all. Even for the early twentieth-century First Ladies before Lou Henry Hoover, there is only scattered documentation. What documentation that does exist is mainly at the Library of Congress. It was not until the 1930s, with the growth in importance of the role of the First Lady and her staff, that separate papers documenting the First Lady and her function emerged. Coinciding with the growing importance of the First Lady was the establishment of the National Archives and its Presidential Library system in 1934 and 1939, respectively.

The system of Presidential Libraries, which is part of the National Archives and Records Administration (NARA), was started when President Roosevelt donated his papers, some land, and a building for a Presidential Library. President Hoover liked the model that President Roosevelt established and later decided to donate some of his Presidential papers, land, and a building for a Hoover Presidential Library. In 1955, Congress passed the Presidential Libraries Act, which is the basic charter on which the system now rests. This legislation authorizes the government to accept land and a building for use as a Presidential Library. As specified in the Act, the Libraries are built with private and/or non-federal funds. With the 1986 amendments to the Presidential Libraries Act, Presidential Libraries (beginning with the George H. W. Bush Library) are required to raise at least an additional 20 percent endowment based on the cost of the building and land to help offset the cost of running the Library. When completed, the Libraries are then donated or leased to the federal government, which is responsible for staffing and running the Library.

With the establishment of the Presidential Library system, the papers of First Ladies from Lou Henry Hoover through Rosalynn Carter have been donated to the Presidential Library of their husbands, as either a separate collection or as discrete parts of the President's collection. There are currently ten Presidential Libraries: covering Presidents Hoover through Bush, and the new Clinton Project. A presidential "Project" is the government facility that houses the Presidential records and artifacts before a Library has been built and turned over to the Archivist of the United States. All of the Presidential Libraries, with the exception of the private Nixon Library, are part of the National Archives and Records Administration. The Nixon presidential materials are in the custody of the National Archives and are located in the Archives facility at College Park, Maryland. Each Library and Project contain the official (and most also have the personal) papers for their First Lady.

The National Archives and Records Administration has traditionally provided advice and assistance to the First Lady on issues related to her files and records. In 1997, the Presidential Materials Staff was created as part of the Office of Presidential Libraries. The primary responsibility of this staff is to serve as a liaison to the White House providing guidance, technical assistance, and courtesy storage for Presidential records (including those of the First Lady), gifts, and historical materials created or received by the President and his staff. The Presidential Materials Staff has assisted the previous First Lady's staff and will again be honored to provide additional guidance and assistance on this issue.

THE CURRENT STATUS AND FILING OF FIRST LADY RECORDS

The Presidential Records Act, which was passed as an outgrowth of the Nixon Watergate controversy in 1978, applies to all official Presidential records from January 20, 1981 forward. While the Act does not specifically mention the First Lady by name, it does require that Presidential records, which the government owns and controls at the end of the Presidential Administration, include any records documenting the activities of the President and his staff in discharging any constitutional, statutory, official, or ceremonial duties. At the end of the President's term the legal custody of these records passes to the Archivist of the United States, who deposits these records in the presidential archival depository.

It is important for an incoming First Lady and her staff to be familiar with the requirements of the Presidential Records Act (44 U.S.C. 2201 – 2207). The Act requires separation of personal files from presidential record files. Personal files are defined as records of a purely private or political nature. The First Lady's staff should thus immediately establish a separate filing system for the purely private and political materials. The National Archives and Records Administration are available as soon as the First Lady and her staff wish to receive briefings, advice, and assistance on the proper implementation of this Act concerning the First Lady's files.

SOCIAL FILES

Traditionally, the First Lady's official records are filed in several different key files. As Betty Ford once said: "If the West Wing is the mind of the nation, then the East Wing is the heart." The files (from Truman on) documenting the official workings of the East Wing of the White House – which is where the First Lady's staff offices are located – are called the Social Files. The Social Files document the ceremonial functions of the Presidency, including records on the preparations for all official social events and occasions. The Social Files include invitation lists, entertainment materials, seating charts, background on guests at functions for Heads of State and other official dinners, family weddings, speech and trip files, and some personal and official correspondence files. These files also include some documentation on the increasing activism of twentieth-century First Ladies in such activities as sponsoring social projects. Examples include Mrs. Johnson's "beautification" project, Mrs. Ford's efforts to get the ERA passed, and Mrs. Reagan's campaign to "just say no" to drugs.

PERSONAL DOCUMENTATION

Care should be taken to ensure that any personal documentation is filed separately. An example would be photographs of a small, private dinner given for or by the President or First Lady in the family quarters. This would also be true of family social functions such as a child's graduation party, family weddings, and other personal events.

PRESS SECRETARY FILES

Another key collection of papers of the First Lady has been the Press Secretary's Files. These have traditionally documented more of the policy role and activities of the First Lady, some of which is done on behalf of the President, and some of which is uniquely reflective of the First Lady's own interests and how she defines her role. The Press Secretary's Files normally include speech and trip files and files on major subjects of interest to the First Lady.

MISCELLANEOUS FILES

Other files of the First Lady, such as her own correspondence files and those of the Personal Secretary have mixed a variety of materials and subjects. Once again, care should be taken from the beginning of her First Ladyship to ensure that *Presidential* records and *Personal* records are not intermixed in these files.

The records generated by the First Lady's office can be kept separately from the records of the President. This allows future scholars to study the First Lady in her own right and for her unique contributions. Following this model, the records of the First Lady are retired by the particular First Lady as "Presidential Records of the First Lady's Staff Members" or under the First Lady's own name. As such, when the First Lady's office finishes with files or documents it should retire them to the White House Office of Records Management, the office in the White House that manages Presidential records. However, records generated by the First Lady's office can be interfiled with the President's records when these items pertain to or document a mainly Presidential function. These items should be sent to the White House Office of Records Management on an individual basis for filing in the appropriate Presidential file.

RECOMMENDATIONS TO THE INCOMING FIRST LADY ON HER FILES

Because of the unique function and role of the First Lady, it is important that clear guidance is given to the First Lady's staff on filing practices and procedures, and that personal items such as photographs be clearly designated and separated from the Presidential record file. The files that scholars tend to find particularly useful and of special interest are files on policies that document the First Lady's main projects as well as files on her speeches. These files can either be set up as "policy and speech files," or filed by the staff that create these documents. It is important that the incoming First Lady take care that policy issues and speeches are well documented and easily accessible.

Other files that prove particularly valuable to scholars are the Daily Briefing Book file or a diary which documents on a daily chronological basis the events and meetings of the First Lady. Relatedly, when the First Lady makes a major speech outside of the White House compound it would be useful if an audiovisual copy of the speech could be made. This is done for the President's speeches. Should the First Lady be willing, any file recording her personal thoughts on key events will prove particularly valuable to history.

As the new First Lady comes into office she embarks on a role that has undergone a great deal of change from Mrs. Hoover to Mrs. Clinton. There is much greater media scrutiny and higher public expectations regarding her activities and a highly public role is now expected of her. From Mrs. Kennedy on, First Ladies have chosen a few causes or concerns on which they have focused their public activities. However, the First Ladyship is probably the most unique of all jobs in that it has no formal or legal standing. In 1968, President Johnson considered issuing an executive order to accord a more permanent status to the First Lady's Committee for a More Beautiful Capital, a body charged with beautifying the capital and established by Mrs. Johnson in 1965. A presidential aide reported that one argument against the proposal was that "the First Lady has never been given official duties by law or executive order, and this would be a break with tradition." The order was never issued. Since there is no formally defined role, and the First Lady is not an elected official, the role will always be reflective of the First Lady herself and her special desires, interests, and tastes. A successful First Lady is one that focuses her attention on things she loves and knows and is true to herself; or, to borrow a phrase from Mrs. Johnson, the role of First Lady, is a "journey of the heart" and the new First Lady's files should reflect her passions and interests. While the interests and activities of First Ladies clearly depend on the individual First Lady, any files devoted to such endeavors not only provide insights into this unique institution, the particular First Lady, and her husband, but also offer a mirror into the times, current issues, and the changing role of women in America.

Chapter 14

PRESIDENTIAL WIVES, THE WHITE HOUSE, AND WASHINGTON, D.C.: RECOMMENDED READINGS AND REFERENCES FOR THE FIRST LADY

Elizabeth Lorelei Thacker-Estrada

OVERVIEW

T he following bibliography includes several of the most definitive, useful, and interesting books, journals, and resources on the First Ladies. For ease of use, these recommended sources are listed by category, beginning with collective biographies and studies on the presidential wives, continuing with books about the White House and official Washington, D.C. – the principal settings in which First Ladies perform their roles – and concluding with reference works.

This Report is not an exhaustive resource list. For the sake of conciseness, in all but one category, only books and resources featuring two or more First Ladies are included. The one exception is the section featuring published autobiographies of former First Ladies.

It has been a pleasure to compile this bibliography for you. These resources detail the lives of presidential wives and their contributions to the Presidency and the nation from the inception of the Republic to the present time. These sources also reveal your predecessors' life stories, their varied approaches to the Office of the First Lady, their participation in their husbands' administrations, and their many accomplishments.

THE LIVES OF PRESIDENTIAL WIVES

Since the nineteenth century, authors have presented the lives of Presidents' wives primarily in the context of Washington social life or as individual biographies. Recently, the growing interest in the lives and influence of First Ladies has developed into a scholarly field of study examining the social and political impact of presidential wives and their place in American history.

COLLECTIVE BIOGRAPHIES OF FIRST LADIES

Anderson, Alice E., and Hadley V. Baxendale. *Behind Every Successful President: The Hidden Power and Influence of America's First Ladies*. New York: Shapolsky Publishers, 1992.

Anthony, Carl Sferrazza. *First Ladies: The Saga of the Presidents' Wives and Their Power, 1789-1961*. New York: Quill/William Morrow, 1990.

Anthony, Carl Sferrazza. *First Ladies: The Saga of the Presidents' Wives and Their Power, 1961-1990*. New York: Quill/William Morrow, 1991.

Barzman, Sol. *The First Ladies*. New York: Cowles Book Co., 1970.

Bassett, Margaret Byrd. *Profiles and Portraits of American Presidents and Their Wives*. Freeport, Maine: B. Wheelwright, 1969.

Boller, Paul F., Jr. *Presidential Wives*, 2nd rev. ed. New York: Oxford University Press, 1998.

Diller, Daniel C., and Stephen L. Robertson. *The Presidents, First Ladies, and Vice Presidents: White House Biographies, 1789-2005*. Washington, D.C.: CQ Press, 2005.

Dunlap, Leslie Whittaker. *Our Vice-Presidents and Second Ladies*. Metuchen, N.J.: Scarecrow Press, 1988.

Furman, Bess. *"Ladies of the White House,"* 1936, Bess Furman Papers, Manuscript Division, Library of Congress, Container 75.

Gould, Lewis L., ed. *American First Ladies: Their Lives and Their Legacy*. 2nd ed. New York: Routledge, 2001.

Harris, Bill. *The First Ladies Fact Book: The Stories of the Women of the White House, From Martha Washington to Laura Bush*. New York: Black Dog & Leventhal Publishers, 2005.

Holloway, Laura C. *The Ladies of the White House*. New York: U.S. Publishing, 1870.

Klapthor, Margaret Brown, and Allida M. Black. *The First Ladies of the United States of America*. 11th ed. Washington, D.C.: White House Historical Association, 2006.

Mayo, Edith P., ed. *The Smithsonian Book of the First Ladies: Their Lives, Times, and Issues*. New York: Henry Holt and Company, 1996.

Means, Marianne. *The Woman in the White House: The Lives, Times and Influence of Twelve Notable First Ladies*. New York: Random House, 1963.

Schnieder, Dorothy, and Carl J. Schneider. *First Ladies: A Biographical Dictionary*. 2nd ed. New York: Facts on File, 2005.

Skarmeas, Nancy J. *First Ladies of the White House*. Nashville, Tenn.: Ideals Publications, 2004.

Truman, Margaret. *First Ladies*. New York: Random House, 1995.

Waldrup, Carole Chandler. *Wives of the American Presidents*. 2nd ed. Jefferson, N.C.: McFarland & Company, 2006.

Watson, Robert P. *First Ladies of the United States: A Biographical Dictionary*. Boulder, C.O.: Lynne Rienner Publishers, 2001.

Whitton, Mary Ormsbee. *First First Ladies, 1789-1865: A Study of the Wives of the Early Presidents*. New York: Hastings House, 1948; Freeport, New York: Books for Libraries Press, 1969.

STUDIES AND THEMES ON FIRST LADIES

Adler, Bill, ed. *America's First Ladies: Their Uncommon Wisdom, from Martha Washington to Laura Bush*. Lanham, Md.: Taylor Trade Publishing, 2002.

Anthony, Carl Sferrazza. *"This Elevated Position—": A Catalog and Guide to the National First Ladies' Library and the Importance of First Lady History*. Canton, Ohio: National First Ladies' Library, 2003.

Beasley, Maurine H. *First Ladies and the Press: The Unfinished Partnership of the Media Age*. Evanston, Ill.: Northwestern University Press, 2005.

Burns, Lisa M. *First Ladies and the Fourth Estate: Press Framing of Presidential Wives*. DeKalb: Northern Illinois University Press, 2008.

Caroli, Betty Boyd. *First Ladies*. Expanded and updated ed. Oxford: Oxford University Press, 2003.

Cook, Jane Hampton. *The Faith of America's First Ladies*. Chattanooga, Tenn.: Living Ink Books, 2005.

Garrison, Webb B. *White House Ladies: Fascinating Tales and Colorful Curiosities*. Nashville, Tenn.: Rutledge Hill Press, 1996.

Gawalt, Gerard W. *My Dear President: Letters Between Presidents and Their Wives*. New York: Black Dog & Leventhal in Association with the Library of Congress, 2005.

Gutin, Myra. *The President's Partner: The First Lady in the Twentieth Century*. New York: Greenwood Press, 1989.

Hay, Peter. *All the Presidents' Ladies: Anecdotes of the Women Behind the Men in the White House*. New York: Viking, 1988.

Heckler-Feltz, Cheryl. *Heart and Soul of the Nation: How the Spirituality of Our First Ladies Changed America*. New York: Doubleday, 1997.

Klapthor, Margaret Brown. *The Dresses of the First Ladies of the White House, as Exhibited in the United States National Museum*. Washington, D.C.: Smithsonian Institution, 1952.

Klapthor, Margaret Brown. *The First Ladies Cook Book: Favorite Recipes of All the Presidents of the United States*. New York: GMG Publishing. New York: Parents Magazine Enterprises, 1982.

MacGregor, Jerry and Marie Prys. *Faith of the First Ladies*. Grand Rapids, Mich." Baker Books, 2006.

Marton, Kati. *Hidden Power: Presidential Marriages That Shaped Our Recent History*. New York: Pantheon Books, 2001.

Mayo, Edith P., and Denise D. Meringolo. *First Ladies: Political Role and Public Image*. Washington, D.C.: National Museum of American History, 1994.

Roberts, John B. *Rating the First Ladies: The Women Who Influenced the Presidency*. New York: Citadel Press, 2003.

Rosebush, James S. *First Lady, Public Wife: A Behind-the-Scenes History of the Evolving Role of First Ladies in American Political Life*. Lanham, M.D.: Madison Books, 1987.

Troy, Gil. *Mr. and Mrs. President: From the Trumans to the Clintons*. 2nd rev. ed. Lawrence, K.S.: University Press of Kansas, 2000.

Truett, Randle Bond. *The First Ladies in Fashion*. New York: Hastings House, 1970.

Watson, Robert P. *The Presidents' Wives: Reassessing the Office of First Lady*. Boulder, C.O.: Lynne Rienner Publishers, 2000.

Watson, Robert P., and Anthony J. Eksterowicz, eds. *The Presidential Companion: Readings on the First Ladies.* 2nd ed. Columbia: University of South Carolina Press, 2006.

Wertheimer, Molly Meijer. *Inventing a Voice: The Rhetoric of American First Ladies of the Twentieth Century.* Lanham, M.D.: Rowman & Littlefield, 2005.

Young, Dwight, and Margaret Johnson. *Dear First Lady: Letters to the White House: From the Collections of the Library of Congress & National Archives.* Washington, D.C.: National Geographic, 2008.

PERIODICAL ISSUES ON THE FIRST LADIES

CQ Researcher (Congressional Quarterly). Vol. 6 (June 14, 1996).

Magazine of History (Organization of American Historians). Vol. 15 (Spring 2001).

Presidential Studies Quarterly (Center for the Study of the Presidency). Vol. 20 (Fall 1990).

The Social Science Journal (Western Social Science Association). Vol. 37 (Fall 2000).

AUTOBIOGRAPHIES BY FIRST LADIES

Although Louisa Adams penned autobiographical manuscripts in the early nineteenth century, no book of memoirs written by a First Lady was published until the twentieth century. Some First Ladies, such as Grace Coolidge, wrote autobiographical articles, and the biographies of Bess Truman and Patricia Nixon were written by their daughters and an account of Mamie Eisenhower by her granddaughter. Additionally, the letters of several First Ladies, including Abigail Adams, Dolley Madison, and Mary Todd Lincoln, have been collected and published. Book-length biographies of many, but not all, presidential wives exist. Two series of biographies on First Ladies currently in production will remedy the lack of a scholarly biography on each First Lady: "Presidential Wives Series," Robert P. Watson, Series Editor, Hauppauge, N.Y.: Nova Science Publishers; "Modern First Ladies Series," Lewis L. Gould, Series Editor, Lawrence, KS: University Press of Kansas.

Bush, Barbara. *Barbara Bush: A Memoir.* New York: Scribner's Sons, 1994.

Bush, Barbara. *Reflections: Life After the White House.* New York: Scribner, 2003.

Carter, Jimmy, and Rosalynn Carter. *Everything to Gain: Making the Most of the Rest of Your Life.* New York: Random House, 1987.

Carter, Rosalynn. *First Lady from Plains.* Boston: Houghton Mifflin Company, 1984.

Clinton, Hillary. *Living History.* New York: Simon & Schuster, 2003.

Ford, Betty. *Betty: A Glad Awakening.* Garden City, N.Y.: Doubleday, 1987.

Ford, Betty, *The Times of My Life.* New York: Harper & Row, 1978.

Grant, Julia Dent. *The Personal Memoirs of Julia Dent Grant (Mrs. Ulysses S. Grant).* Edited by John Y. Simon. New York: G.P. Putnam's Sons, 1975. [Published posthumously, these memoirs were the first to be intended for publication by a former First Lady.]

Johnson, Lady Bird. *A White House Diary.* New York: Holt, Rinehart and Winston, 1970.

Reagan, Nancy, and Bill Libby. *Nancy.* New York: Morrow, 1980.

Reagan, Nancy, and William Novak. *My Turn: the Memoirs of Nancy Reagan*. New York: Random House, 1989.

Reagan, Nancy, and Ronald Reagan. *I Love You, Ronnie: The Letters of Ronald Reagan to Nancy Reagan*. New York: Random House, 2000.

Roosevelt, Eleanor. *The Autobiography of Eleanor Roosevelt*. New York: Harper & Brothers, 1961.

Roosevelt, Eleanor. *On My Own*. New York, Harper & Brothers, 1958.

Roosevelt, Eleanor. *This I Remember*. New York: Harper & Brothers, 1949.

Roosevelt, Eleanor. *This is My Story*. New York: Harper & Brothers, 1937

Taft, Helen Herron. *Recollections of Full Years*. New York: Dodd, Mead, 1914. [The first published memoirs of a First Lady.]

Wilson, Edith Bolling Galt. *My Memoir*. Indianapolis: Bobbs-Merrill Company, 1939.

MEMOIRS OF ACQUAINTANCES OF FIRST LADIES

Senatorial wives, journalists, military men, White House employees, and others wrote reminiscences featuring First Ladies and encompassing several presidential administrations.

Adams, John Quincy. *Memoirs of John Quincy Adams, Comprising Portions of His Diary From 1795 to 1848*. 12 vols. Edited by Charles Francis Adams. Philadelphia: J. B. Lippincott & Co., 1874-77. [The son of Abigail Adams and husband of Louisa Adams recorded fifty-three years of his political life and times.]

Bauer, Stephen. *At Ease in the White House: The Uninhibited Memoirs of a Presidential Social Aide*. New York: Carol Publishing Group, 1991. [Nixon to Bush administrations.]

Bryant, Traphes, and Frances Spatz Leighton. *Dog Days at the White House: The Outrageous Memoirs of the Presidential Kennel Keeper*. New York: Macmillan Publishing Co., 1975. [Truman to Nixon administrations.]

Clay-Clopton, Virginia. A *Belle of the Fifties: Memoirs of Mrs. Clay of Alabama, Covering Social and Political Life in Washington and the South, 1853-66.* New York: Doubleday, Page & Co., 1905. [Senator's wife recalls antebellum First Ladies.]

Crook, William H. *Memories of the White House: The Home Life of Our Presidents From Lincoln to Roosevelt*. Compiled and edited by Henry Rood. Boston: Little, Brown, and Co., 1911. [The Colonel worked at the Executive Mansion for forty-six years.]

Davis, Varina. *Jefferson Davis: Ex-President of the Confederate States of America, A Memoir by His Wife*. 2 vols. New York: Belford Co., 1890. [The future First Lady of the Confederacy was the confidante of Margaret Taylor and Jane Pierce.]

Fields, Alonzo. *My 21 Years in the White House*. New York: Coward-McCann, 1961. [White House Chief Butler's memoirs recalling every First Lady from Lou Henry Hoover to Mamie Eisenhower.]

Foraker, Julia B. *I Would Live It Again: Memories of a Vivid Life*. New York: Harper & Brothers, 1932. [Senator's wife recalls late nineteenth and early twentieth century presidential wives.]

Fremont, Jessie Benton. *Souvenirs of My Time*. Boston: D. Lothrop and Co., 1887. [The wife of the first Republican presidential candidate, John Charles Fremont, describes several nineteenth century presidential wives.]

French, Benjamin Brown. Witness to the Young Republic: A Yankee's Journal, 1828-1870. Edited by Donald B. Cole and John J. McDonough. Hanover, N.H.: University Press of New England, 1989. [The Assistant Clerk in the House of Representatives and the Commissioner of Public Buildings records observations on antebellum first ladies and Mary Lincoln.]

Gobright, Lawrence A. *Recollection of Men and Things at Washington: During the Third of a Century*. Philadelphia: Claxton, Remsen & Haffelfinger, 1869. [Newspaper man's view of the administrations from Andrew Jackson to Andrew Johnson.]

Gouverneur, Marian Campbell. *As I Remember: Recollections of American Society During the Nineteenth Century*. New York: D. Appleton & Co., 1911. [The granddaughter-in-law of Elizabeth Monroe and mother of Rose Gouveneur Hoes, one of the founders of the Smithsonian collection of First Ladies' gowns, remembers presidential wives.]

Hoover, Irwin Hood. *Forty-Two Years in the White House*. Boston: Houghton Mifflin Company, 1934. [Chief Usher Ike Hoover worked at the Executive Mansion from the administration of Benjamin Harrison to that of Franklin Roosevelt.]

Keckley, Elizabeth. *Behind the Scenes, or, Thirty Years a Slave and Four Years in the White House*. New York: G. W. Carleton & Co., 1868. [The dressmaker created gowns for Mary Todd Lincoln, Varina Davis, and Martha Johnson Patterson, daughter of Andrew Johnson.]

Keyes, Frances Parkinson. *Capital Kaleidoscope: The Story of a Washington Hostess*. New York: Harper & Brothers, 1937. [The novelist and senator's wife writes of early twentieth century First Ladies and vice-presidential wives.]

McClure, Alexander K. *Colonel Alexander K. McClure's Recollections of Half a Century*. Salem, M.A.: The Salem Press Company, 1902. [This Colonel reminisces about nineteenth century presidential wives.]

Montgomery, Ruth Shick. *Hail to the Chiefs: My Life and Times with Six Presidents*. New York: Coward-McCann, 1970. [Syndicated columnist writes of every First Lady from Eleanor Roosevelt to Lady Bird Johnson.]

Parks, Lillian Rogers. *My Thirty Years Backstairs at the White House*. New York: Fleet Publishing Corp., 1961. [A White House maid writes about the First Ladies, from Helen Taft through Mamie Eisenhower, known to her and her mother, who was also a White House maid.]

Pendel, Thomas F. *Thirty-Six Years in the White House*. Washington, D.C.: Neale Publishing Co., 1902. [The door-keeper kept watch from the Lincoln through Theodore Roosevelt administrations.]

Pierpoint, Robert. *At the White House: Assignment to Six Presidents*. New York: G. P. Putnams's Sons, 1981. [The White House correspondent devotes some attention to First Ladies, from Mamie Eisenhower to Rosalynn Carter.]

Poore, Benjamin Perley. *Perley's Reminiscences of Sixty Years in the National Metropolis*. 2 vols. Philadelphia: Hubbard Brothers, 1886. [The journalist and *Congressional Directory* editor discusses presidential wives of the nineteenth century.]

Randolph, Mary. *Presidents and First Ladies*. New York: D. Appleton-Century Co., 1936. [White House secretary writes of Grace Coolidge and Lou Henry Hoover.]

Smith, Ira R. T., and Joe Alex Morris. *"Dear Mr. President...": The Story of Fifty Years in the White House Mail Room*. New York: Julian Messner, 1949. [The White House Chief of Mails delivers an account of the McKinley through Truman administrations.]

Starling, Edmund W., and Thomas Sugrue. *Starling of the White House: The Story of the Man Whose Secret Service Detail Guarded Five Presidents from Woodrow Wilson to Franklin D. Roosevelt*. New York: Simon & Shuster, 1946.

Thomas, Helen. *Front Row at the White House: My Life and Times*. New York: Scribner, 1999. [The doyenne of White House journalists has covered every President and First Lady from the Kennedys to the Clintons.]

Thomas, Helen. *Dateline: White House*. New York: Macmillan Publishing Company, 1975.

Walters, Barbara. *Audition: A Memoir*. New York: A. A. Knopf, 2008. [The prominent television interviewer recalls presidents and first ladies of the past forty years.]

West, James B., and Mary Lynn Kotz. *Upstairs at the White House; My Life with the First Ladies*. New York: Coward, McCann & Geoghegan, 1973. [This Chief Usher knew every presidential couple from the Franklin Roosevelts to the Nixons.]

THE WHITE HOUSE

Every First Lady since Abigail Adams, with the exception of Anna Harrison, has resided in the Executive Mansion. Presidential wives have usually borne the responsibility of managing "The First Lady's House," and many, such as Abigail Fillmore who established the permanent White House library, have substantially changed and improved this historic site.

History of the White House

Angelo, Bonnie. *First Families: The Impact of the White House on Their Lives*. New York: Morrow, 2005.

Anthony, Carl Sferrazza. *America's First Families: An Inside View of 200 Years of Private Life in the White House*. New York: Simon & Schuster, 2000.

Caroli, Betty Boyd. *Inside the White House; America's Most Famous Home, the First 200 Years*. New York: Canopy Books, 1992.

Clinton, Hillary Rodham. *An Invitation to the White House: At Home with History*. New York: Simon & Schuster, 2000.

Freidel, Frank and William Pencek, ed. *The White House: The First Two Hundred Years*. Boston: Northeastern University Press, 1994.

Furman, Bess. *White House Profile: A Social History of the White House, Its Occupants and Its Festivities*. Indianapolis, I.N.: Bobbs-Merrill Company, 1951.

Jeffries, Ona Griffin. *In and Out of the White House, from Washington to the Eisenhowers; an Intimate Glimpse into the Social and Domestic Aspects of the Presidential Life*. New York: Wilfred Funk, 1960.

Jensen, Amy La Follette. *The White House and Its Thirty-Five Families*. New York: McGraw-Hill Book Company, 1970.

Johnson, Haynes Bonner. *The Working White House*. New York: Praeger Publishers, 1975.

Lewis, Ethel. *The White House: An Informal History of its Architecture, Interiors and Gardens*. New York: Dodd, Mead & Co., 1937.

Monkman, Betty, and Lonnelle Aikman. *The Living White House*. 12th ed. Washington, D.C.: White House Historical Association with the cooperation of the National Geographic Society, 2007.

Ryan, William, and Desmond Guinness. *The White House: An Architectural History*. New York: McGraw-Hill, 1980.

Seale, William. *The President's House: A History*. 2nd ed. Baltimore, M.D.: Johns Hopkins University Press; Washington, D.C.: White House Historical Association, 2008.

Singleton, Esther. *The Story of the White House*. 2 vols. New York: McClure Company, 1907.

Truman, Margaret. *The President's House: A First Daughter Shares the History and Secrets of the World's Most Famous Home*. New York: Ballantine Books, 2003.

Watson, Robert P. *Life in the White House: A Social History of the First Family and the President's House*. Albany: State University of New York Press, 2004.

Whitcomb, John, and Claire Whitcomb. *Real Life at the White House: Two Hundred Years of Daily Life at America's Most Famous Residence*. New York: Routledge, 2000.

The White House: An Historic Guide. 22nd ed. Washington, D.C.: White House Historical Association with the cooperation of the National Geographic Society, 2003.

Special White House Topics

Kirk, Elise Kuhl. *Music at the White House: A History of the American Spirit*. Urbana: University of Illinois Press, 1986.

Klapthor, Margaret Brown et al. *Official White House China: 1789 to the Present*. 2nd ed. New York: Barra Foundation, Inc., in association with Harry N. Abrams, 1999.

Kloss, William, and Doreen Bolger. *Art in the White House: A Nation's Pride*. 2nd ed. Washington, D.C.: White House Historical Association, 2008.

Landau, Barry H. *The President's Table: Two Hundred Years of Dining and Diplomacy*. New York: Collins, 2007.

Monkman, Betty C. *The White House: Its Historic Furnishings and First Families*. Washington DC: White House Historical Association, 2000.

Sadler, Christine. *Children in the White House*. New York: G.P. Putnam's Sons, 1967.

Seale, William. *The White House: Actors and Observers*. Boston: Northeastern University Press, 2002.

Seale, William. *The White House Garden*. Washington, D.C.: White House Historical Association, 1996.

Smith, Marie D. *Entertaining in the White House*. Rev. and updated ed. New York: Macfadden-Baptell, 1970.

Smith, Marie D., and Louise Durbin. *White House Brides*. Washington, D.C.: Acropolis Books, 1966.

Spillman, Jane Shadel. *White House Glassware: Two Centuries of Presidential Entertaining*. Washington, D.C.: White House Historical Association in cooperation with the National Geographic Society and the Corning Museum of Glass, 1989.

Periodicals about the White House

White House History (White House Historical Association), 1983-.
White House Studies (Nova Publishers), 2001-.

OFFICIAL WASHINGTON

Many of the works featuring presidential wives have placed them in the larger context of the social life of the capital city. First Ladies have frequently exerted both social and political influence in Washington.

Allgor, Catherine. *Parlor Politics: In Which the Ladies of Washington Help Build a City and a Government.* Charlottesville, V.A.: University of Virginia Press, 2000.

Ames, Mary Clemmer. *Ten Years in Washington: Life and Scenes in the National Capital as a Woman Sees Them.* Cincinnati, O.H.: Queen City Publishing Company, 1874.

Briggs, Emily Edson. *The Olivia Letters: Being Some History of Washington City for Forty Years as Told by the Letters of a Newspaper Correspondent.* New York: The Neale Publishing Company, 1906.

Daniels, Jonathan. *Washington Quadrille; the Dance Beside the Documents.* Garden City, N.Y.: Doubleday, 1968.

Ellet, Elizabeth F. *Court Circles of the Republic, or, the Beauties and Celebrities of the Nation: Illustrating Life and Society under Eighteen Presidents, Describing the Social Features of the Successive Administrations from Washington to Grant.* Hartford, C.T.: Hartford Publishing, 1869.

Ellet, Elizabeth F. *The Queens of American Society.* Philadelphia: Porter & Coates, 1867.

Graham, Katharine. *Katharine Graham's Washington.* New York: Knopf, 2002.

Green, Constance McLaughlin. *Washington: A History of the Capital, 1800-1950.* Princeton, N.J.: Princeton University Press, 1962.

Hurd, Charles. *Washington Cavalcade.* New York: E.P. Dutton, 1948.

Logan, Mrs. John A. [Mary Simmerson Cunningham Logan]. *Thirty Years in Washington; or, Life and Scenes in Our National Capital.* Hartford, C.T.: A.D. Worthington & Co., 1901.

McLendon, Winzola, and Scottie Smith. *Don't Quote Me: Washington Newswomen and the Power Society.* New York: Dutton, 1970.

Smith, Margaret Bayard. *The First Forty Years of Washington Society in the Family Letters of Margaret Bayard Smith.* Edited by Gaillard Hunt. 1906. Reprint, New York: Frederick Ungar Publishing Company, 1965.

A Smithsonian Book of the Nation's Capital. Washington, D.C.: Smithsonian Books, 1992.

Wharton, Anne Hollingsworth. *Social Life in the Early Republic.* Philadelphia: J.B. Lippincott, 1902.

REFERENCE SOURCES ON FIRST LADIES

Brogan, Hugh, and Charles Mosley. *American Presidential Families*. New York: Macmillan Publishing Co., 1993.

Clotworthy, William G. *Homes and Libraries of the Presidents: An Interpretive Guide*. 3rd ed. Blacksburg, VA: McDonald & Woodward Publishing Co., 2008.

The First Ladies Index. Compiled by Cynthia Polhill. July 1983. Library of Congress, Manuscript Reading Room, Washington, D.C.

Guidas, John et al. *The White House: Resources for Research at the Library of Congress*. Washington, D.C.: Library of Congress, 1992.

Hinding, Andrea, ed. *Women's History Sources: A Guide to Archives and Manuscript Collections in the United States*. 2 Vols. New York: R.R. Bowker, 1979.

Innis Pauline, et al. *Protocol: The Complete Handbook of Diplomatic, Official, and Social Usage*. 25th Anniversary ed. Dallas, TX: Durban, 2002.

James, Edward T., Janet Wilson James, and Paul S. Boyer, eds. *Notable American Women, 1607-1950; A Biographical Dictionary*. Cambridge, M.A.: Belknap Press of Harvard University Press, 1971.

Sayler, James, comp. *Presidents of the United States & Their Written Measure: A Bibliography*. Washington, D.C.: Library of Congress, 1996.

Schick, Frank L., Renee Schick, and Mark Carroll. *Records of the Presidency: Presidential Papers and Libraries from Washington to Reagan*. Phoenix, A.Z.: Oryx Press, 1989

Smith, Nancy Kegan, and Mary C. Ryan, eds. *Modern First Ladies: Their Documentary Legacy*. Washington, D.C.: National Archives and Records Administration, 1989.

United States. National Archives and Records Administration. *Guide to Federal Records in the National Archives of the United States*. Compiled by Robert B. Matchette. 2nd ed. 3 vols. Washington, D.C.: National Archives and Records Administration, 1998.

United States. National Park Service. *First Ladies National Historic Site, National First Ladies' Library, Ohio*. Washington, D.C.: National Park Service, U.S. Dept. of the Interior: GPO, 2005.

Veit, Fritz. *Presidential Libraries and Collections*. New York: Greenwood Press, 1987.

Watson, Robert P., ed. 2nd ed. *American First Ladies*. Pasadena, C.A.: Salem Press, 2006.

Chapter 15

NATIONAL FIRST LADIES' LIBRARY

Pat Krider

HISTORY AND BACKGROUND

The National First Ladies' Library was founded in 1995 by Mary A. Regula, wife of Congressman Ralph Regula, and incorporated as a non-profit corporation in the District of Columbia on September 16, 1997. All living First Ladies are honorary chairs of the Library. A National Board of Directors as well as a National Advisory Board oversees the operations. The membership of these boards includes representatives from the Smithsonian and Library of Congress, members of the U.S. Senate and U.S. House of Representatives, as well as noted journalists and authors. There is also a committee of First Ladies of the states and a congressional committee.

The Library serves as a central repository for information about the First Ladies of the United States and other women who have played prominent roles in American history and culture. To that end, the Library's functions include the following: (1) develop a research facility and educational center for scholars of all ages interested in First Ladies of the United States and other prominent women; (2) develop and maintain an on-line bibliographic database of written materials about First Ladies of the United States; and (3) engage in other activities intended to raise public awareness of the important achievements and contributions of First Ladies and other notable American women. In October 2000, the National First Ladies' Library was named the First Ladies National Historic Site by the 106th Congress.

The Library intends to focus its initial efforts largely on developing and maintaining a physical library and educational center which will house resources regarding First Ladies and other women who have played important roles in American history and culture. The physical library is located in the Saxton McKinley House, which was home to First Lady Ida Saxton McKinley. The Grand Opening of this location was celebrated on June 8, 1998. The Library will expand to include an educational and research center that will be located in the restored 1895 historic City National Bank Building.

In addition to establishing the physical facility, the Library will also devote a substantial amount of time and effort to the development of on-line electronic resources concerning First

Ladies and other prominent women. A web site (www.firstladies.org) was officially dedicated by First Lady Hillary Rodham Clinton in a ceremony at the White House in February 1998. The web site contains a 40,000 entry bibliography of books, articles, manuscripts, and other media on each of our First Ladies, the only one of its kind in existence. This bibliography will be updated annually. Finally, the Library will continue to take steps to increase public awareness concerning the contributions of First Ladies and other prominent women in American society, including establishing an annual national award for women who have been the first to achieve leadership positions of national significance in their chosen professions. This annual recognition – First Ladies Salute First Women – is in its second year, having honored Madeleine Albright, Sandra Day O'Connor, Shirley Chisholm, Gwendolyn Brooks, and Elizabeth Campbell in 1999, and Althea Gibson, Antonia Novello, Kathy Sullivan, Frankie Hewitt, and Helen Thomas in 2000.

The main activities of the Library include an online bibliographic database and a library educational center which will eventually include a collection of out-of-print books, letters, and manuscripts, a collection of audio recordings, a photo collection, a research center, both temporary and permanent exhibits, a media/theater center, and an educational outreach center. Other projects include developing a curriculum and units of study for grades K-12 on the contributions of our nation's First Ladies and public awareness initiatives.

MISSION

As the first and only facility of its kind, the National First Ladies' Library serves as a unique, national resource for patrons from school children to serious scholars. As a national archive devoted to educating people about the contributions of First Ladies, the Library's holdings will fill an informational void that has long frustrated academicians and armchair history buffs alike. The Library will fulfill this mission by serving as both a physical educational facility and an electronic virtual library, in an effort to educate people in the United States and around the world.

GOALS

– To update each year a complete, annotated bibliography developed on First Ladies, from Martha Custis Washington to Hillary Rodham Clinton. Restore and historically document all the public rooms located in the home of First Lady Ida Saxton McKinley.

– Compile, assemble, and produce complete educational units and study guides for classroom students K through 12 on the contributions of First Ladies to American History. (Curriculum and teachers' guides to be available by the year 2001.)

– To restore and renovate a historic office building built in 1895 into a modern research electronic library and an educational center dedicated to the history of women in America.

– Continue the national First Ladies Salute First Women Awards honoring women in the nation who are first in their field or pioneers in the field of their careers.

- To plan and conduct seminars, workshops, and lectures on the role of First Ladies and how it has changed over two centuries.
- To collect all the out-of-print books by and about First Ladies, as well as films, documentaries and other media.
- To collect copies of all First Ladies' letters and manuscripts dealing with the major social issues of the time, now scattered throughout the country.

CITY NATIONAL BANK BUILDING RENOVATION/RESTORATION PROJECT

The National First Ladies' Library is renovating the City National Bank Building located on Market Avenue just a block north of our home at the Ida Saxton McKinley house. It is our plan to adapt the building for the Library's growing need for space. On July 23, 1999, this project was designated as an Official Project of Save America's Treasures, a Millennium Council initiative created by President and Mrs. Clinton.

The building was constructed in 1895 and has seven floors with approximately 20,000 square feet of usable space. Architectural proposals for its restoration and renewal are most encouraging. A goal of five years for completion was established with a completion date for the first four floors of 2001. This building will become the National First Ladies' Library's Educational and Research Center and a state-of-the-art electronic library. It will include research facilities, auditorium/seminar facilities, exhibit rooms, video/teleconferencing facilities, as well as lease opportunities including offices, classrooms, and conference rooms for 501 (c) (3) non-profit organizations on the upper floors of the building.

CURRICULUM PROJECT

It is a goal of the National First Ladies' Library to create a curriculum and units of study on the contributions of the First Ladies of the United States. It will be designed to raise the awareness of students to the role the First Ladies have played and to the impact they have had on the nation's history.

The need for a curriculum project such as this is multi-faceted. In a time when schools are seeking age-appropriate ways to integrate the study of prominent women into an already crowded curriculum, the infusion of selected units on the First Ladies meets many needs. Women's studies issues are addressed by close examination of the changing role and activities of women in American society at large during our 225-year history as a free nation.

These changes are mirrored in the continual alteration of the First Ladies' duties during their period of service. In addition, the selection of these particular women helps students to make a personal connection with each woman and with her unique place and time in history. This sense of connectedness can enhance not only the individual student's knowledge of a certain period of American history but also his/her awareness of the efficacy and power of one single individual as they take a stand on an issue of public concern.

The curriculum is designed for grades K-12, with units of study specifically for the elementary, middle, and secondary levels. They are designed to be integrated into the social studies or history courses and takes into account the requirements of proficiency tests at the appropriate levels of learning. The units of study will be made available on the National First Ladies' Library web site free of charge. In addition, printed versions of the study guides, along with teacher's guides, will be made available for a small charge. The aim of the study units is to provide a variety of biographical information about each First Lady, as well as provide general information about the period in which she lived, a bibliography for further research, activities that can be completed by the students, and links to other relevant web sites.

Each of the units, regardless of its subject, was based on the Vision of Powerful Social Studies Teaching and Learning, as outlined in the National Council for the Social Studies in their publication *Expectations of Excellence* (1994). Briefly stated, these five key features are essential components of outstanding social studies instruction. This form of teaching and learning is powerful because it is meaningful to both learners and teachers; it is integrative within the social studies and across the curriculum; it is value-based on the enduring ethical dimensions of a representative democracy; it is challenging through thoughtful participation in lessons, activities, and assignments; and it is active through the application of new skills and learning.

This project began in May 1999, with the development of a pilot program that was tested in twelve fourth-grade classrooms, including an inner-city, rural, and a private school as well as a gifted class in the 1999-2000 school year. It will be followed by a middle- and secondary-school pilot project. It is anticipated that the entire program was completed in 2003.

VISIT THE NATIONAL FIRST LADIES' LIBRARY

Currently, the Library is open to the public, by reservation, only for guided tours that are conducted two days a week. Costumed docents, dressed as first ladies, conduct the tours that last approximately one hour. We average 7,500 tour visitors per year. Our visitors have come from forty-four different states and six different foreign countries.

The Library also has a virtual presence with its web site. This web site contains extensive information on the organization, as well as a 40,000-entry, annotated bibliography on all the first ladies. The web site receives 9,000 – 12,000 hits per month. The site has been accessed from 95 different foreign countries.

The National First Ladies' Library can be reached by mail at 331 Market Avenue South, Canton, Ohio 44702; by phone at 330-452-0876; or by fax at 330-456-3414. The web site address is www.firstladies.org.

ADVICE TO THE FIRST LADY

Chapter 16

My Advice to the Next First Lady[*]

Eleanor Roosevelt

Whichever party wins this month's election, the next First Lady will be a young woman. And she will find herself in a position that is often extremely difficult as well as extremely interesting. Her official role, the only role required of her as the President's wife, is that of official hostess for the United States Government. But, of course, she does have to confront a wide range of unofficial responsibilities. What actually is expected of the First Lady? What will she find on entering the White House? Her first task, of course, must be undertaken before the inauguration: She will visit the White House, acquaint herself with the second and third floors, which are set aside as the private apartments of the President and his family, and decide how to allot the rooms to meet the demands of her own family and what changes she wants to make in the rearrangement of furniture.

She does not have to bring with her any furniture, china, glass, silverware or linen. All these are provided in abundance. But she is free to use her own fancy and her own taste in the arrangement of the family rooms. There are, however, certain traditions which every First Lady has been hesitant about breaking. For instance, one treats the Lincoln bedroom with respect and is reluctant to move the furniture. The Oval Room, which is used by the President as his study, reflects the interests of the incumbent in its books and pictures, but the general arrangement will be much the same.

There is a storehouse of White House furniture and an allowance for buying what is needed by the new First Lady, so there is no need to bring personal belongings. All of us, however, have special things we like to live with and any family will move these into their new surroundings.

It is also important that the President's wife know the kind of wardrobe, at least in its basic essentials, required in this new and exacting position.

Inaugural day is full of activity and is tiring. The inauguration itself is followed by an official parade, a luncheon at the White House, a reception in the late afternoon and the

---

[*] *Editor's note:* This essay is reprinted from Redbook 116 (November 1960): 18-21, 95-96. Eleanor Roosevelt's words are timeless, as much of what she had to say to the prospective First Ladies in 1960 – Jacqueline Kennedy and Pat Nixon – is still quite pertinent. I thought you might enjoy these words from the longest serving First Lady in U.S. history.

inaugural balls in the evening. The fairly warm dress and coat – for it is cold in Washington in January – may be worn right through the day until time to dress for dinner. But – and I am reminded of one horrible occasion – it is wise to arrange to have a complete replacement wardrobe waiting for you at the White House.

One unforgettable inauguration day my husband and I drove in an open car through a downpour and arrived at the White House with our clothes sodden. To make matters worse for me, the dye in my hat had run down my face in a startling fashion. My only relief was that the dye did not touch my hair and have any effect on it!

The President and his wife go out rarely in the evenings. Most of their formal social life is confined to the White House. A basic minimum wardrobe would comprise three or four formal evening dresses, half a dozen afternoon dresses, a couple of suits and a few silk dresses with lightweight coats for the early spring.

One of the most exhausting duties of the First Lady is to stand in reception lines, often for two hours at a time. In order to survive this it is most helpful to abandon fashion for the occasion and wear low-heeled shoes. I still suffer from what I call my "White House" feet.

It is important to be more conscious than ever before in your life that your accessories must all match, that they belong with the dress or suit that you are wearing. For though you may theoretically be prepared for the fact, you will still discover with a shock of dismay that henceforth you are not a private person. Every move you make will be photographed, every piece of clothing will be watched with a critical eye and there will be someone to write immediately and caustically if the handbag did not match the shoes or the necklace was wrong for the dress. You will feel that you are no longer clothing yourself; you are dressing a public monument.

It is assumed that the apartments on the second and third floors of the White House are a place where the family can live its private life. But even with the most strenuous efforts it is almost impossible to achieve a truly private life. You must be prepared for the fact that you will rarely during your occupancy of the White House sit down to a family meal, whether breakfast, luncheon or dinner. There are always people with whom the President needs to talk, people for whom the brief appointment time during the day is not sufficient.

My aunt Edith, who was First Lady while Theodore Roosevelt was President, told me that it was a terrible job to bring up small children in the White House. People made too much fuss over them and spoiled them and it was a losing battle to try to keep them disciplined and without self-consciousness. When my daughter, Anna, left the White House she said she knew it would be much better for her small children. Only the day before, her son had said, "Why do people stare at us through the fence? Are we different in some way?"

The children risk something more grave than the danger of too much publicity and too much attention. That is having too little of their father's time and attention. There are simply not enough hours in the day. The President must make grave personal sacrifices when he becomes a public servant, and one is that there is little leisure for his children and their problems.

Along with the publicity attending the First Lady's movements and the discovery that even mealtimes are no longer an occasion for the family to be together in a simple way and the problem of coping with the excessive attention paid the children, she will discover two other real losses in her personal life. The first is the fact that it is not judicious for her to carry on her old friendships. From now on each person she sees acquires a fictitious prominence, meaning is read into a simple walk or a luncheon or a chat over a tea table. "Is this woman trying to make it easy for her husband to meet the President through the First Lady?"

This applies with even greater force to one's foreign friends. A White House wife must observe protocol, and it is impossible for her to call on people in diplomatic circles, even though they may be old and warm friends, more than a limited number of times. The moment it is noticed that one group or one individual has an advantage over another, there is jealousy and there may even be serious international repercussions. You must remember that from now on anything you do, however innocent, however trivial, is blown up to huge proportions by publicity and speculation. Whether you know it or not someone, somewhere, is watching you.

The most serious loss, however, is the fact that the President is the most occupied man in the world. His attention is claimed by every quarter hour of the day. So many appointments crowd his time that much of his serious work must be done at night. And with momentous issues at stake, with his thoughts necessarily claimed by basic and far-reaching decisions, he inevitably has less time for personal relationships. This is the biggest sacrifice which the First Lady has to make but she must be prepared to do it, and cheerfully.

No two First Ladies have ever coped with their problems in the same way. It would be absurd to try, for they are all different people, living under different circumstances.

My own personal activities outside the White House, which caused some comments while I was First Lady, were an effort to bring my husband firsthand accounts of conditions and places that he could not observe personally. If he could have made these trips himself, mine, of course, would not have been required. But those were exceptional days and his were exceptional circumstances.

While he and I always discussed my impressions, the result was merely the addition of more data for his consideration and not an attempt to shape his opinion. That was not the job of a President's wife.

Varied as the tastes and interests of each First Lady are bound to be, the general routine of running the White House remains fairly static through all changes in administration. Usually the first duty in the morning is to see the housekeeper and go over the menues; then see the head usher to tell him what people are coming or going, what transportation must be arranged for the family and for visitors; and finally discuss with her social secretary those interminable seating charts for any kind of party which is to be given.

All this seems formidable, particularly for a person who has had no experience with protocol, but here the First Lady will find able and trained assistance at hand. The State Department's official in charge of protocol is prepared with advice on the seating charts and he also informs the First Lady of what indispensable official entertaining must be done.

My suggestion to the next First Lady would be to get in touch with this State Department official before moving to the White House to get the whole situation clear.

In fact, if the head usher and the major-domo can take over all the arrangements for inauguration day, it will make life much easier for the new incumbent and his wife, for whom the day will be full enough without being cluttered by perplexing details of protocol.

The White House belongs to the people of the United States. This point must never be forgotten. Before long the new official hostess will feel that she is being bombarded with requests to receive large groups of women. Practically every feminine group meeting in Washington asks to be received, and usually the women who attend men's conventions. This is a constant swallower of one's time and a drain on energy, but it seems to me that whenever possible such a request should be granted.

To give two or even three afternoons a week to receiving large numbers of strangers is extremely difficult at first. In the past, anyone leaving a card at the White House expected to be invited to a reception. Two things I learned from these functions. One was to stop the receiving line for five minutes at the end of an hour and sit down quietly, even though people were waiting restively in the East Room and on the staircase. At least when they passed me I would be able to see them and greet them with some park of intelligence instead of becoming entirely glassy-eyed. There were times when I did not stop the line, and greeted some of my closest friends without even being aware that they were there and that I had gone through the motions of shaking hands with them.

The other thing I learned was that the people whom one receives in this way are only too aware that the White House is theirs and they keep a stern eye on detail. Mrs. Hoover told me that she had received a sharp letter of complaint because of a darn in a curtain, and people reproached me because they got dust on their white gloves from the stair railing. If I stayed at home, these people implied, I could keep an eye on the housekeeping. I explained – but rather helplessly – that the railing is dusted every half hour.

The degree of formality or informality of what may possibly be termed family life is determined by the wishes of the incumbent. My husband disliked dressing for dinner when we were not entertaining formally, and we used the small dining room, as a rule. In fact, we never used the big state dining room except for formal parties.

Perhaps I carried informality too far, and I know that I often shocked the head usher. I was told gently that the President's wife was not supposed to run the elevator for herself, but this I obstinately insisted on doing. I am inclined to believe that the young woman who becomes the White House hostess will not bother much, either, about restrictive rules of this kind.

Another thing that would be helpful for the First Lady would be to meet as soon as possible the young military and naval aides who are at her disposal in filling out dinner parties. She has ten – or used to have – on whom she can call at any time. Nothing, I imagine, short of death or sudden emergency excuses an aide from accepting a White House invitation.

And while she is becoming acquainted with the people who are available for social occasions, it would be wise to meet and know, as far as possible, all the individuals who make up the complicated staff of the White House. If they feel that they can speak to her, it will relieve a great deal of friction, which is bound to arise form time to time no matter how expert the housekeeper may be.

Sooner or later the First Lady is going to have to contend with the problem of gifts, masses of them, and of the strangest variety, which come from people whom she will rarely know or even have heard of. Sometimes these are bona fide, sometimes not. Occasionally a gift will be followed after a couple of weeks or months by a demand for payment. I found that the best way to cope with the situation was to have bins built in a large closet. Here we placed everything that came in as a gift, arranged by months, which we kept for a year as a safeguard against a demand for payment.

But there is no safeguard, alas, against gossip, personal criticism and, more painful, the criticism of one's husband and children. There is no way to clear the record, to straighten out the facts, to stop the flood of rumor and conjecture and malice that breaks like a wave over anyone in public life. If you cannot stop it or alter it, then it seems to me wisest, and least painful, to try to remain as ignorant of it as possible. Of course, injustice to one's children and one's husband is much harder to bear than criticism of oneself, but none of it is pleasant to hear.

The job of the President's wife is in many ways quite an onerous one, restricting her private life and turning her slightest act, her most trivial word, into a public action.

It is also tremendously interesting. One is living at the very heart of great events. One constantly meets some of the most fascinating and valuable people in the world. The next First Lady can never be sure what excitement or what unforeseen problems each day will bring. The only thing, in fact, that she can be sure of is that her job will never be an easy one.

Chapter 17

LOOKING BACK: LESSONS FOR THE FIRST LADY – AND HER HUSBAND – FROM HISTORY

Gil Troy

OVERVIEW

I wish I could tell you what most First Ladies tell their successors: this position is what you make it, so "make the choices that are right" for you. As the father of a young girl growing up in a world still lacking many positive female role models, I wish I could say what most historians of the First Ladyship say: seize the power, tackle challenging policy issues, show the world how a woman can lead. I even wish I could offer the rationalizations many of your predecessors have used when they ran into the inevitable firestorms: what do you expect? Americans remain sexist and uncomfortable with powerful, independent women.

Unfortunately, such advice and rationalizations reflect wishful thinking not historical reasoning. In truth, this role, while elusive, has clear protocols, clear DOs and DON'Ts. Americans have spoken loud and clear: they want joint image-making and not power-sharing at 1600 Pennsylvania Avenue. And while sexism is a factor, consider also the complexities of the position itself – this is a job you get as "the wife of" and not on your own; this is a job with a rich but complicated history; this is a job based on your unique proximity to the most powerful man in the world, who is leading a country deeply ambivalent about presidential power, and terrified of anyone, male or female, spouse or staffer, who gets too close to the President.

As First Lady of the United States, you will have vast fame and, yes, influence. You will be a modern queen, surrounded by courtiers, courted by all, whisking by mere mortals. Do not let the illusion of power go to your head. Do not let the access to Barbara Streisand and Barbara Boxer, to Queen Elizabeth and Elizabeth Taylor, fool you. You are bound by gossamer shackles, silk handcuffs that reflect the great potential you have to do good, and the limitations that can lead to disaster if ignored.

Think about Hillary Clinton, Barbara Bush, Nancy Reagan, and Rosalynn Carter. Two Democrats, two Republicans. Four very smart, very strong, and very different women. Yet each of them ended up regressing toward the mean, acting similarly. The converging public images of these four underline the First Lady's unspoken yet definitive job description. Politically, First Ladies can do more harm than good – failures can lose many more voters than successes can gain. Those First Ladies who violated the protocols risked the kind of witch hunts Nancy Reagan and Hillary Clinton endured. It is worthwhile to study your predecessors' experiences and avoid a painful readjustment. First Ladies can succeed – even thrive – if they learn the right lessons from history.

1. *Don't be yourself – Be Who They Want You to be.* While it is best not to be a phony, presidential couples must accept their roles as cultural leaders weaving together a national fantasy. First Couples should provide the love story the American people desire. Mrs. President needs to humanize Mr. President, symbolizing the warm, traditional marriage he has established despite working around-the-clock to get elected. The First Lady also offers a warm-hearted facade to a welfare state that has grown increasingly complex, bureaucratic, and impersonal.

    Furthermore, do not forget your constituencies. Reporters have particular demands, as do the white-gloved brigade for Republicans and working women for Democrats. Noting the growing demands on political wives thanks to feminism, no wonder Helen Jackson, the wife of the presidential aspirant, Senator Henry Jackson, sighed in 1976: "It takes a lot more energy now than when all we did was drink tea and shake hands with the ladies."

2. *Support Each Other, Cooperate, but Don't Forget Who's Boss.* With the President "living above the store" and having the "loneliest job in the world," most presidential marriages have thrived. Mamie Eisenhower, Lady Bird Johnson, and Betty Ford were particularly pleased to have their peripatetic husbands home for dinner most nights. Beset by jockeying staffers and groveling visitors, Presidents need their spouses as a "safe haven." A supportive spouse provides what the President needs: Eleanor Roosevelt was her handicapped husband's roving "eyes and ears"; Lady Bird Johnson offered her volatile husband "se-ren-i-ty." Nancy Reagan saw that aides often clammed up in her husband's presence, so she passed on essential information to her passive husband. All these women remembered that their primary task was to support the President. When Bess Truman went off for weeks to Missouri, when Hillary Clinton created an alternative power center with aides more devoted to her than him, their respective husbands – and the nation – suffered.

3. *Let the White Glove Pulpit Resonate with the Bully Pulpit.* The outpouring of public affection after her mastectomy taught Betty Ford to use what Nancy Reagan would call the "white glove pulpit" to inspire Americans. Mrs. Ford's pulpit at times undercut her husband's pulpit. First Ladies have a critical role as the president's chorus. Jackie Kennedy's call for a stylish America echoed Jack's call for a new frontier; Hillary Rodham Clinton's "politics of meaning" tried to illustrate her husband's call for individual responsibility and a "third way" between 1960s libertinism and 1980s selfishness. Mrs. Clinton's characteristic error – at first – was to emphasize her views rather than *their* views, *their* vision, as central to *his* administration.

4. *The Spouse's Project is an Integral Part of the Administration.* Modern First Ladies have learned that to help define their husbands they need to define themselves, usually with a special project. The project should be uncontroversial at worst. At

best, it should illuminate an aspect of the President's agenda, just as Lady Bird Johnson's beautification campaign advanced LBJ's Great Society with a clever program that was more radical than it appeared, or Nancy Reagan's "Just Say No" campaign advanced Ronnie's conservative restoration. The project should touch on an area of interest to women, allowing the First Lady to function as a special emissary to them, offering uplift and self-fulfillment.

5. *The Less Power You Seem to Want, the More You will Get and the More Popular You Shall be.* For someone derided as an anti-feminist throwback, Barbara Bush understood the sexist discomfort with powerful women – and especially with powerful First Ladies – better than many feminists. Many female politicians have succeeded in overcoming the Lady Macbeth stereotype; it is harder for the First Lady, considering her unelected, pseudo-monarchical position in a democracy terrified of government power and monitored by a media addicted to controversy. By explaining that she never meddled in George's affairs, and he never meddled in hers, Mrs. Bush became one of the most popular and effective First Ladies ever.

    It is understandable why these constraints would frustrate many modern First Ladies. But therapists teach that "the unit of decision making is one." Ultimately, the President cannot share power with the First Lady or anyone else. However, "the unit of intimacy is two": the First Lady is uniquely positioned to help the President as no one else can, as a peer and partner whose relationship transcends the insanity of White House life.

6. *Never Criticize the President, Unless You Both Agree it's Convenient to do so.* Both Rosalynn Carter and Pat Nixon long frustrated reporters by refusing to criticize their husbands. When Rosalynn finally criticized Jimmy during the 1980 campaign, it was a ploy to build him up as a statesman. She chided him for spurning her advice and sticking to principle despite the political consequences. The Nixons were more subtle. Dick had Pat confront him about not appointing a woman to the Supreme Court and dithering on the Equal Rights Amendment to help women feel that someone in the White House represented their interests.

7. *Pioneers Belong in the Wild West, and Possibly the West Wing, but Certainly not the East Wing.* Considering that she is an unelected figure, he is the head of state, and they live in a political culture most comfortable with consensus, the First Couple should play to the cultural center. In a nation wracked by "culture wars," the presidential couple should find a DMZ. Offer a benign, soothing role model. The safety zone to which the First Couple retreats can remind Americans of common ties and central values.

8. *Nothing is Trivial and the Personal is Political, but do not take the Political Personally.* Hillary Clinton was teased for teasing her hair, Barbara Bush was deified for wearing fake pearls, and Nancy Reagan changed her image with a two-and-half-minute self-deprecating skit. Mrs. Clinton attributed the obsession with minutiae to "24 hours news filling all those minutes and hours, so that things that would never have been paid attention to … 10 years ago, are now more important than they should be." But in 1945 Harry Truman's mother had asked him about the hordes of reporters who greeted her in Washington: "Harry, if you are President, why can't you shoo all these people away?"

In a therapeutic celebrity culture where personal tidbits are considered revealing, the First Couple must always be on guard. When the inevitable leaks occur, do not overreact. Reporters are only doing their jobs and will dig deeper if they get a rise out of you or you dare to confront them.

9. *To Build a Zone of Privacy just say no – Surgically, Sparingly.* The First Couple can protect what Hillary Clinton called their "zone of privacy" by creating an illusion of exposure. You can simply say NO to certain topics, as long as you appear forthcoming in other matters. The Clintons protected Chelsea more effectively than the Carters protected Amy by defining boundaries. They also distracted reporters with tidbits about their own marriage. Even the reclusive Bess Truman realized the need to purchase privacy when she told one reporter about Margaret's plans to stay longer in Missouri, muttering, "God only knows what they may be saying. I'd prefer telling her it's *none of their d---- business.*"

10. *You get One Mea Culpa, Use it Well.* Petty scandals and minor controversies are inevitable. Fortunately, Americans, especially reporters, are suckers for confessionals. The Clintons could have derailed the Whitewater inquisitors with a suitably weepy press conference in which they volunteered embarrassing information and asked for forgiveness. Instead, they repeatedly confessed retroactively to each disclosure, altering their stories so many times that a special prosecutor was hired and a stench of dishonesty lingered.

11. *Take the Long-Term View on Your Marriage.* While reporters describe marriages in all-or-nothing terms as wonderful or horrible, most marriages lie somewhere in between (except for this author's truly idyllic match!). Marriages ebb and flow, rupture and heal. The Eisenhowers survived the war; the Nixons survived Watergate; the Trumans survived the White House.

    The President should acknowledge the many sacrifices the presidential spouse makes but defer most payment until after the administration ends. Dwight Eisenhower thanked Mamie with the extravagant Gettysburg renovations during the presidency. Harry Truman mollified Bess by retiring to Independence rather than running for the Senate. Bill Clinton helped Hillary run for Senate. And Richard Nixon did penance for some of his high marital crimes by excusing Pat from any public appearances after the resignation, be it hosting one of his elder statesman "comeback dinners" or greeting trick-or-treaters at Halloween.

12. *Keep up Appearances – You set the Standard Now, and your Marriage Belongs to History.* In America today, the presidency and marriage are undergoing similar credibility crises. Both institutions are enduring a manic-depressive phrase, romanticized yet denigrated, aggrandized yet trivialized. Just as husbands and wives choose to build useful fictions about each other, about their relationships, so too do citizens need useful fictions about their leaders and their government. Presidential marriages resonate and can alter many people's futures. Rather than confirming our culture of negativity, lead toward a culture of faith. As the Reagans discovered after their rocky marital start, your marriage and our country just might live up to the billing.

13. *Have Fun!* This job or role or position can be frustrating, exhausting, and heartbreaking. But it can also be satisfying, challenging, enriching, and epoch-making. Do not let critics like me bug you. Enjoy it.

Chapter 18

20 TIPS: WALKING IN THE FOOTSTEPS OF HISTORY

Robert P. Watson

THE CHALLENGE BEFORE YOU

One thing that all First Ladies have in common – apart from being married to the President – is that they have been the targets of criticism. The First Ladyship is arguably the most demanding and challenging unpaid "job" there is. A fine line exists between what the public sees as acceptable and what they deem to be unacceptable behavior for the presidential spouse. For instance, many felt Betty Ford was too outspoken, while Pat Nixon did not have enough to say. Nancy Reagan was criticized for dressing too elegantly, while Rosalynn Carter was criticized for her drab wardrobe. Jane Pierce was too dour, while, unbelievable as it may seem, some said that Harriet Lane (niece of and hostess for bachelor James Buchanan) was too happy. And Mary Lincoln was seen as unfaithful to the Union by northerners and unfaithful to the Confederacy by southerners. Indeed, the fickle winds of pubic opinion are forever changing and, to complicate matters further, it would appear that the American public has not yet decided what they want in a First Lady.

But there are lessons to be gleaned from history. The monumental task before you has been undertaken by others who, in general, discharged their duties with dignity and competence.

So, while there is the challenge of walking in footsteps of the likes of Martha Washington, Abigail Adams, Dolley Madison, Eleanor Roosevelt, and your more immediate predecessors, most of whom enjoyed considerable popularity during and after their First Ladyships, solace can be taken from the trails they have blazed, the prestige they have instilled in the institution, and the lessons one finds in their example. So, let the guidance of history and the highly capable women in whose footsteps you now follow work on your behalf.

What follows are 20 lessons which can be found in the study of the first 39 First Ladies and handful of nieces, sisters, and daughters that served as White House hostess.

1. *Expect Criticism.* The First Lady should not expect to please all of the people all of the time. The office is filled with daunting challenges and the paradox of, technically, not actually being an "office" per se. Nevertheless, she is expected to act, but is often criticized when she does. First Ladies dare not cross that near-invisible and shifting line between being a supportive spouse and being an influential spouse. On the other hand, the First Lady should not respond by criticizing public figures or the press because the public does not take kindly to such actions by their First Lady; unless such action is directly in defense of her husband.

2. *All Things in Moderation.* Considering the first point, the First Lady would be wise to seek moderation when determining her role, which activities to undertake, and how to balance her time between the various political and social requirements of the office. The First Lady should play it safe by not taking on too much of any one approach or activity. Yet, she should avoid being portrayed as uni-dimensional by restricting herself to a single role or activity.

3. *Promote Yourself and Your Accomplishments, However...* The First Lady should hire good public relations people and promote her causes, travels, and appearances. Of course, it is wise to practice moderation and humility in these endeavors and not appear vain. However, the country wants to get to know its First Lady, and the appearance of an active, dedicated, hardworking spouse will bring support for the First Lady and for the President. It will also prevent the media or the First Lady's critics from defining her because she will already have defined herself and established a rapport with the public.

4. *Balance the Social and Political.* The public permits and, indeed, now expects First Ladies to be involved in a variety of political and social activities such as campaigning, meeting the public, advocating social causes, and presiding over White House social events. However, if the public perceives the First Lady to be solely a political player, the public will view her as they do other politicians. If, however, a First Lady pays at least as much attention to the social roles of the office as she does politics, it reduces her vulnerability to criticism of her power or political activism. Both roles are important and First Ladies should attempt to achieve a balance in their prioritization of these two areas of service.

5. *Select a Project, Promote It, Enjoy It.* Recent First Ladies have been identified with a "pet project" or cause. These projects improve the First Lady's image and allow her to make many meaningful contributions to worthy issues. The First Lady should select a project that supports her husband's platform (it would be a lose-lose situation should a First Lady select a project at odds with the President's or party's agenda) and something about which both the President and the First Lady feel strongly. Preferably, the project should be something in which the First Lady was affiliated prior to her White House years and something that does not require the formal machinery of government to accomplish. Promote the project and enjoy it. In the harsh world of presidential politics, a meaningful project can be a relief from the grind of politics and can be personally rewarding. Such projects are also unique because they bypass the usual bureaucracy of government and often allow for immediate impact. With the credibility of the First Lady's reputation behind them, such projects can make a difference.

6. *Practice Making Speeches.* A First Lady will be required to make many speeches, even if she is reluctant to do so. As with the President's "bully pulpit," the First Lady's "white glove pulpit" is often a source of great power. In the present mass media age, it is

paramount for all public figures to master the media, the visual image, and public opinion in order to be successful.

7. *Travel with and Campaign for the President.* The public has grown to expect First Ladies to support the President and his endeavors, political or otherwise. This does not mean that a spouse must announce her support of his policies to the public or debate the details of them. Rather, the appearance of support is made through the symbolic act of appearing with him or on his behalf. Through such appearances, the First Lady can be a major benefit to the President's popularity (and such appearances will aid her own agenda).

8. *It is Okay to be Politically Active, as Long as You are Frank about it.* The public is not afraid of a politically active First Lady per se, but it is concerned about unchecked power and influence that occurs beyond the purview of public introspection. Oftentimes the media and the public assume the worst. Perception is reality in politics and even suspicion fuels criticism. A First Lady can thus be active in political and policy affairs, but only as long as she is forthcoming about it, the activism is not on behalf of an issue that is highly controversial, and the matter is kept within the perspective of the First Lady's realm. Participation in political matters can also occur under the guise of loyal support of her husband.

9. *Be yourself – to a Degree.* The First Lady should approach the office in a way in which she is comfortable. She should not try to be Eleanor Roosevelt if she is not Eleanor Roosevelt, she should not try to be Jacqueline Kennedy it she is not Jacqueline Kennedy. If a First Lady explains her approach to the people, they will understand. Yet, within the individualized conceptualization of the office, there must be room for functioning according to the precedents set by history and the basic expectations of the public.

10. *Respect and Give Credit to the Public.* Too many political figures err by not giving the public credit. The public will understand, forgive, and support a public figure as long as it perceives that someone is being forthright and honest with them. The public is capable of understanding issues better than is often believed and they deserve to know what is going on. Relatedly, the public wants to get to know their First Lady on a personal level. If the First Lady obliges this interest, she will earn their trust and support.

11. *White House Social Affairs are Important.* The nation still loves a good and gracious hostess. Social hosting is a win-win situation: It is rarely controversial and it generally receives positive media coverage. The First Couple also has an obligation to continue the tradition of hosting social affairs. Only in times of war and economic crisis should these affairs be minimized. Such events can often fulfill a viable political role, improving political relations with guests, foreign nations, and the public.

12. *Make the White House the People's House.* The First Lady should try not to limit the public's access to this national monument and living museum. It is incumbent upon the First Couple to tend to necessary White House renovations and restorations. Many First Couples have reaped considerable political mileage by showcasing a restored White House. All guests and visitors to the White House remember the experience.

13. *Create a Private Life for You, the President, and Your Family.* The demands of the White House are considerable for not only the President but the President's family. To be most effective, the President needs to have a private life and a relaxing environment to distract him from the challenges of governing the nation. This is also true for the First Lady and the entire First Family, as may be the case. The living quarters of the White House must be a place where the First Family can escape the pressures of politics. On the same note,

as much as possible the First Family should try to retain their hobbies, take vacations together, eat meals together, and anything to create some semblance of normalcy in the White House.

14. *Assist the President with Cabinet Selections and Staffing, but Only in an Advisory Role.* Presidents often form committees to assist them with staffing. Successful staffing is a key to a successful administration. In politics, however, everyone has a political agenda, and there are consequences and reasons behind every staffing decision and piece of advice offered to the president by aides. The President might not have the "distance" from the matter to spot potential problems, especially in the matter of selecting a staff that works well together. The First Lady is one of the few confidants of the President who really knows him and his weaknesses, can say NO to him, and can offer advice with no political strings attached. As such, her advice in politically sensitive staffing decisions is invaluable. But her hand in such matters should not appear to be too heavy-fisted.

15. *Be the President's Confidante.* Many aides find it difficult to disagree with the President, to be completely frank with him, or to offer advice irrespective of the political consequences. Yet, the President needs precisely such counsel. The President must also worry about the loyalty of aides, his advisers' ulterior political objectives, and the possibility that an aide will leak a story or write a tell-all book after leaving office. In the First Lady the President finds his most loyal, trusted confidante, someone with whom he can discuss sensitive matters openly, someone who will say NO to him, and someone who will keep the conversation confidential. The First Lady can help the President by being his top political confidante and sounding board.

16. *Beware of the President's Enemies.* First Ladies must be aware that some presidential aides (and enemies and the press) will use the First Lady to get to the President. Advisers recognize that the First Lady influences the President and therefore may try to influence the First Lady in hopes of ultimately influencing the President. Likewise, the President has many political enemies and the media is always looking for an interesting story. First Ladies should be careful of the veritable pack of wolves in sheep's clothing one finds in the capital city.

17. *Be an Advocate for Women.* Women are beginning to turn out to vote in greater numbers than men. By giving voice to women's issues – providing they are consistent with the President's agenda – a First Lady can build support among women for her husband. She can accomplish this through her political activities, her social causes, and social hostessing. The First Lady should appear at women's events and organizations. Given the comparative lack of women in positions of power, the First Lady is in a unique position to also make a difference on important issues of interest to women.

18. *Know the Institution of the First Lady.* The First Lady should study the history of the office. She can learn from the experiences, stories, and successes of previous First Ladies and avoid the old adage that those who fail to study the mistakes of history are doomed to repeat them. The institution has a proud heritage and it should be seen as an honor to follow in the steps of such legends as Martha Washington, Abigail Adams, and Eleanor Roosevelt.

19. *Surround Yourself with a Good Staff.* This advice is true of anyone in a position of leadership, power, or public trust: Find energetic, competent, politically astute, and loyal staffers. The First Lady should attempt to hire a staff that shares her vision for the office, has the necessary political experience, and feels free to give the First Lady honest advice,

however painful it might be. Included within the staff should be someone who knows the First Lady well and aides responsible for the duties associated with the office, such as public and media relations, the First Lady's project, speech writers, scheduling and advance aides, and individuals with a talent for organization.

20. *Enjoy the Front-row Seat to History in the Making!* If a First Lady is enjoying her service, this will become apparent to her staffers, the press, and, more importantly, the public and it will work to her benefit. The First Lady has the unparalleled opportunity of living in a national museum, to witness firsthand history in the making and the unfolding of the affairs of a nation, to travel and meet interesting people from around the country and world, and to experience the luxury of living in the White House. Perhaps most importantly, she has the honor of serving the American public and opportunity to make a difference. Most first ladies have done so and the nation is all the better for it!

Good luck!

Chapter 19

WOMEN AND POLITICAL LEADERSHIP

Lori Cox Han

The traditional view of politics suggests that those with political power are those who hold specific leadership positions within government. However, only in recent years have women in the United States begun to make inroads in achieving both elected and appointed political office. Currently, more women hold positions of political power than ever before in all three branches of government at both the national and state level. Yet, there is a long way to go before gender parity is reached, particularly in executive political positions. The dearth of women executive leaders in government—whether as president, vice president, cabinet members, top presidential advisors, state governors, or mayors—suggests a difference in how executive leadership is defined from a woman's perspective.

INTRODUCTION

In general terms, leadership is defined as the ability to encourage, influence or inspire others to act in pursuit of a common goal or agenda. However, as the work of many scholars has pointed out in recent years, the definition of leadership is fluid—it can change based on the context and situation in which the term is used. While a universal and precise definition of "effective" or "successful" leadership may not exist, we know that historically, leadership has always been defined on male, as opposed to female, terms. In American politics, business, and military circles, strong leadership is defined as an attempt to exert one's will over a particular situation. This conceptualization of leadership on male terms has often served as a barrier for women in politics, not only for those seeking elected office, but those holding political office as well.

The policymaking process in the United States is viewed as the reallocation of resources within society, with the winners exerting their power and influence over the losers within the political arena. Since men are traditionally expected to be competitive, strong, tough, decisive, and in control, the male view of leadership better fits the American political model.

Women, on the other hand, are expected to exhibit traits that are cooperative, supportive, understanding, and show a willingness to serve others. Other female characteristics of leadership include using consensus decision-making, viewing power as something to be shared, encouraging productive approaches to conflict, building supportive working environments, and promoting diversity in the workplace. Gender, socialization, and chosen career paths all play an important role in defining leadership and in explaining the differences in the leadership styles of women and men.

Scholars interested in studying gendered differences in leadership show that in some areas, particularly politics and business, women often bring a more open and inclusive style to leadership positions. That is not to say that men cannot also exhibit a more inclusive and participatory approach to leadership, and with so few women in executive positions, a broad categorization of leadership styles based on gender is elementary at best. Differences between male and female leadership styles are sometimes subtle and should not be overstated. It is also important to point out that a "generic woman" does not exist when attempting to determine such differences, since race, class, ethnicity, age, and sexual orientation also play an important role when determining the context of one's actions or behaviors in the political arena. Nonetheless, using other countries as an example, women national leaders have exhibited diverse leadership styles—some more traditionally "male," like former British Prime Minister Margaret Thatcher, and some more traditionally "female," like former Philippine President Corazon Aquino.

WOMEN AS EXECUTIVE LEADERS

The job of the American president is often compared to that of a chief executive officer of a large corporation. Unlike positions in legislatures, which by their very nature require cooperation on some level with other members in an equal position, a president or CEO has no counterpart within the organization and is ultimately responsible for making the executive decisions. Several politicians in recent years have sought either the presidency or the position of state governor based on their successful business careers as corporate executives. Former business executives often reason that if they can run a major corporation that those same skills should transfer into running a government bureaucracy. For example, in 1992, H. Ross Perot received 19 percent of the popular vote in the presidential election based on his approach for fiscal responsibility in handling the federal budget, a skill he attributed to his long career as a leader in the corporate world.

Whether or not a successful CEO could also effectively run the executive branch of the federal government remains to be seen. However, both the political and business sectors share many masculine traditions in their structure, environment, and culture. Women have also been slow to make substantial gains in each field, if for no other reason than not enough time has passed since the women's movement of the late 1960s began to break down many of the social and cultural barriers for women seeking executive positions. Women need both time and credentials to work their way up in both business and political leadership positions. Executive positions of power have always been male dominated, and as a result, gender plays an important role in determining successful leadership traits.

How do women business executives fare in a male dominated arena, and are there instructive comparisons for women governors, women cabinet members, or a future woman president or vice president? In recent years, much has been written about how women's leadership styles in the business world — those based on building inclusive relationships — was better for business than the traditional, hierarchical system. Management literature has embraced the notion of women's unique leadership qualities, as well as their emotional intelligence (the ability to recognize and control one's emotions). However, many women in the corporate world fear that acknowledging a difference exists between male and female leadership traits will be the same as admitting to inequality. As a result, they try to act more like their male colleagues and avoid their inherent female traits.

The old paradigm of leadership, defined as masculine within a hierarchical, command-and-control structure, shows an opposition to change. This style of leadership is also defined by individual (as opposed to group) efforts, with indirect communication trickling down through the organization's vertical structure. However, many successful women in business have adopted a new paradigm of leadership that has moved away from this more traditional approach. According to Esther Wachs Book, author of *Why the Best Man for the Job is a Woman*, women used to try to succeed by trying to be more like men, including dressing like men and managing in a structured, top-down approach that limited their access to colleagues and customers – a "command-and-control style long associated with the masculine mind-set." But by the mid-to-late 1990s, successful female corporate executives, like Meg Whitman of eBay, Inc. and Marcy Carsey of Carsey-Werner Company, had developed new strategies to grow their businesses. These new paradigm leaders are "noted for their abilities to blend feminine qualities of leadership with classic male traits to run their companies successfully, and become some of the most powerful women in American business."

Book states that these women who adopt the new paradigm of leadership succeed for three main reasons: Self-assurance compels new paradigm leaders to stay motivated and take risks; an obsession with customer service helps them anticipate market changes; and new paradigm leaders use "feminine" traits to their advantage (empathy, collaboration, cooperation — acknowledging differences between men and women and their leadership styles make more approaches available). She also identifies seven key characteristics of new paradigm leadership: selling the vision; reinventing the rules; a laser focus to achieve; maximizing high touch in an era of high tech; turning challenge into opportunity; an obsession with customer preferences; and courage under fire.

Like women in politics, women in business careers also face barriers in reaching the top of the corporate ladder. Childrearing and other family responsibilities top the list, as well as incorrect stereotypes that women just are not tough enough, aggressive enough, or ambitious enough to make it to the corner office. Studies have also shown that men are often reluctant to place women in positions of power over others in work settings. Perhaps the most notable current woman CEO is Carly Fiorina of Hewlett-Packard, who has a leadership style that even other women corporate officers admit is a tough act to follow. Fiorina has succeeded not by promoting her difference as a woman but in following the more traditional male path to power through drive and ambition, not the new paradigm of leadership. But most women in business have not followed Fiorina's model. Currently, women hold only eight percent of the top-level jobs in major U.S. companies.

According to Marie Wilson, founder of the White House Project, a non-partisan organization dedicated to placing more women in top leadership positions within government and business, "Ambition in men is an expectation and a virtue. In women, it can be a kiss of death, guaranteeing isolation, ending relationships (personal and professional), pushing entire families into therapy, and making even the most self-assured CEO wonder what she was thinking." As Wilson writes in her book, *Closing the Leadership Gap: Why Women Can and Must Help Run the World*, women, more often than men, are not willing to make family sacrifices in order to climb the corporate ladder. While women today are equal competitors with men in terms of education, experience and skill, success is based more on how hard a person chooses to compete rather than gender discrimination, and "the folks who tend to compete the hardest are generally the stereotypically manly men." Recent studies have also suggested that women may be happier if they give up positions of power in return for more quality time in their lives for family, friends, and other non-business pursuits. Nonetheless, women are often conflicted about such decisions, believing that they have somehow failed other women in their profession if they choose family over career.

WOMEN IN THE EXECUTIVE BRANCH

While no woman has yet served as president or vice president, women have taken an increasingly prominent role in other positions throughout the executive branch. Beginning in the 1960s and continuing through the 1970s, the link between the presidency and women—both in terms of appointments within the executive branch and in terms of policies relevant to women—became much stronger. During the 1980s, in spite of Ronald Reagan's appointment of the first woman to the U.S. Supreme Court, the number of overall appointments of women to positions within the administration declined. With George H.W. Bush's election in 1988, the numbers again increased, as well as the attention paid to women's issues. And the two most recent presidents, Bill Clinton and George W. Bush, have appointed women to executive posts in record numbers, in part as recognition for the political importance of women voters and interest groups devoted to women's issues. Three avenues of influence for women within both the White House and the federal bureaucracy include presidential appointments to cabinet and other cabinet-level positions, posts within the White House as presidential advisors, and the unofficial yet sometimes powerful role of the First Lady.

Since the presidential cabinet was established in 1789, only 21 women have served in these positions. Frances Perkins became the first woman to ever serve in the cabinet when Franklin D. Roosevelt appointed her as Secretary of Labor. Madeleine Albright, who served as Secretary of State during Bill Clinton's administration (1996-2001), became the highest-ranking woman to ever serve in the cabinet. The rank of cabinet offices is based on presidential succession, as well as the four "inner" cabinet positions that have been designated as such by presidency scholars in recent years due to the influence of the positions in national policymaking. The "inner" cabinets include the Departments of State, Justice, Defense, and Treasury. According to the Presidential Succession Act of 1947, cabinet members follow the Vice President, Speaker of the House of Representatives, and the President Pro Tempore of the Senate based on the date their offices were established. The first four cabinet members in line for succession include, in order: Secretary of State, Secretary of Treasury, Secretary of Defense, and the Attorney General. However, Albright could not have served as president due to the constitutional requirement that presidents must be natural born citizens, since she was born in Czechoslovakia.

During the mid-part of the twentieth century, women cabinet appointments were usually viewed as tokenism within an administration. By the 1990s, however, the political climate had changed and public expectations had shifted as women cabinet appointments began to be seen as a more routine presidential practice. At the start of his administration in 2001, George W. Bush appointed three women to his cabinet — Elaine Chao (Labor), Gale Norton (Interior), and Ann Veneman (Agriculture) — as well as appointing Christine Todd Whitman to the cabinet-level position as head of the Environmental Protection Agency. Bush sought to follow the example set by his predecessor, Bill Clinton, in appointing a cabinet that looked like America in terms of gender and ethnic diversity. A total of five women served in cabinet positions during Clinton's two terms in office, including Albright, Janet Reno (Justice), Donna Shalala (Health and Human Services), Alexis Herman (Labor), and Hazel O'Leary (Energy).

The size of the White House staff has grown dramatically during the past century. With the creation of the Executive Office of the President in 1937, a formal staff put in to place during Franklin Roosevelt's second term in office to help with the implementation of New Deal policies, the president's inner circle of advisors has grown in both numbers and influence. With the increase in the role of the federal government in policymaking in the post-New Deal era, White House staffers now perform influential roles in the policymaking process. Women have made substantial gains in obtaining White House staff positions in recent years, particularly during the administrations of Bill Clinton and George W. Bush. However, a glass ceiling still seems to exist in allowing women access to the president's inner circle of closest advisors. Even when women are appointed to White House staff positions, their positions tend to be more political than related to the policymaking process within the White House.

As Bush's national security advisor, Condoleezza Rice is a prominent exception to that rule, but no woman has yet served as a chief of staff and only a handful of women have ever earned the title "special assistant to the president." Even Dee Dee Myers, who served as Clinton's first press secretary (and the first woman to ever hold the job), had difficulty performing her duties as she was routinely excluded from the inner-circle access to information found among Clinton's closest advisors. Situational and structural barriers also exist for women seeking top staff positions within the White House. Not only do women with family responsibilities realize many political career opportunities somewhat later in life than their male counterparts, much of the White House staff comes from the president's campaign staff, where women rarely play a major role. Karen Hughes, who was a close advisor to Bush in her capacity as communications director in both his 2000 campaign and in the first two years of his administration, opted to leave her position to return to her home state of Texas during her son's high school years. (She did, however, continue to play an advisory role from afar during the President's reelection campaign during 2004).

WOMEN AS STATE GOVERNORS AND MAYORS

Women have historically not had an easy time winning their state's highest political office, and many women gubernatorial candidates have been harmed by negative attitudes and stereotypes that suggest a woman cannot succeed in such a powerful executive position. However, the face of the state governor is finally starting to change. As of 2004, a total of eight women were serving as state governors, which is the most women who have ever served in this position simultaneously. A total of 26 women have served as governor in twenty-one states (seventeen Democrats and nine Republicans). Of those, seventeen were elected in their own right, three replaced their husbands, and six became governor by constitutional succession. Arizona is the only state where a woman governor has ever been succeeded by another woman, and boasts the largest number — three — of women to hold the position. Rose Mofford, a Democrat, was elected Secretary of State in 1986, and succeeded to governor in 1988 after the impeachment and conviction of Governor Evan Mecham. Mofford served as governor until 1991. Jane Dee Hull, a Republican, also began her ascent to governor as the Arizona Secretary of State, and succeeded to governor in 1997 upon the resignation of Fife Symington, who had been convicted of fraud. Hull was elected to a full term in 1998 and served through 2003. Janet Napolitano, a Democrat, succeeded Hull as governor in 2003.

While the governor's office of large states is often considered a stepping stone to the White House, only one of the six largest electoral states (California, New York, Tex as, Florida, Illinois, and Pennsylvania) has ever elected a woman as governor — Democrat Ann Richards served one term as Texas governor, elected in 1990 but defeated by George W. Bush in her reelection effort in 1994. (Richards is the second woman governor in Texas; Miriam Amanda "Ma" Ferguson, a Democrat, served as governor from 1925-1927 and 1933-1935, replacing her husband, who was impeached). Nellie Tayloe Ross, a Wyoming Democrat, became the nation's first woman governor in 1925 when she replaced her husband after he died in office. Ross served for two years, and later became vice chair of the Democratic National Committee and director of the U.S. Mint. At the 1928 Democratic National Convention, she received 31 votes on the first ballot for Vice President. Ella Grasso, a Democrat from Connecticut who served from 1975-1980, was the first woman elected as governor in her own right. Republicans would not elect their first woman governor until 1986 with the election of Kay A. Orr of Nebraska.

Historically, women have played a much larger role in the political process at the local level. Many women who would go on to have successful political careers at a much higher level began their careers in elected positions at the city level. In 1887, Susanna Salter was elected mayor of Argonia, Kansas to become the nation's first woman mayor. Bertha K. Landes, the Republican city council president at the time, became acting mayor of Seattle in 1924, the first woman to lead a major American city. Two years later she was elected mayor in her own right in a campaign run by women, but lost in her bid for a second full term. As of June 2003, a total of 188 women were serving as mayors of cities with a population of 30,000 or more. Of these, the woman who heads the largest city within that group is Laura Miller of Dallas, which has a population of more than 1.18 million. (The next largest city on the list is Portland, Oregon, whose mayor is Vera Katz).

CONCLUSION

While women have certainly made progress during the past decade in breaking down more barriers to executive positions of political power, reaching gender parity within these leadership positions is still many years away. However, having women in such integral national positions such as Secretary of State (Madeleine Albright), Attorney General (Janet Reno), and National Security Advisor (Condoleezza Rice) can go a long way in changing social and cultural attitudes towards women in positions of power within our government. The election of more women state governors is also crucial to increase the number of women in the "on-deck circle" for potential presidential or vice presidential candidates in future campaigns. Recent studies have begun to focus more intently on the consequences of masculinism dominating executive politics. These consequences include a loss of talent by limiting the candidate pool to men only; a constrained worldview with a limited set of experiences for solving problems; and a loss of legitimacy for the government itself with women voters. An absence of women in executive political positions also perpetuates the myth that this is a male-only arena.

Despite all the progress for women seeking political careers, the United States still lags behind several other countries, some with much more conservative political cultures, in terms of electing women to executive leadership positions. While no other national system of government matches the constitutional uniqueness found within the American system of government, other countries have nonetheless selected women as their chief executives (including Great Britain, Ireland, the Philippines, Israel, Argentina, Iceland, Pakistan, Nicaragua, and Sri Lanka). Many of these women were elected prime minister through a parliamentary system of government, which means that they did not have to win election through the support of a national constituency of voters. However, different societal expectations are beginning to emerge for women in American politics, and the recent trend of women entering more executive political positions, whether through election or appointment, suggests that America may be moving closer to its first woman president.

Chapter 20

LEGAL CONSIDERATIONS FOR A NEW FIRST LADY

Sindee Kerker

INTRODUCTION

A transition to the White House is an exciting time that will present many opportunities as well as challenges for the First Lady. Undoubtedly, this transition will raise a number of questions, many of which will have some legal ramifications. For example, is the First Lady required to release to the public homemade videos of her daughters? Can the President appoint the First Lady to chair an advisory committee on health care reform? Must these meetings remain open to the public? Can the First Lady receive compensation for serving on an advisory committee? Can the First Lady seek outside employment and pursue her successful private career? These are just some of the legal issues that the First Lady will have to consider as she settles into her new role.

PRESIDENTIAL RECORDS ACT OF 1978 (PRA)

It is necessary for the First Lady to become familiar with the requirements of preserving presidential records as set forth in the Presidential Records Act (44 U.S.C. sections 2201-2207). The term "presidential records" includes any documentary materials created or received by the President, his immediate staff or a unit or individual of the Executive Office of the President whose function is to advise and assist the President in conducting any activities that relate to constitutional, statutory, or other official or ceremonial duties of the President. Clearly, the First Lady, while not specifically mentioned in the Act, falls under "a unit or individual" of the Executive Office.

The PRA governs the official presidential and vice presidential records created or received after January 20, 1981. Prior to the PRA, the President and Vice President legally owned their private records even if such records related to the official or ceremonial duties of the President. As long as such records were deemed private and personal, the President and Vice President were exempt from releasing these records to the public.

Congress passed the PRA in response to the Watergate scandal in order to avoid future problems with the Executive Branch destroying the records at the end of their terms. The public has the right to access and review the actions of past administrations through the Freedom of Information Act (5 U.S.C. section 552) commencing five years after the end of the Administration. However, the President can invoke any of six specific restrictions to public access for up to twelve years. These restrictions include any information relating to: (1) an Executive Order to be kept secret in the interest of national defense or foreign policy; (2) appointments to federal office; (3) any statute that specifically exempts disclosure; (4) privileged or confidential trade secrets and commercial or financial information obtained from a person; (5) confidential communications requesting or submitting advice either between the President and his advisors or between such advisors; and (6) personal and medical files, and similar files, the disclosure of which would constitute an unwarranted invasion of privacy.

Pursuant to the PRA, the United States shall reserve and retain complete and public ownership of the records. The President is responsible for the custody and management of the records. The PRA specifically defines the terms "documentary records," "personal records," "archivist," and "former president." The Act allows the incumbent President to dispose of records that no longer have administrative, historical, informational, or evidentiary value after he has obtained the views of the Archivist on the proposed disposal of records. The Act further requires the President and his staff to take all practical steps to file personal records separately from presidential records and establishes a procedure for restriction and public access to these records, including specific procedures for Congress, courts, and subsequent administrations to obtain special access when such records are closed to the public. The Act states that the vice presidential records should be treated in the same manner as presidential records and are not to be archived separately from the President's records. It is assumed that the same standard applies to a First Lady's records.

AMENDMENTS TO THE PRESIDENTIAL RECORDS ACT OF 1978

It is important to note that, since the enactment of the PRA in 1978, there have been two amendments by way of Executive Orders, as well as amendments passed by House and Senate committees. President Ronald Reagan issues Executive Order 12667 on January 18, 1989 to establish the policies and procedures governing the assertion of Executive Privilege by incumbent and former Presidents in connection with the release of presidential records by the National Archives and Records Administration (NARA). President George W. Bush issues Executive Order 13233 on November 1, 2001, revoking President Reagan's Executive Order by allowing Presidents, Vice Presidents, and their heirs or representatives to prevent most documents from becoming public. Bush's Executive Order, in effect, reversed the procedures for releasing presidential records and granted unbridled authority to the former and incumbent President to withhold presidential records or delay their release indefinitely.

On March 14, 2007, the House of Representatives passed the Presidential Records Act of 2007 (H.R. 1255) to invalidate Bush's Executive Order and restore public access to presidential records. H.R. 1255 limits the authority of former presidents to withhold presidential records, requires the President to assert Executive Privilege claims personally and not through his heirs or representatives and eliminates Executive Privilege claims for Vice Presidents. The Senate version of the Bill (S. 886) passed on January 13, 2007 by a voice vote in committee. Since President Bush threatened to veto the legislation and the Senate Democratic leadership was not confident that there were enough votes to override a presidential veto, the Bill has been placed on the Senate Legislative Calendar under General Orders and has yet to be considered by the Senate as a whole.

PERSONAL RECORDS

Personal records, as defined by the PRA, are documentary materials of a private or non-public character that do not relate to the constitutional, statutory, or other official or ceremonial duties of the President. Documentary materials include books, correspondence, memoranda, documents, papers, pamphlets, maps, films, motion pictures, and any other electronic or mechanical recordings (44 U.S.C. section 2201). Personal records also include diaries, journals, or other personal notes serving as the functional equivalent of a diary or journal, as long as they are not prepared for the purpose of transacting government business.

Other items that are deemed personal records include materials pertaining to personal political associations that are not directly related to the constitutional, statutory, or other official or ceremonial duties of the President. This includes materials relating exclusively to the President's own election to the office or the election of an individual to federal, state, or local office as long as there is no relation to the constitutional, statutory, or other official or ceremonial duties of the President.

First Lady Hillary Rodham Clinton preserved approximately two million pages of records relating to constitutional, statutory, or other official or ceremonial duties. Mrs. Clinton's diaries, telephone logs, daily planners, and schedules may soon be released to the public. Pages can be partially redacted or withheld entirely if the archivists determine that such material contains classified communications on policy or security matters. For example, the health care papers that were released not long ago have been redacted. In addition, a number of records involving First Lady Clinton have been kept closed to the public because they contain confidential advice between presidential aides.

There are some First Lady records now open to the public at presidential libraries. About 75,000 pages of First Lady Rosalynn Carter's records are publically available including scheduling and social files. First Ladies Nancy Reagan and Barbara Bush also have records released to the public at their husband's presidential libraries.

IS THE FIRST LADY AN OFFICER OR EMPLOYEE?

The First Lady is not elected, receives no compensation, and cannot be impeached. She is not granted power by statute or the Constitution. However, the spouse of the President plays an important role in American society and at the White House. Her involvement in serving as the President's official hostess for state functions is, for example, a longstanding tradition in public service. The First lady acts as an advisor and personal representative of her husband; she is expected to support her husband and expand his public image. Whether she is intelligent and educated, shy and soft-spoken, frumpy or sophisticated, disciplined or undisciplined, glamorous or private, the individuality of the First Lady is what makes her and her office unique. Since there is no official or even magical formula for how to function, the First Lady can strive to be herself.

The U.S. Court of Appeals for the District of Columbia in the case Association of American Physicians and Surgeons, Inc. versus Hillary Rodham Clinton (813 F. Supp. 82, 1993), held that Mrs. Clinton was a "*de facto*" officer or employee of the federal government. This case involved a dispute between the AAPS and First Lady Clinton over access to meetings held by the Task Force for National Health Care Reform, which was chaired by Mrs. Clinton. The 12-member Task Force was appointed by President Bill Clinton on January 25, 1993 and included six Cabinet secretaries and several White House officials. The purpose of the Task Force was to listen to all interested parties and prepare legislation for health care reform. The Task Force held an open meeting in March of 1993, but later meetings were held in closed hearings to develop options and recommendations for the President.

The AAPS requested that its members be permitted to attend the Task Force meetings pursuant to the provisions of the Federal Advisory Committee Act (FACA). The President's legal counsel denied AAPS access to the meetings on the basis that the Task Force was not an advisory committee subject to FACA requirements. Counsel asserted that the First Lady was the "functional equivalent of a federal employee" rather than an outsider who could unduly influence the committee.

Congress enacted FACA in 1972 to govern the creation and operation of advisory committees from meeting in secrecy and to prevent undue influence from outside lobbying groups. The statue exempts from its public disclosure requirements of advisory committees that are composed entirely of full-time officers or employees of the federal government. By declaring the First Lady to be a federal officer, the court avoided applying the provisions of FACA. The Task Force could continue its closed meetings and there were no constitutional restrictions on the President's ability to seek and accept advice.

Judge Buckley wrote a concurring opinion stating that the First Lady should not be deemed a government officer or employee, but agreed with the court's conclusion that FACA should not apply to the Task Force. Judge Buckley concluded that the 1972 law was "unconstitutional as applied to the Task Force" because it interfered with the confidentiality of presidential communications. The Constitution imposes certain requirements upon its federal officers; Judge Buckley determined that First Lady Clinton failed to satisfy those requirements.

An officer of employee is defined as an individual who is: (1) appointed to civil service; (2) engaged in a federal function; and (3) subject to supervision by a person authorized to make such an appointment (5 U.S.C. sections 2104-2105). The Supreme Court has consistently held that an officer must be appointed by the President, the courts, or the head of a department, and that the officer must receive compensation for his services and that such duties are continuing and permanent and not occasional and temporary. First Lady Clinton engaged in a federal function by gathering facts and proposing health care legislation while chairing the Task Force and she was subjected to the supervision of both the President and Congress. However, she was not appointed to civil service since she was not confirmed by the Senate. Her duties as Chair of the Task Force were limited in duration to four months and she was never compensated for her services. Had she been compensated for her services, she would have been in violation of the Anti-Nepotism Act of Title 5 that prohibits a public official from appointing or employing a relative in an agency in which he is serving or over which he exercises control (5 U.S.C. section 3110(b)).

CAN THE FIRST LADY SEEK OUTSIDE EMPLOYMENT?

It is unclear whether the First Lady should have to sacrifice a successful career in the private sector or in government because her husband is the President. The Ethics in Government Act of 1978 places limits on outside earned income for certain upper-level officers or employees of the federal government (5 U.S.C. section 501). If the First Lady is not deemed a federal official or employee, or if she is considered to be a federal official or employee but does not receive compensation, she would be exempted from this ban on outside employment. Notwithstanding the federal official or employee designation, the First Lady should avoid employment in the private sector so as not to cause an appearance of impropriety.

It is certain that this issue will be tested at some point and, to a lesser degree, similar questions exist for the President's children and relatives.

CONCLUSION

A First Lady is expected to be an assistant to the President. From time to time, a President can use his spouse to carry out a task that might otherwise be delegated to one of his White House aides. According to case law, the First Lady, when assisting the President on an advisory committee, is considered a *de facto* officer or employee of the federal government. However, from a constitutional perspective, the First Lady is not considered a federal officer or employee because she is not confirmed by the Senate, is not hired, and does not receive compensation for her services. There is also a long history – as is discussed in this Report – of First Ladies serving on behalf of their husbands in matters of politics and policy.

Since private personal records that are not prepared for the purpose of transacting government business do not need to be released to the public, the First Lady can rest assured that the homemade videos of Malia's school play or Sasha's birthday party will remain private. The First Lady should also take comfort in knowing that any private thoughts written in her diary can remain just that.

BIOGRAPHIES OF RECENT FIRST LADIES

Chapter 21

BESS TRUMAN

Raymond Frey

UPBRINGING

Elizabeth Virginia Wallace was born on February 13, 1885 in Independence, Missouri, the oldest child of Margaret (Madge) Gates and David Wallace. As a young girl, Bess chose sports as the way to assert herself. She played third base on her brothers' sandlot baseball team, and was their best hitter. In high school, besides being an outstanding student, she was considered to be the best tennis player in Independence – male or female – as well as an excellent ice skater and horseback rider.

When she was eighteen years old, Bess's life was shattered by the violent death of her father. David Wallace was one of the most popular men in town, but his life was deeply troubled. He held a succession of minor political patronage positions that never produced enough income to support his extravagant wife and their five children. Although Bess's mother continued to employ several servants, he could not afford to send Bess to college. Becoming increasingly depressed, Wallace began drinking heavily. On the morning of June 17, 1903, 43 year old David Wallace committed suicide by shooting himself with a revolver in the bathroom of his house. His violent death by his own hand profoundly influenced Bess for the rest of her life; after her father's death she became much more reserved, private, and pessimistic.

Bess first met Harry Truman at Sunday school in 1890, when he was six years old and she was five. Although Harry was absolutely infatuated with her, she always considered him to be just a friend, and they saw little of each other during their school days. In 1906, however, they began seeing each other more frequently. He would often travel to visit her and they wrote to each other almost every day. Mother Wallace strongly disapproved of the growing relationship, but Harry was determined to win Bess's hand in marriage. In June 1911, he finally summoned up the courage to propose, but she refused. Bess knew that her mother was almost totally dependent upon her, which had discouraged other suitors, but not Harry. Afraid that he would take Bess away from her, Mrs. Wallace told her that "You don't want to marry that farmer boy, he's not going to make it anywhere." Finally, in 1917, after seven years of courtship, and just before Truman joined the army and was to be shipped overseas, Bess accepted his proposal. She wanted to get married at once, but now Harry refused, telling her that she must not tie herself to a man who might not come home at all.

MRS. TRUMAN

Truman returned safely from World War I and, on June 28, 1919, he and Bess were married. They moved in with her mother at 219 North Delaware Street in Independence, Missouri. Harry and a war buddy, Eddie Jacobson, opened a men's haberdashery in Kansas City, but it went bankrupt in 1921. Unemployed and in debt, he decided to try his hand at politics, accepting the support of the powerful Pendergast political machine of Kansas City, much to the dislike of Bess. She always believed that her father's lack of success in politics had much to do with his depression, alcoholism, and suicide, and she remembered the public humiliation of her family by the press following his death. Bess had no desire to be a politician's wife.

Truman was elected county judge of the eastern district of Jackson County in 1922, but was defeated in 1924. This placed a considerable strain on their marriage, as Margaret Truman, their only child, was born at home on February 17, 1924, four days after Bess's 39th birthday. At the age of 40, Harry Truman was out of a job.

In 1926, after a few unsuccessful business ventures, the Pendergast machine agreed to support Harry for presiding judge of the county court. After talking it over with Bess, he accepted the offer. The salary was modest, but this was an important decision, and they both knew it. Truman was now 42 years old, and getting past the time of seriously thinking of switching careers.

He took Bess along to political meetings and speaking engagements, possibly in an effort to interest her in his work, but she seemed aloof. Quietly and behind the scenes, however, she worked both to aid and protect her husband's reputation. Truman easily won the election and Bess was now a professional politician's wife. She considered herself to be an equal partner in her husband's political career, but kept a low profile in public. Her family was her life, and beyond assisting her husband in his job, she had no desire for public attention or acclaim.

Truman had much success as a county judge, and soon there was talk of him becoming a candidate for governor of Missouri – "You may yet be the First Lady of Missouri," he told Bess. He was, however, passed over for the nomination, and was certain his political career was over. But Missouri political boss Tom Pendergast did have plans for Harry – a run for the U.S. Congress. Bess did not approve. Concerned about her ailing mother, she was not eager to leave Independence, Missouri for Washington. Meanwhile, Pendergast had changed his mind and picked another candidate. Harry was dejected and nearly out of money, but a few weeks later would receive some astonishing news – Pendergast had chosen him to run for the U.S. Senate.

Bess Truman supported her husband's decision to accept the nomination, but her heart was troubled. She did not want to live in Washington, and was not certain she could endure the personal and political attacks sure to come their way. Truman waged a relentless campaign across the state of Missouri, often speaking as much as sixteen times in a single day. Bess would frequently appear with him on the platform, but never said a word on his behalf. Political speeches, she told her husband, were not her style. Truman won an overwhelming victory in the November, 1934 election and, in January of 1935, Harry and Bess, along with their ten-year-old daughter Margaret and Mother Wallace, boarded a train for Washington, D.C. Bess was not at all happy about moving to the nation's capital. Their small town, mid-American values and lifestyle did not mesh well with Washington high society, and they had little money to keep up with the pace of Washington social life. Bess enrolled Margaret in Gunston Hall, a private school for young girls, where she would spend the school year and then return home with her mother for the summer.

Whenever they could, Bess and Margaret stayed in Independence. Harry missed having Bess by his side, but he understood her homesickness. She missed him, too, and would occasionally adjust her schedule when his pleas became frantic. Although she preferred to stay home as long as possible, the fact was that he was relying on her more and more. Senator Truman called his wife a "genius" at handling reporters, and she became his favorite speechwriter. When Bess was away from Washington, Harry constantly kept her informed of events in the Senate, and she, in turn, was his eyes and ears at home. He often used his letters to her as an opportunity to clarify his thoughts, although he rarely asked her for advice.

During Truman's second term in the Senate, Bess became such an important partner – and their finances were so low – that he put her on the Senate payroll as his secretary. As his work on the "Truman Committee" required frequent travel to visit arms factories and military installations, Bess became more involved in the daily operation of the office. Truman was quite content being a senator, but by the summer of 1943, rumors about a possible vice-presidential candidacy began to circulate. "I don't want to be the Vice President," he said, "the Vice President simply presides over the Senate and sits around hoping for a funeral... It is a very high office which consists entirely of honor and I don't have any ambition to hold an office like that." And besides, he added, "The Madam (Bess) doesn't want me to do it."

Privately, many of the Democratic Party bosses knew Roosevelt was dying, and their choice for Vice President would very likely become FDR's successor. Truman knew perfectly well what his nomination meant. A reporter remarked to him that as Vice President he might "succeed to the throne." Truman replied, "Hell, I don't want to be President." He was very concerned about Bess and Margaret's privacy, and the fact that his wife was on his Senate office payroll would surely surface. And Bess very much feared that her father's suicide – that disgraceful event that had so strongly affected her as a young girl – would become public.

But on the convention floor, the momentum was building for a Truman vice-presidential nomination, although he continued to insist that he was not interested. On the afternoon of July 19, 1944, he was summoned to a hotel room where the party bosses were waiting. They had Roosevelt on the phone, where he told them "you tell the Senator that if he wants to break up the Democratic Party in the middle of the war, that's his responsibility." A stunned Truman replied, "Well, if that's the situation, I'll have to say yes."

Bess was very unhappy about the sudden turn of events. After Harry delivered his brief acceptance speech, the Trumans made their way to a waiting car through a crush of reporters and photographers. As they got into the car, Bess glared straight at Harry. "Are we going to have to go through this for the rest of our lives?" she asked. It was not a good beginning.

Truman tirelessly campaigned for Roosevelt in 1944, traveling thousands of miles around the country. Throughout most of the campaign, Bess had remained so obscure as the future Vice President's wife that reporters knew virtually nothing about her. At one point her job as

Truman's Senate secretary was made an issue, but he vigorously defended his wife, telling the press that it was no secret Bess was on the Senate payroll. "She's a clerk in my office and does much of my clerical work," he said. "I need her here and that's the reason I've got her there. I never make a report or deliver a speech without her editing it...There's nothing secret about it." This would be the only time during the campaign that the press would scrutinize Bess. To their immense relief, nothing was said about the death of her father.

FIRST LADY

On April 12, 1945, Roosevelt died of a massive brain hemorrhage. That evening, Harry S. Truman took the oath of office as the thirty-third President of the United States. Bess and Margaret stood next to him as he solemnly took the oath of office. That evening, Bess recounted that she spent most of the night thinking about how their lives would change. "I was very apprehensive," she admitted. "The country was used to Eleanor Roosevelt. I couldn't possibly be anything like her. I wasn't going down in any coal mines."

A few days later, the new First Lady held her first press conference, which, she announced, would also be her last. A reporter asked, "Mrs. Truman, how are we ever going to get to know you?" She quickly replied, "You don't need to know me. I'm only the President's wife and the mother of his daughter."

During Harry Truman's first years as President, Bess held no press conferences, made few public appearances, and expressed few personal opinions. "People don't warm up to her easily," one article said. "Her inability to unbend before strangers and her resolute silences do not win friends. She rarely gets a hand when she makes a public appearance...Mrs. Truman's mien suggests to many that she is digging her heels in and saying to people, 'I dare you to like me.' People, in turn, respect her integrity and recognize her determination to measure up to the requirements of her position, but they do not enthuse about her."

In private, Bess was a completely different person. Her Washington friends, mostly senators' wives she befriended during Harry's Senate years, were extremely fond of her. They said that she was kind, considerate of others, a gracious hostess, and an entertaining conversationalist, although she almost never discussed public affairs. Old friends from Independence or members of the White House staff who saw her on an almost daily basis would speak warmly of her kindness.

The newspaperwomen who had the run of the White House during Mrs. Roosevelt's regime were incredulous and enraged at Bess's public silence. They protested, they objected, they tried to bring pressure, and some swore privately to wear her down. But all of their words and wrath failed to lift the veil Mrs. Truman had lowered. She flatly refused to be interviewed. Finally, after months of trying, Washington women reporters persuaded Mrs. Truman to answer a series of written questions in 1947. Her extremely brief, written, penciled replies were read aloud by two White House secretaries.

Long-time White House servant J.B. West, who wrote a book about his service in the Truman White House, commented that "Bess guarded her privacy like a precious jewel, yet within that privacy played a prominent role far exceeding what any but a few suspected. She did advise Truman on decisions. And he *listened* to her." But to the American public, Bess remained a mystery. It would take some time for her to warm up to the press and the public.

She attended hundreds of dinners, teas, and receptions, and hosted dozens more for various associations. She found hosting to be exhausting work, greeting scores of people and shaking thousands of hands. Soon she came to dread what she called "one of those dismal teas."

The Trumans' private life in the White House was simple. In the evenings Harry, Bess, and Margaret would chat, play the piano, and enjoy each other's company. Mrs. Truman was also a baseball fan, and liked to listen to the broadcasts of the Washington Senators' night games. Sometimes Bess and Margaret would play ping-pong. Many evenings the President would work in his study, assisted by Bess.

Bess's part in the hard-fought presidential campaign of 1948 was considerable. Harry called her his "chief advisor," and she was. Every decision he made was her personal concern. "She was a one-woman Gallup poll and audience-reaction tester," *Newsweek* reported, "keeping a sharp watch on the crowds which listened to her husband's oratory. She was also the careful censor of the President's occasional lapses into humorous over-exuberance." Frequently the President would use some rather caustic language, and the First Lady, fearful that reporters would write negative stories, would remind him to be careful with his words.

Newsmen told of seeing her sitting at a window of the train, busily blue-penciling Harry's speeches. At every stop the routine was the same: they would appear together on the rear platform of their private car, Harry would deliver a few words and then introduce Bess as "the boss," (a title which she quickly came to detest), and then Margaret as "the boss's boss." This homespun display of family solidarity helped to portray Truman as a decent and devoted family man to the small-town crowds of the American heartland, and was considered by many to be a decisive factor in Truman's remarkable election victory in 1948.

The final two years of Truman's administration were the most difficult of his entire Presidency, and physically, he was beginning to feel the stress. And yet early in 1952, he was still toying with the idea of running for another term. Bess told him that she feared he could not survive another term, and she did not think that she could either. She reminded him that he would be 73 at the end of another term. Pulitzer Prize-winning Truman biographer David McCullough believes that Bess would even have left him if he had chosen to run in 1952.

LIFE AFTER THE WHITE HOUSE

On March 29, 1952, Truman announced to the American people what most had already suspected – he would not be a candidate for President. Bess was both happy and relieved. In most of the photographs of the First Lady, there is no hint of a smile, but on that day she looked, one of Truman's aides told him, "like you do when you draw four aces."

After the inauguration of President Eisenhower, Bess and Harry returned to 219 North Delaware Street in Independence, Missouri to live much as they had before they had left for Washington – just ordinary citizens. Harry S. Truman died on December 26, 1972 at the age of 88. Bess continued to live in the Independence house for another ten years, still doing her own shopping at Milgram's Supermarket and keeping her weekly appointment at Miller's Beauty Shop. She died on October 18, 1982, at age 97.

Unlike Eleanor Roosevelt who preceded her, Bess Truman preferred to remain in the background. Bess would see her most important role as being the President's sounding board and confidante. There is no doubt that she was the most important person in Harry Truman's life.

Chapter 22

MAMIE EISENHOWER

Robert E. Dewhirst

UPBRINGING

Mamie Geneva Doud was born on November 14, 1896 in Boone, Iowa, one of four daughters of a wealthy businessman. Born at the close of the "Victorian Era," which spanned part of the lengthy rein of Britain's Queen Victoria, Mamie was very much a product of that period in time and its expected pattern of behavior, featuring in part what observers have described as reserved, prim, and genteel manner of what was though to be "proper" behavior of men and women. Her formal education was minimal, completed at Miss Walcott's Fashionable School in Colorado.

She spent her early childhood in small towns in Iowa, before moving to Denver, Colorado. The family also spent winters at the family winter home in San Antonio, Texas. In October 1915, while visiting a relative in San Antonio, Mrs. Eisenhower met Dwight Eisenhower, an Army lieutenant stationed at Fort Sam Houston. They were engaged on Valentine's Day in 1916 and were married in Denver on July 1 of that year.

MRS. EISENHOWER: ARMY WIFE

Mamie's married life was defined through her role as an "Army wife," a role in stark contrast to the comfortable, affluent life of her upbringing. Dwight Eisenhower's Army career paid little and the Eisenhowers were forced to live on a modest salary. Additionally, the demands of Ike's career required them to live in 25 different locations, seven of them coming within one year. During World War II, they were separated from 1942 to 1945, and saw him only once during the period. They lived in Army posts in western and southern parts of the United States and overseas in the Panama Canal Zone and the Philippines as well. She endured these long separations by writing him daily letters, but she did go with him to Manila, Philippines, from 1936 to 1939. Most often, living conditions were cramped, uncomfortable, remote, and dirty.

Throughout this time she developed skills at making their marriage work and living on a limited budget. The first of their two children, Doud Dwight, lived from 1917 to 1921, dying of scarlet fever. Their second son, John Sheldon Doud, was born in 1922. Because of the demands of his military career, the Eisenhowers did not buy their first house until 1950, in Gettysburg, Pennsylvania. It is not surprising then that she viewed the prospect of living from four to eight years in one place – the White House — as a comforting refuge from the challenges of the nomadic life as a dutiful Army spouse. She finally had her husband to herself.

Although Mrs. Eisenhower apparently enjoyed accompanying her husband on campaign trips, she never wanted to give a speech. But, she did enjoy being introduced and waiving to the crowds. Her role in his campaign was highly public, but only as a supportive wife who appeared at her husband's side, smiling and applauding. Republican strategists recognized her popularity and scheduled many public appearances during the 1952 campaign in an effort to contrast the Eisenhowers with Adlai Stevenson, the recently divorced Democratic presidential nominee.

Mrs. Eisenhower suffered from health problems, which were exacerbated by the strenuous campaigns and demands of travel. Her preferred mode of travel tended to be by either train or automobile. Although she did travel by aircraft, she was limited from doing so because of her lifelong struggle with Meniere's Syndrome, a carotid sinus condition causing lightheadedness when a vein would press against the inner-ear. She also reportedly suffered from claustrophobia. The lightheadedness cause by her inner-ear and carotid sinus affliction often cause her to stagger in public, and this in turn spurred rumors that she had a drinking problem. She did drink alcohol on social occasions, but there is no evidence that she had an alcohol problem. Because of these reoccurring health issues she made fewer public appearances during Eisenhower's second term, and declined to accompany the President on major overseas trips in both 1959 and 1960.

FIRST LADY

Unquestionably, Mrs. Eisenhower enjoyed being First Lady – but only within an approach defined solely as wife and spouse. She managed the family matters and the social obligations of White House activities. Although many new First Ladies found the transition to living in the White House difficult, Mrs. Mamie Eisenhower possessed several tools for dealing with the challenges. Indeed, few incoming First Ladies were ever better prepared for being married to the President than Mrs. Eisenhower. First, she had overcome many trying times earlier in her marriage, including the death of her first son which left emotional scars which remained with her the rest of her life. The demands of being wife of an Army officer and moving so many times also toughened her. Most significantly, her lengthy experience as the wife of an Army officer – and particularly the years when her husband served at the highest levels – provided Mrs. Eisenhower with countless opportunities for planning and managing large formal social gatherings.

Of particular note in helping Mrs. Eisenhower develop her skills as hostess were her husband's overseas Army assignments, especially to the Philippines in 1936 as an aide to General Douglas MacArthur and after the Second World War when he was appointed

Supreme Commander of North Atlantic Treaty Organization (NATO) forces in Europe. In both instances Mrs. Eisenhower was put in charge of extensive domestic staffs assigned to a large home which served as both living quarters for the Eisenhowers and as the site for large social events over which Mrs. Eisenhower presided. The NATO assignment provided Mrs. Eisenhower with extensive opportunities to plan and carry out large social events attended by an array of important international guests. The couple lived in a 14-room villa at Marnes-la-Coquette just outside Paris where she was often the hostess for gatherings of more than 100 guests, including European royalty.

A second way her life before the White House contributed to Mrs. Eisenhower's preparation for becoming First Lady came from her experience overseeing a large number of aids assigned to carry out an event. The social obligations of military officers expanded with promotions; generals, particularly those assigned to major commands overseas, were expected to entertain important military, economic, and political figures. As her husband's career-related social obligations increased, so did Mrs. Eisenhower's comfort in giving orders to support staff, supervising the execution of those plans, and making immediate corrections if she thought they were needed. A third important factor was that Mrs. Eisenhower was comfortable with being married to a powerful husband. She understood politics and power and knew she might have to endure overly harsh criticisms of either herself or her husband. Mrs. Eisenhower was used to guarding her public and private actions so as to not embarrass her husband or harm his career. She adopted the practice of avoiding saying or doing anything controversial and always maintaining a gracious appearance.

Another strength Mrs. Eisenhower brought with her to the White House was an apparent determination to create what later might have been called an appropriate "image" which would support the position of her husband. She was passionately devoted to her family and provided the public with countless images of a caring wife, mother, and grandmother. She also sought to present a fitting picture of a president's wife and was successful in doing so. Mrs. Eisenhower was named to several "best-dressed" lists of prominent Americans. Her favorite color was pink and she wore it often and in a variety of ways. She also popularized bangs to the point that they became known as "Mamie bangs."

Mrs. Eisenhower did not participate in politics and policy issues. Not only did she not take public positions on contemporary issues, she eschewed even talking about politics and issues with her husband during their private personal times together. "It wasn't my business anyway – he was President and I wasn't," she explained to an interviewer. Likewise, she completely avoided giving public speeches and news conferences. The First Lady entered the Oval Office itself only four times during her husband's eight years in the Presidency. And she did on those occasions only after being invited to do so, she reported.

Aside from attending to personal family matters, Mrs. Eisenhower devoted her time as First Lady to planning and carrying out the myriad of social obligations associated with the White House. By all accounts she excelled at all of the duties associated with such activities. She planned each occasion, particularly those held in the White House itself, down to the smallest detail, seeing to the receptions, parties, state dinners, and other social gatherings in the White House. With the White House staff, Mrs. Eisenhower quickly established a reputation of being the lone person in charge, who saw her as a forceful yet fair manager who paid great attention to the countless details of overseeing the operation of the White House.

Mrs. Eisenhower welcomed life in the White House, as it was the most permanent address she had enjoyed since their marriage in 1916. She enjoyed being able to have her family live in one location for the longest time in their marriage. Her mother, Mrs. Elivera Carlson Doud, also lived with them until periodically and Mamie's son John and his family were frequent guests for fairly lengthy stays. The sights and sounds of grandchildren playing in the hallways and on the White House grounds was comforting and uplifting for both the President and the First Lady.

LIFE AFTER THE WHITE HOUSE

The Eisenhowers had a long and generally happy marriage which survived powerful obstacles presented by a career as an Army officer – long workdays; frequent household moves; living in cramped, uncomfortable, and at times harsh conditions; and several lengthy separations caused by duty. While such factors would severely strain any marriage, the Eisenhowers overcame occasional disagreements triggered by his career demands and arrived at a mutually-acceptable arrangement. Indeed, there is substantial evidence suggesting that they had a generally strong marriage. For example, each of them exchanged lengthy and frequent letters when they were apart. Many of these letters suggest a healthy marriage, marked by occasional disagreements. The most serious threat, the rumored "affair" between Ike and Kay Summersby, was never documented and vigorously denied by the general.

Like their husbands, First Ladies have been subjected to analysis. In the handful of ratings of First Ladies that exist, Mrs. Eisenhower has tended to be ranked near the middle of most classification schemes, which tend to focus primarily on Twentieth Century First Ladies. A poll conducted in 1980 by *Good Housekeeping* Magazine had Mrs. Eisenhower ranked in a tie for 13th place with Mrs. Grace Coolidge. A survey of presidential scholars by R. P. Watson found Mrs. Eisenhower ranked 33rd and she was rated 17th in a survey conducted by the Siena Research Institute.

In conclusion, perhaps the motto of Mrs. Eisenhower as First Lady would be "dutiful service." Her clear preference was to remain in the background and do whatever necessary to support her husband in meeting his responsibilities as President of the United States. While she valued her privacy and her family relationships above all else, she also felt obligated to meet the challenges of her position as the wife of the President. She remained an exceptionally strong presence in those areas in which she thought proper for a First Lady – managing the social side of the White House and tending to family matters. Mrs. Eisenhower died on November 1, 1979 in Washington, D.C.

Chapter 23

JACQUELINE KENNEDY

Gil Troy

CAMELOT

She was a most unlikely politician's wife. The elegant pearls, the soft "babykins" voice, the stolen moments reading Proust at campaign stops, all suggested that Jacqueline Bouvier Kennedy was too blue-blooded to be her husband's cheerleader. Even John Kennedy worried in the 1950s that his "fey" wife had "too much status and not enough quo" to be politically useful.

And yet, Jackie Kennedy may have been America's most compelling First Lady. She was the first, and so far only, "superstar" First Lady. She shaped the image of her husband's administration more than any presidential wife including Eleanor Roosevelt. From her inaugural star-turn as the chic 31-year-old fashion plate, to her poignant performance as the grieving widow one thousand days later, Mrs. Kennedy helped generate the Kennedy "magic" that entranced America from 1961 to 1963.

Serving at the height of the Cold War, she and her husband Jack dazzled the world. In De Gaulle's France, Jackie proved so popular that the leader of the free world introduced himself as "the man who accompanied Jacqueline Kennedy to Paris." Uninterested in policy and ambivalent about her role, Jackie Kennedy nevertheless played her part magnificently. With her White House renovation, she proved that a First Lady needed a useful project, and positioned the presidential spouse as a key public relations partner in the media age. Fittingly, in those awful days after her husband's murder, Mrs. Kennedy immortalized his administration- and their joint accomplishment – by calling their "brief, shining moment... Camelot."

Nearly four decades later it is easy to overlook how hard both Kennedys worked to project their aura of effortless glamour. It is also easy to forget how rocky Mrs. Kennedy's tenure was, as she balanced her professed desire to be "just" a mother to her children, the traditional white-gloved demands that the President's wife be genteel, reporters' calls for an activist and accessible First Lady, and her own attraction to the spotlight.

UPBRINGING

Like Jack Kennedy, Jacqueline Bouvier was raised in a world of wealth and elegance that emphasized appearances over integrity. Born to John Vernon Bouvier III and Janet Norton Lee in 1929, Jacqueline Lee Bouvier was the oldest of two sisters. The Bouviers' marriage was a decadent upper-class alliance between his social standing and her newer money. Jackie's parents divorced when she was eleven.

Especially after her mother remarried, Jackie lived amid great splendor yet somehow felt deprived. She was educated at the finest institutions: Miss Porter's School for Girls, Vassar, George Washington, and the Sorbonne. These schools drilled her in the fine points of the domestic ideal, bred her for aristocratic living, and honed her considerable intelligence.

Jackie could be haughty; her classmates nicknamed her "Jacqueline Borgia." But she could also be saucy and funny. In June 1947, Jacqueline vowed in her senior yearbook "Not to be a housewife." And for all her girlish iconoclasm, Jackie was thrilled when Igor Cassini, the Hearst gossip columnist, named her "The Queen Deb" of 1947. Jackie was flirtatious yet prim. A breathy and little-girlish way of talking masked her intelligence. She received her B.A. in 1951 and in 1952 Jackie became the *Washington Times-Herald's* "Inquiring Photographer."

MRS. KENNEDY

Jackie met Jack Kennedy in 1951 at a dinner party. The 34-year-old Congressman invited the 20-year-old brunette for a drink. She demurred. A boyfriend had snuck into her car and was waiting for her. Over the next two years, they had "a very spasmodic courtship," Jackie would recall. If Jackie was moodier than Jack would have liked, she was at least cultured and intelligent. If Jack was less romantic than Jackie would have liked, he was at least successful and sober. He had money, she had class, and both were Catholic. On September 12, 1953, 1400 guests attended the Kennedys' "storybook wedding." This marriage was made in public. Jackie's private life would be public fodder for the rest of her days.

Alas, the marriage was no fairy tale. In their first two years, Jackie miscarried and Jack suffered from Addison's disease and two spinal operations. He missed the entire 1955 Senate session. Jackie resented her husband's roving eye and single-minded ambition. She dreamed of "a normal" nine-to-five life. Still, "The Deb" displayed resilience underneath the porcelain. She changed Jack's oozing wound, buoyed his spirits, and inspired him to write *Profiles in Courage*, which won the Pulitzer Prize.

Caroline's birth in November 1957 belied the rumors of a doomed marriage. The next year, the "team of Jack and Jackie" campaigned in almost 200 cities for Jack's reelection and a Democratic Congress. When Jackie stumped, the crowds doubled. Like good makeup, Jackie highlighted Jack's best features. Her breeding brought class to his wealth, her glamour made him look cool but not cold, her Continental ways added some *savoir-faire*.

Although John Kennedy won the presidency in 1960 by packaging his persona, he dismissed all the hoopla. "When you run for the Presidency your wife's hair or your hair or something else always becomes of major significance," Kennedy sighed. "I don't think it's a great issue, though, in 1960." Jackie remained unconventional. She often bristled on the campaign trail. Tensions between the two sometimes surfaced. Before one of their rare joint appearances, one aide reminded the Senator to "turn to her with a gesture or a smile."

FIRST LADY

The Kennedys were playing a dangerous game. The celebration of "youth, babies and beauty" generated excitement. Her poise and her interest in the arts would give the administration a sophisticated sheen. But the Kennedys had to live up to the legend and avoid appearing too callow or too calculating.

Barely three weeks after her husband's victory, Jackie gave birth to John F. Kennedy, Jr. John Junior's birth gave Jackie more cover as she entered the White House. She wanted to be First Wife and First Mother, not First Lady. Yet Jackie seemed more like a movie star than "an old fashioned wife." The "Jackie look" swept America. She became America's favorite cover girl.

Jackie Kennedy tried to separate her official and personal roles. She rejected the title of "First Lady" as suited to "a saddle horse." She preferred the more democratic "Mrs. Kennedy." The "President's wife should be just that – his wife," she insisted. "People must be as sick of hearing about us and (Caroline's pony) Macaroni as I am," she snapped. While commanding her press secretary to give reporters "minimum information – with maximum politeness," Mrs. Kennedy sometimes lapsed and lashed out at the "harpies" covering her.

Nevertheless, the thirty-one-year-old Jackie Kennedy revolutionized the role of First Lady. Rather than playing to America's matrons she played to the cameras, and the middle class masses. She combined the well-bred woman's interest in philanthropy, the arts, and entertaining with the suburbanite's zeal for home improvement and PTA meetings. Her four major projects – the White House restoration, a more elegant social season, support for the arts, and Caroline's nursery school – illustrated the mix. Jackie would not humor garden clubs or help the poor. Her efforts revealed a penetrating and effective executive beneath the girlish facade.

The First Lady's reserve enhanced her appeal. Mrs. Kennedy had everything – money, brains, sex appeal – yet she wanted to be a mom. "If you bungle raising your children I don't think whatever else you do well matters very much," she preached. This reformed career girl validated other "Happy Housewives'" choices. Reporters went wild. "We interviewed Jackie's hairdresser, her pianist, her caterer ... even ... the owner of the local diaper service," Helen Thomas of UPI recalled. Once, Thomas called the Kennedy press secretary, Pierre Salinger, at 3 A.M. to inquire whether one of Caroline's hamsters had died.

Scrutiny of Jack's weekend activities, Jackie's purchases, Caroline's jokes, John-John's first steps, overwhelmed the White House press office. Salinger "found it impossible to jump from an announcement on nuclear testing to a precise description of Mrs. Kennedy's latest hat." He consigned "all questions involving society, zoology, and millinery" to the East Wing. Forty people now helped the First Lady cope with her public duties.

Unlike Mrs. Kennedy, Jack Kennedy and his men indulged reporters. They believed that, as Arthur Schlesinger, Jr., would say, "His 'coolness' was itself a new frontier." Kennedy worried about Jackie's hostility to the press. "Poor Jack," she sneered, "he thinks if I ignore them he'll be impeached." At one dinner, the President grabbed the First Lady by the arm, dragged her across the hall and commanded: "say hello to the girls darling." Jackie renounced many of the First Lady's matronly duties. She often spurned invitations at the last minute with feeble excuses. She spent weekends on Cape Cod and in Palm Beach, holidayed on the Riviera, and lobbied for assignments to romantic places. When she announced her pregnancy in 1963, the President joked, "Now, Jackie will have an excuse to get out of things."

For all her popularity, Jackie Kennedy had little impact on policy. Echoing Mrs. Eisenhower, Mrs. Kennedy said she talked to the President "about family matters, never about matters of state." Jackie said, "Jack has always told me the one thing a busy man doesn't want to talk about at the end of the day is whether the Geneva Convention will be successful or what settlement could be made in Kashmir or anything like that."

To millions, Jackie symbolized all that was wrong with the Kennedys – their arrogance, wealth, and dynastic ambitions. Jackie Kennedy was caught in a culture clash. Many renounced a celebrity culture valuing fame for fame's sake. Leaders, especially First Ladies, were supposed to represent tradition.

Jackie remained defiant. "People told me 99 things that I had to do as First Lady, and I haven't done one of them," she boasted. A month before the 1962 elections, a Gallup Poll showed that Mrs. Kennedy remained popular. Respondents most often mentioned her "good looks," her "good personality," and her intelligence. But her actions attracted criticism. Asked "what are the things you like least about her," respondents mentioned her travels away from her family, her love of the limelight, her hairdo, her clothes and her undignified behavior.

In August 1963, Jackie gave birth five weeks prematurely. Jackie was vacationing on Cape Cod and Jack was working in Washington. Jack was with Patrick Bouvier Kennedy when he died two days later at the Children's Medical Center in Boston. Jackie was recuperating on the Cape. Two months later, Jackie was off cruising the Mediterranean aboard the 303-foot yacht *Christina,* owned by the notorious Greek shipping magnate, Aristotle Onassis. When she returned, Jack exploited "Jackie's guilt feelings" to get her politicking. By November 1963 his approval ratings were down to 43 percent.

Jackie's concession placed her by her husband's side in Dallas when a bullet shattered his brain. Her presence in the convertible united the two in death as nothing had done in life. The assassination, and the spectacle that followed, retroactively exorcised any public doubts about the Kennedys or their marriage. Widowhood made Jacqueline Kennedy the primary keeper of Jack's flame. No longer a thorn in his side, no longer a potential political liability to be neutralized, she guarded Jack's image. Troubled by the meaninglessness of the death, she helped make his death a monument to American idealism. Retroactively labeling her husband's administration "Camelot," was a masterstroke. One of the most influential actions of a First Lady in American history, Jackie's labeling proved stronger than all the ugly revelations that followed.

The Cold War's lifestyle battle focused on the First Couple at a time when other presidential weapons like party loyalty were being dulled. First Couples came to epitomize the country. Just as late twentieth century Presidents would strive to do right by Roosevelt in the Oval Office, all succeeding presidential couples would strive to succeed as the Kennedys appeared to have at home. Jackie Kennedy would live out her days as the Greta Garbo of American politics, always watched, rarely heard. For all her imperfections, for all her husband's scandals, the two would epitomize the great hopes, great faith, and great power Americans felt at the start of the 1960s.

Chapter 24

LADY BIRD JOHNSON

Claudia Wilson Anderson

INTRODUCTION

Long after returning to Texas from the White House, Lady Bird Johnson wrote about her role as First Lady, saying, "The Constitution of the United States does not mention the First Lady. She is elected by one man only. The statute books assign her no duties; and yet, when she gets the job, a podium is there if she cares to use it. I did. The public nature of the White House allowed me to focus attention on the environment, especially on plantings for roadsides and parks. But my story begins long before that – with a love of the land that started in my childhood."

UPBRINGING

Lady Bird Johnson's parents, Thomas Jefferson Taylor and Minnie Lee Patillo Taylor, were married in Alabama, in 1900. T. J. Taylor, as he was known, had moved to the east Texas town of Karnack from Alabama and was a merchant and "dealer in everything." He returned briefly to Alabama to marry his sweetheart, and the couple settled in Karnack. The Taylors had two sons in the early years of their marriage. Their third child was born in Karnack on December 22, 1912, and named Claudia Alta Taylor. When Claudia was two, her nursemaid remarked that she was as "purty as a lady bird," giving the child her well-known nickname.

When Lady Bird was only five years old, her mother died. As the child grew, her father realized that he needed help, and Lady Bird's aunt – her mother's sister – Effie Patillo, came to Texas from Alabama to help raise the young girl. Mrs. Johnson credits Aunt Effie with instilling in her the love of nature. She says of Aunt Effie: "She was the sweetest person, generally, but she had no idea of discipline, no idea of how to choose the right clothes or how to put a girl in the right society. She did, however, love beauty and nature, and she spent hours explaining how lovely the fields and meadows could be. She taught me how to listen to the wind in the pine trees and to the way birds sing."

Lady Bird's two brothers were much older and often away at school. She has said, "People always assume my childhood was lonely. To me, it definitely was not. I lived in a country of farm lands and pine forests and little country lanes. In the spring there were wild cherokee roses along the fence rows, and in the woods there were violets.... I spent a lot of time just walking and fishing and swimming." She developed an awareness of the environment very early in life. In her interviews and writings, she frequently refers to the East Texas of her childhood: Caddo Lake, "enchanted bayous," "picturesque gnarled cypress trees," and the "first wild violets" of spring. She speaks of a "love affair with nature" that began as a child.

Lady Bird attended a small rural elementary school and often visited relatives in Alabama with Aunt Effie during the summer. At age fifteen, she graduated from Marshall High School in Marshall, Texas, and went on to attend Saint Mary's Episcopal School for Girls in Dallas for two years before entering the University of Texas in Austin in 1930. In 1934 she received a bachelor of arts degree with a major in history. She remained at the University an additional year to earn a second degree in journalism.

MRS. JOHNSON

On August 31, 1934, a mutual friend introduced Lady Bird to Lyndon Johnson. The next morning the two met for breakfast, spent the day together, and Johnson proposed marriage. A week later, he returned to Washington, D. C., and his job as secretary to Congressman Richard Kleberg from South Texas. The two wrote a series of love letters over the next few weeks, and in November Lyndon Johnson returned to Texas, still proposing marriage. On November 17, 1934, Johnson finally persuaded Lady Bird to marry him, and they were married that very evening at St. Mark's Episcopal Church in San Antonio. After a brief honeymoon in Mexico, the newlyweds settled into an apartment in Washington, D. C. During their short courtship, they wrote a series of love letters. The letters from Lyndon Johnson show a dynamic young man full of energy. The letters from "Bird" Taylor show a young woman with a strong interest in the environment, but little enthusiasm for a life in politics. In one letter she wrote, "Lyndon, please tell me as soon as you can what the deal is .... I am afraid it is politics. Oh, I know I haven't any business – not any 'proprietary interest' – but I would hate for you to go into politics." Lady Bird was soon reconciled to Lyndon's ambitions and supported his run for the House of Representatives less than three years after their marriage.

By 1937, the Johnsons had returned to Austin from Washington, D. C., and Lyndon was the Texas State Director for the National Youth Administration. When the Congressman from the 10th District of Texas died in office, it presented the opportunity for Lyndon Johnson to enter politics. Lady Bird Johnson borrowed $10,000 from her share of her mother's estate to help finance her husband's campaign for the House seat. He won and spent the next twelve years in the House of Representatives.

In 1943, Lady Bird invested part of her inheritance in a small radio station, KTBC, in Austin, Texas. In the months following the station's purchase, Lady Bird spent much of her time in Austin, getting the business on its feet. With Lady Bird as chairman of the board, KTBC grew and became, with television station KTBC, the foundation of the Johnsons' financial interests. The Johnsons' first child, Lynda Bird, was born in 1944; their second, Luci Baines, was born in 1947. The year after Luci's birth, Lyndon Johnson decided to run for the Senate. He became the Democratic nominee by winning the Democratic primary by 87 votes, earning the nickname, "Landslide Lyndon." As the Democratic candidate, he easily won election to the Senate that fall. In 1955, Johnson became the Senate Majority Leader. During LBJ's years in the House and Senate, Mrs. Johnson's interest in the environment continued to mature. She frequently drove between Washington and Texas observing the nation's countryside, maintained a garden, and planted wildflowers at their home in Texas, the LBJ Ranch.

At the Democratic Convention in July 1960, John F. Kennedy selected Senator Johnson as his running mate. Lady Bird became the most visible woman on the campaign trail because Jacqueline Kennedy was pregnant and not able to actively campaign. Mrs. Johnson campaigned with LBJ across the Deep South and toured Texas with John Kennedy's sister, Eunice Shriver, and his sister-in-law, Ethel Kennedy, hosting a series of tea parties. After LBJ's election as Vice President, the Johnsons purchased a larger home, "The Elms," which was well-suited for entertaining. During this period Mrs. Johnson had the opportunity to travel extensively with LBJ, who made a number of foreign trips as Vice President representing the Kennedy administration.

FIRST LADY

On November 22, 1963, with the assassination of President Kennedy, Lyndon Johnson assumed the Presidency, and Mrs. Johnson was catapulted into the position of First Lady. At that moment, her priorities were to "ease Mrs. Kennedy's burdens, if she could," and "to make a comfortable, peaceful place" for her husband "to work and prepare to carry all the heavy load of public service." Throughout the administration she continued to see her primary role as one of creating a warm and comfortable environment for the President. Near the end of the administration when a reporter asked Mrs. Johnson about the role of a First Lady, she reiterated the theme, saying, "her role principally, is to support and give solace and companionship to her husband ... to give him an island of serenity in which to work, to do his job." While she felt strongly that this was true, Mrs. Johnson also seized the opportunity to use her position to speak for the issues that were close to her heart.

During the first year of the Johnson administration, as the President pressed for legislation to eliminate racial injustices and aid those in poverty, Mrs. Johnson too focused on poverty and prejudice. She made several high profile trips, including a tour with President Johnson of desperately poor areas of Appalachia. The trips highlighted the need for more educational aid and better health care for the poor, as well as the dangers that racial inequity posed for the nation. Soon after be coming First Lady, Mrs. Johnson inaugurated a series of "Women Doers Luncheons" at the White House. These luncheons, which continued throughout the Johnson Presidency, highlighted issues of concern to women and recognized women's accomplishments. During that first year, Mrs. Johnson also addressed a number of women's groups and organizations, including the graduating class at Radcliffe College. Many of these speeches were compiled into a booklet distributed in the 1964 campaign under the title, "It is a good time to be a Woman ... . It is a good time to be Alive." The speeches encouraged women to value education, be active citizens, and to work for better lives for their families and communities.

At the time of the Kennedy assassination, the White House renovation that Mrs. Kennedy began was well underway, but not complete. On November 26, 1963, four days after the assassination of President Kennedy, Mrs. Kennedy invited Mrs. Johnson to tea to discuss housekeeping details. During the visit, Mrs. Kennedy gave Mrs. Johnson a handwritten memo about the things she had done in restoring the White House. She asked Mrs. Johnson to safeguard and continue her work. The next March, President Johnson signed an Executive Order establishing a Committee for the Preservation of the White House to continue Mrs. Kennedy's work and ensure the proper care of the White House and its many artifacts. Mrs. Johnson served as an active member of the Committee wanting to ensure "continuity in all of the good things that have been done, preservation of everything that has gone forward."

Throughout the Johnson administration, Mrs. Johnson maintained a diary. When she had quiet time available, she would record her thoughts on a tape recorder and later have the recordings transcribed. She frequently saved clippings, programs, and bits of memorabilia in large envelopes filed by day; she used these to jog her memory when, maybe several days later, she was able to find the time to record her thoughts and deeds. After leaving office, she selected the most interesting days from the transcripts and published them in *A White House Diary*.

The campaign of 1964 brought new opportunities for Mrs. Johnson to help the President. She became the first wife of a President to campaign by herself for her husband. In October 1964, Mrs. Johnson traveled 1,682 miles in four days on a train dubbed the "Lady Bird Special." The train went from Alexandria, Virginia, to New Orleans, Louisiana, making 28 scheduled stops along the way. Johnson's civil rights legislative agenda was unpopular in the South, and Mrs. Johnson wanted to campaign there. She explained her reasons in a speech to the crowd as she departed Alexandria, Virginia, "I want to tell you from Alexandria to New Orleans that to this President and his wife the South is a respected and valued and beloved part of the country. I know that many of you do not agree with the Civil Rights Bill or with the President's support of it, but I do know the South respects candor and courage and I believe he has shown both." During the trip, Mrs. Johnson endured the boos and yells of hecklers, but the trip successfully illustrated the Johnsons' regard for the South. Following the "Whistle Stop Campaign," Mrs. Johnson made a plane trip to campaign at stops in Texas, Oklahoma, Arkansas, Indiana, and Kentucky.

FIRST LADY OF THE ENVIRONMENT

At the time of the Kennedy assassination, Lady Bird Johnson told a friend, "I feel like I am suddenly on stage for a part I never rehearsed." In spite of her reservations, Lady Bird had been well-prepared for the part by her experiences as a businesswoman, campaigner, and hostess, and by her travels abroad during her husband's years as Vice President. Not only was Mrs. Johnson well-prepared for the role of First Lady, but the nation was receptive to the environmental agenda that Mrs. Johnson would decide, by 1965, to pursue. Rachel Carson had published *Silent Spring* in 1962, President Kennedy had called a White House Conference on Conservation in 1962, and Secretary of the Interior, Stewart Udall, published a book called *The Quiet Crisis* in 1963. At the time of the assassination, a Wilderness Bill and a Land and Water Bill were pending before Congress and had White House support. There was a growing recognition in the nation of the importance of conservation.

As the 1964 campaign had approached, Mrs. Johnson began to consider what she wanted to do if the President were elected to a full term. On May 22, 1964, President Johnson delivered what has become known as his "Great Society Speech." In this speech, President Johnson clearly linked the country's natural splendor to his vision of the Great Society. Recalling the speech, Mrs. Johnson wrote, "... as I began to see the things he was applying himself to, there emerged the interests that made my heart sing, the ones that I knew most about and cared most about. Those were the environment and beautification."

In August 1964, Mrs. Johnson made a trip to Montana, Utah, and Wyoming with Interior Secretary Stewart Udall. The trip was multipurpose: to campaign, dedicate a dam, visit Indian reservations and speak at the University of Utah. Although the trip occurred before Mrs. Johnson took up the banner of "beautification," her speeches were peppered with references to the environment, and in many ways this trip was a precursor of trips made later to highlight the country's natural wonders and national parks. It was on this trip that Secretary Udall realized the First Lady had an extraordinary interest in conservation.

With the landslide election of her husband in November 1964, Mrs. Johnson began to seriously evaluate her own role in the new administration. She has spoken often about wanting to choose some of those things that made her "heart sing," and in 1965, Mrs. Johnson centered her attention in two areas, an interest in children and education through Project Head Start and conservation through her "beautification" campaign.

The first priority of Mrs. Johnson's beautification campaign was an effort to beautify the nation's capital. Mrs. Johnson headed the First Lady's Committee for a More Beautiful Capital, bringing together a number of philanthropists, community leaders, and experts interested in the environment. The Committee was responsible for many landscaping and architectural projects, including planting thousands of the bulbs and flowering trees that still blossom every spring in the capital. Next was a visible campaign to clean up the nation's countryside and cities. The infectious movement spread to communities all across the nation. That year, President Johnson submitted the Highway Beautification Bill to Congress. The bill, which many thought of as "Lady Bird's bill," called for restrictions on billboards and junkyards along highways. Mrs. Johnson lobbied for the bill and has said, "This was one instance when I gathered up enough courage to call a few key people in Congress to urge passage of this bill!"

To highlight beautification, Mrs. Johnson made trips to a number of scenic areas of the country. She treated the pubic to delightful press photos of her rafting down the Rio Grande River in Big Bend National Park, walking on Texas seashores, and hiking through California Redwoods. Her journeys had the added dimension of supporting the Johnson administration's "See America First" campaign, which was designed to help with the foreign balance of payments deficit.

Although beautification consumed much of Mrs. Johnson's time from 1965 to the end of the administration, she also devoted considerable energies to Project Head Start. After a tea at the White House for the Advisory Council of the War on Poverty on February 3, 1965, Sargent Shriver, head of the Office of Economic Opportunity, asked Mrs. Johnson to serve as honorary chairman for Head Start. That night Mrs. Johnson recorded in her diary, "After this heady meeting I am more inclined to say 'Yes,' although I don't like being just 'honorary' anything. If I take it on, I want to work at it." She became an active honorary chairman, traveling to New Jersey to observe Head Start in operation and hosting White House events to underscore her interest in Head Start and in underprivileged children.

In 1965, the Johnsons began to consider plans for a Presidential Library in Texas. Mrs. Johnson took much of the burden of planning off of the President's shoulders, meeting with experts, helping select the architect, and traveling to existing Presidential Libraries. After returning to Texas, and later after President Johnson's death, Mrs. Johnson continued to have a strong interest in the LBJ Library's programs.

LIFE AFTER THE WHITE HOUSE

On March 31, 1968, President Johnson announced that he would not accept the nomination for another term as President. This was a decision that Mrs. Johnson strongly supported, and on January 20, 1969, with the inauguration of President Richard Nixon, the Johnsons returned to Texas. There President Johnson died on January 22, 1973. Mrs. Johnson has continued to lobby and campaign for the environment. She worked on the beautification of Town Lake in Austin; she sponsored highway awards for Texas Highway Department workers; and, at seventy, she founded the National Wildflower Center. In 1988, with co-author and horticulturist, Carlton B. Lees, she wrote a book on wildflowers.

Mrs. Johnson now lives in Austin, Texas, and often enjoys the company of her seven grandchildren and five great-grandchildren. During retirement she has served on numerous boards, committees, and commissions; she served on the University of Texas Board of Regents, was appointed to the Commission on White House Fellows by President Carter, and was the honorary chairman of the LBJ Memorial Grove on the Potomac in Washington, D.C. In 1977, President Ford awarded her the Medal of Freedom and, in 1988, she received the Congressional Gold Medal from President Ronald Reagan.

Chapter 25

PAT NIXON

Mary Linehan

UPBRINGING

Thelma "Pat" Ryan was born on March 16, 1912, in the Nevada mining town of Ely. As a child, she moved with her family to a small truck farm in Artesia, California. A tomboy whose nickname was "Buddy," Pat also worked hard on the farm. She picked tomatoes and cauliflower and drove the team of horses. When Pat was fourteen her mother died of cancer and she took over as housekeeper for her father and two older brothers. Despite long hours in the kitchen and fields, Pat was an excellent student and just missed being valedictorian of her class. When she was a senior in high school, her father became seriously ill and she added nursing to her responsibilities. Before her graduation, Pat's father died. She later admitted, "as a youngster life was sort of sad, so I had to cheer everybody up. I learned to be that kind of person." Such fortitude would serve her well later in life.

Young Pat Ryan did have dreams. She yearned to travel to faraway places. She also dreamed of getting a college education and broadening her horizons. "I always wanted to do something besides be buried in a small town," she told a reporter. To finance her education at the University of Southern California, Pat worked as a cleaning woman, chauffeur, stenographer, X-ray technician, store clerk, telephone operator, and movie extra. In 1937, she graduated *cum laude* with degrees in education and business. She wanted to be a department store buyer but, with the country in economic depression, she gratefully took a teaching job when it was offered to her. At Whittier High School, Pat taught typing and shorthand. She also directed the school plays and coached the cheerleaders.

MRS. NIXON

In the fall of 1938, Pat tried out for a role in a play being produced by the Whittier Community Players. She earned the part and met an ambitious young attorney named Richard Nixon. That evening, he told Pat he intended to marry her. Pat recalled, "I thought he was nuts." Nonetheless, Nixon pursued a courtship. He took up ice-skating and dancing to impress her, wrote poems for Pat, graded her students' assignments, and even drove her to dates with other men. Eventually the stubborn suitor wore down her resistance. By the time Nixon proposed in March 1940, Pat was in love and readily accepted. They were married in a simple Quaker service on June 21, 1940.

The outbreak of World War II brought the young couple to Washington, D.C. where they worked for the Office of Price Administration. When her husband requested active duty in the Navy, Pat moved to San Francisco and was promoted within the OPA. The Nixons wrote to each other everyday when he was overseas. He praised her contributions, writing: "I am really *very* proud. I like to tell the gang how smart you are as well as being the most attractive person they'll ever see."

After the War, Nixon entered politics instead of practicing law. Pat was not thrilled with his choice, but said, "I could see it was the life he wanted, so I told him that it was his decision and I would do what he liked." Pat did give her husband two conditions: One, that there would be no politics at home so that their children (Tricia born in 1946 and Julie in 1948) could have a normal life; two, that she would not have to make speeches. Both promises were soon broken, but the "Dick and Pat" team was born. While he stumped for votes, she worked in the campaign headquarters. During the 1946 race for Congress, Pat sometimes made appearances with her husband. Though it was obvious to the staff that she was "nervous, uptight and tense," they agreed that – with her warmth and charm – Pat Nixon was "a hell of an asset." As she would do throughout Richard Nixon's career, Pat's charisma softened his dour personality and made him more human and accessible to voters.

A friend said of Pat Nixon, "she didn't want politics ever. She hated the idea of facing another campaign. Every time Nixon entered one she was in deep despair." Nonetheless, with each campaign her contributions became more significant. When he ran for reelection to the House in 1948 and for election to the Senate in 1950, she worked in the office, helped prepare his speeches, and made campaign appearances on her own. In 1952, when her husband was nominated for the Vice Presidency by the Republicans, Pat proudly announced, "we work as a team." She handled mail and news releases, attended women's meetings, and made informal non-political speeches. A party official claimed, "she's the best one on the whole ticket." Because of her graciousness, her simplicity, and her spontaneity, "the crowds just love her."

When the Eisenhower-Nixon ticket won the presidential election, Pat became the most politically involved Second Lady to date. She made frequent goodwill tours with her husband. They paid official visits to Asia, Africa, England, and the Soviet Union. Pat studied the countries she was to visit and, while there, tried to avoid ceremonial functions. She preferred to see schools, hospitals, and orphanages. She insisted on meeting women's groups in every country the Nixons visited. Pat wanted to bring attention to women's accomplishments and their problems, especially in nations where women's status was low. State Department officials and President Eisenhower praised Pat's diplomatic successes. This was especially true in May 1958 when the Nixons were the targets of death threats and violent anti-American demonstrations in Peru and Venezuela. One of the Secret Service agents said Pat displayed, "more guts than any man I've ever seen." The press called her "magnificent."

The Second Lady was so popular that when Richard Nixon ran against John F. Kennedy in the 1960 presidential election, the Republicans made Pat an important part of the campaign. "When you elect a President, you are electing a First Lady whose job is more than glamour," they announced. "The First Lady has a working assignment. She represents

America to all the world. Pat Nixon is part of the experienced Nixon team. She's uniquely qualified for the position of First Lady." Pat attended coffees and rallies in her honor and forcefully spoke out, encouraging women to engage in the political process. She described herself as "reflective of women all over America taking an active part, not only in political life, but in all activities." Perhaps because of her activism in the 1960 campaign, Pat was especially bitter when her husband lost the election. Her distaste for politics increased when Nixon lost his 1962 campaign for Governor of California.

Six years later, with Pat's encouragement, Nixon re-entered the presidential fray. She took a very active role in the campaign. Pat sought vindication for past losses and she was genuinely convinced that "he alone was capable of solving some of the problems we were facing in the country." During the race, Pat asserted her interest in women's issues. She told a reporter she gave her husband advice on "what women think." In light of the Vietnam War and her husband's promise that he had a "secret plan" to end hostilities, she explained, "they are thinking peace at home and peace abroad." Pat rejoiced at the Republican victory and told her daughter, "I felt at last that Daddy was where he could really be of value to the country and to the world."

FIRST LADY

Pat Nixon made valuable contributions to the nation and the world. As First Lady, she was a superb hostess. She liked entertaining, not only dignitaries and celebrities, but also people from orphanages, hospitals, and nursing homes. She continued her involvement with women's groups and frequently hosted luncheons and receptions for them. The women of the press corps were especially impressed. Helen Thomas explained, "she is warm and kind and goes the extra mile to shake a hand and greet a stranger. She is concerned about people's feelings." Her graciousness and warmth also extended to her correspondence. Pat received an overwhelming volume of mail. At first she tried to read every letter. When this task became too burdensome, she coached her staff to respond with promptness and courtesy even to her critics.

As First Lady, Pat Nixon continued to travel on behalf of the country. She created good feelings wherever she went – the Soviet Union, China, Africa, Europe – by her knowledge of the countries she visited and her interest in their customs and culture. In May 1970, after a terrible earthquake destroyed large parts of Peru, Pat – in spite of the hostile reception she received on her last visit – insisted on flying to Lima with tons of relief supplies. The Peruvian government rewarded her with their highest national honor and relations between the United States and Peru dramatically improved. In 1972, after she represented the United States at the inauguration of the Liberian President, the President's aides (who had previously been hostile to the First Lady and her staff) conceded, "Mrs. Nixon has now broken through where we have failed." They wrote to the President, "she has come across as a warm, charming, graceful, concerned, articulate, and most importantly, a very human person. People identify with her and in return with you."

Pat Nixon's special project as First Lady was to encourage volunteerism. She explained, "government is impersonal, and to really get our problems solved we need to have people too. We need the personal touch." She especially encouraged women to become involved in volunteer service to their communities. In March 1969, Pat traveled across the country to study and publicize voluntary efforts on behalf of the poor, the disabled, and children. When she visited colleges and universities, Pat was confronted by student protesters opposed to Richard Nixon's Vietnam policy. She often silenced her critics with kindness. One demonstrator stated: "she wanted to listen. I felt like this is a woman who really cares about what we are doing. I was surprised. I didn't expect her to be like that." Once again, pat softened her husband's image and brought credit to his administration.

Pat Nixon could not, however, save her husband from his greatest political crisis. When she first heard reports of the bungled burglary of the Democratic headquarters in Washington, she thought they were "blown all out of proportion." When it became clear that Nixon had tried to block an investigation of the Watergate break-in, she claimed, "it's right out of *The Merchant of Venice*. They're after their last pound of flesh." Convinced that the growing scandal was a Democratic ploy to destroy her husband, Pat remained fiercely loyal. She told one reporter, "I have great faith in my husband... [and] I love him." There were rumors that Pat had become an alcoholic as a result of the scandal and that the Nixons were planning to divorce. These stories were false. Pat's loyalty never failed, even as the House Judiciary Committee considered articles of impeachment, she believed he would win. The Nixon women wanted the President to fight on, but when he decided on resignation Pat declared, "we're all proud of you Daddy."

LIFE AFTER THE WHITE HOUSE

In retirement the Nixons settled in San Clemente, California. Pat, in deep despair, became a recluse. She refused to do interviews, serve on charity boards, or see her friends. Nonetheless, she remained one of the most admired women in America according to a "Ladies Home Journal" poll. In July 1976 Pat suffered a stroke that left her partially paralyzed and with a slight speech defect. As she recovered, and resumed gardening and reading, "McCall's" called her the "unsinkable Pat Nixon." As she explained to her daughter Julie, "Watergate is the only crisis that ever got me down." Pat continued to be bitter that the scandal was the only thing people remembered about the Nixon administration. She blamed White House aide Robert Halderman for Watergate and believed her husband would eventually be vindicated.

In the 1980s, the Nixons moved to the New York City area to be closer to their children and grandchildren. A second stroke in 1983 left her in frail health. Although she never permitted herself to be seen smoking in public, Pat was a lifelong smoker. In her later years she suffered from lung problems and emphysema. Pat Nixon died of lung cancer on June 22, 1993. She was 81 years old, and had fulfilled her childhood dreams of seeing the world and making a difference.

Chapter 26

BETTY FORD

Jeffrey S. Ashley

UPBRINGING

Betty Ford was born Elizabeth Bloomer on April 8, 1918 in Chicago, Illinois. She was a typical child with a normal upbringing – something she emphasizes to this day. According to Mrs. Ford herself, both she and President Ford were everyday people who came from common middle-class backgrounds. Nevertheless, these common people were thrust into the spotlight during uncommon times. The post-Watergate political environment provided a setting which made an inherently difficult and stressful job even more taxing. The "common" background of Mrs. Ford must have instilled in her something special in order for her to survive – by most accounts, flourish – under such circumstances. However, while her background as a dancer, model, professional woman, mother, and congressional wife were all crucial to her development as a person, this essay will focus on her approach to the office of First Lady and the ways she used the office as well as her life after the White House.

FIRST LADY

Family and Personal Identity

First and foremost, Mrs. Ford entered into the office intent on maintaining family relations. To her, family had always been of the utmost importance. Beyond the inherent ties that a mother has with her children, Mr. and Mrs. Ford were true companions and confidants. President Ford's oath of office provides some insight into the importance of the partnership that the Fords had developed over the years. When he stated that, "I am indebted to no man and only one woman – my dear wife," it became clear that Mrs. Ford was much more than a social companion. She and Mr. Ford had done their best to maintain a normal family life during his years in Congress, and she was not about to see that disappear. While she knew that job pressures would undoubtedly put some strain on the family and that time would be hard to come by, she set out to maintain stability in any way possible. One seemingly small attempt at normalcy actually created a minor stir when Mrs. Ford insisted that she and the President would not be sleeping in separate bedrooms and that they would be bringing their own bed into the White House. She was accused of being immoral but did not worry about such comments. She was perfectly willing to take on the duties of First Lady but was not about to give up a part of herself and the things in which she cared in the process.

In addition to caring for her family and Mr. Ford, Mrs. Ford was careful to take care of herself and to keep her sense of humor. At one point in her life, she buckled under the strain of raising children, keeping an active social and political calendar, and managing the house while her husband was away much of the time. After seeking some help, Mrs. Ford realized that she was not superhuman and that she occasionally needed to take some time for herself. She also realized that maintaining her individuality was of vital importance and that becoming active in things that mattered to her was crucial. Above all, she learned humility – a trait that would later endear her to those around her and to a healing nation. She brought this philosophy into the White House and it not only helped her, but it helped the President and those around her. One cannot help but think that the free-spirited Mrs. Ford had a positive influence on the White House staff by treating them as family and jokingly placing cigarettes in the hands of otherwise stately statues for the unsuspecting to find. The unpretentious atmosphere created by Mrs. Ford was a breath of fresh air in a troubled time and was very well received. As ex-Beatle George Harrison put it, "I feel good vibes about this White House."

Life was not all fun and games, however. Mrs. Ford also realized that the office required a certain seriousness and that the citizenry was scrutinizing the entire Ford administration, the First Lady included. Mrs. Ford was placed center stage and was asked to perform without time to truly prepare. Her approach: she believed that the best way to deal with public matters was to avoid skirting issues and to be as honest as possible.

Honest

Having spent a number of years in Washington prior to assuming the office, Mrs. Ford had friends and role models who had preceded her. From their experiences, she knew that there would be press conferences, questions, and constant attention. It was decided from the outset that her approach to the Office of the First Lady would be direct. In discussing her view on the position, Mrs. Ford stated that, "my approach was I will just be open and not beat around the bush and answer questions as best I can." The Ford Presidency came at a time when the citizenry was questioning the integrity of government and Mrs. Ford believed that candor and honesty would be crucial to the healing process. Such an approach was not especially difficult since it was in her nature. However, her openness was enhanced by the fact that she knew most of the members of Washington's press corps personally. All of the years spent in and around Washington had allowed Mrs. Ford to cultivate relationships with the press and, when thrust into the spotlight, she felt comfortable dealing with them. Even with personal relationships in place, however, the candor initially caught many in the media off guard. According to Mrs. Ford, "it was not what they expected and I think they were not only surprised but they were pleased. I didn't know how it was going to come out [the honest approach], but I felt I got good grades on that." Good grades indeed! According to one *Washington Post* columnist at the time, "she is too honest. Mrs. Ford wears her defects like diamonds. And they dazzle."

Of course there were times when the honest, candid approach led to controversy but Mrs. Ford stayed the course and never swayed from being as forthright as possible. From her views on abortion rights and the Equal Rights Amendment to marijuana, premarital sex, and other socially sensitive issues, Mrs. Ford was never shy about her position. To a small segment of the population, the honesty was too much and they felt she had overstepped her bounds. Fortunately, the vast majority of Americans embraced the honest approach embodied by Mrs. Ford. The general sentiment is best illustrated by the following letter of support:

I am 83 years old and one of my friends calls me the last of the Puritans. I haven't been able to decide what our society should do about abortion, and sex relations, and marijuana. But I do know what I think about honesty. I'm for it. And I am deeply grateful that we have someone in the White House who thinks integrity is more important than political advantage. Many thanks for your refreshing example.

The public support allowed Mrs. Ford to endorse and push for many of the programs that were important to her. She was not simply Mrs. Gerald Ford, but she was Betty Ford – a woman with her own identity and base of support. According to her former assistant, Sheila Weidenfield, "people liked her honesty, her sparkle, her frankness. What's more, as First Lady, she had some national influence. She could push causes and areas she believed in. For the first time in her life she was in the spotlight because of her *own* characteristics."

Mrs. Ford's Causes

Upon entering into the Office of the First Lady, Mrs. Ford was asked about her "program." She replied that she did not really have a program but that she had a number of interests that she planned to pursue. Among those interests were the arts and placing more attention on the neglected segments of society whom she felt were generally mistreated – primarily the elderly, the poor, and children with disabilities. Although she had no "program," Mrs. Ford attacked these issues with vigor and ended up addressing them all. She spent countless hours in local hospitals visiting sick children and fought to improve the condition of elderly persons living in nursing homes. As for the arts, Mrs. Ford had a particular fondness, especially for dance. As a child and young woman, she had dreamed of a career as a dancer and had even spent time in New York studying under Martha Graham. As First Lady, she had various people from the arts and humanities invited to the White House and fought for increased funding for the National Endowment for the Arts. Mrs. Ford even convinced President Ford to bestow the Presidential Medal of Freedom on her old dance instructor, Martha Graham – the first dancer ever to receive the prestigious honor. However, the issue that Mrs. Ford felt the strongest about – the issue for which she initially gained the most notoriety – was the promotion of equal rights for women.

Early in the Ford Presidency, Mrs. Ford clearly set the tone for things to come when, at the first full-fledged press conference by a First Lady in more than twenty years, she announced to reporters that she wanted to encourage greater political participation by women, endorsed the Supreme Court decision in *Roe v. Wade*, and would be actively campaigning for the Equal Rights Amendment. Mrs. Ford was true to her word. She made speeches in support of the ERA, openly discussed equal rights for women in interviews, and even contacted legislators across the country encouraging them to vote for the Amendment – and if they could not openly endorse the measure, she wanted them to at least allow it to come to a vote. So powerful was her message that she became the target of Phyllis Schafly, one of the primary players in the crusade against the passage of the ERA. Schafly, from the group STOP ERA, was so concerned that Mrs. Ford was having an impact that she (Schafly) demanded an accounting of how much federal money was being spent on the endorsement – either through telephone bills, staff time, or salaries of other federal officials working on the issue. Not to be dissuaded, Mrs. Ford carried on and pushed forward with true style. She even had an ERA flag (designed by one of her Secret Service agents) that was placed on her car. She had jokingly mentioned that the President and other dignitaries had flags but she did not. She said, "If the President gets flags, why shouldn't the First Lady?" What better way to announce *her* motorcade than with a bright red, white, and blue flag emblazoned with ERA?

In addition to supporting women's rights publicly, Mrs. Ford worked on the issue in private. Her so-called "pillow talk" resulted in the appointment of a female cabinet member and she tried to get President Ford to appoint the first woman to the Supreme Court. When they ran for reelection in 1976, she even pressed for a female running mate but stated, "there were too many men involved." To this day, both Mrs. and President Ford are advocates of women's rights in every way possible.

Perhaps Mrs. Ford's most lasting impact came in the area of breast cancer awareness – an issue she clearly had not intended to take on. She began her monumental fight on September 26, 1974, the day she was diagnosed with breast cancer. When a tumor was discovered, the entire Ford family was in shock. However, despite the very private nature of the situation, Mrs. Ford made an important decision which would have tremendous social impact: she decided to make her condition known to the public. This, of course, coincides with her philosophy of an open, honest, First Ladyship. While she could have quietly had the tumor removed and gone on with her life, giving the appearance that nothing had happened, she decided to discuss the uncomfortable issue of breast cancer and mastectomy. While such a decision was undoubtedly difficult, Mrs. Ford, being a very unassuming and humble person, acted as if she had no choice at all. According to her, "I got a lot of credit for having gone public with my mastectomy, but if I hadn't been the wife of the President of the United States, the press would not have come racing after my story, so in a way it was fate." She adds, "there had been so much cover-up during Watergate that we wanted to be sure there would be no cover-up in the Ford administration." Even if that meant exposing such a personal and sensitive issue. It must be remembered that, at the time, this was an issue that was not to be discussed in private, much less in public. These are very modest statements which tend to underplay the heroics of her decision and the impact that the decision had.

By going public with her cancer and mastectomy, Mrs. Ford was personally responsible for increased awareness and she became fully aware herself of the power that the First Lady holds. After she went public to alert as many women as possible of the benefits of early detection, millions of women scheduled appointments at breast cancer clinics across the country. According to Lisa Liebman, "her courage and candor not only removed the stigma from the topic but also saved countless lives." Physicians still refer to the "Betty Ford effect" and the number of diagnosed cases directly attributable to Mrs. Ford's speaking out.

There is no telling what other issues Mrs. Ford might have taken on, or whether the ERA might have had success, if Gerald Ford had won the 1976 election. Mrs. Ford most likely would have addressed and embraced issues as they arose, as that was her style. Nevertheless, Mrs. Ford continued to be a social activist after leaving the White House and continues her fight today, speaking out on cancer, reproductive rights, equal rights for women, social problems, and, of course, addiction.

LIFE AFTER THE WHITE HOUSE

Shortly after leaving the White House, Mrs. Ford once again found herself the unintended spokesperson for an illness that people never discussed openly. Instead of breast cancer, this time it was alcoholism and addiction. True to form, Mrs. Ford openly discussed her problem with reporters and the world, holding nothing back. Once again, her action had a tremendous spillover effect – if Betty Ford could have this problem, then it was less stigmatizing for others to have it too. She brought the topic to the forefront and made it safe for people to discuss the topic of addiction and to seek out help. As if this were not enough, Mrs. Ford went on to help countless other addicts by co-founding the Betty Ford Center on October 3, 1982.

Currently, Mrs. Ford can be found spending time with her husband, children, and grandchildren and she continues to oversee the operations of the Betty Ford Center in Rancho Mirage, California. She is also active in promoting women's rights, health care, and funding for substance abuse and has testified before Congress on several occasions. Her activism and social impact has been profound. By continuously giving herself, Mrs. Ford has been the recipient of over twenty prestigious awards including the Freedom of Human Spirit Award (International Center for the Disabled), the Hubert Humphrey Inspirational Award (The American Cancer Society), the Gold Key Award (National Council on Alcoholism), and the Presidential Medal of Freedom (awarded by President George Bush).

Finally, on October 17, 1999, she received the Congressional Gold Medal – something she considers to be one of her proudest moments. This award has been given to Presidents in the past but has not been bestowed upon presidential spouses. In this case, those in attendance were effusive in their praise for both President and Mrs. Ford with regard to their collective efforts to heal "a nation in torment."

With everything Mrs. Ford has accomplished – both in and out of the White House – it is easy to see why some scholars assert that "Betty Ford was, and is, the bridge to the modern first lady."

Chapter 27

Rosalynn Carter

Virginia A. Chanley

Overview

In December of 1980, as First Lady Rosalynn Carter neared the end of her time in the White House, the District of Columbia City Council met to honor the First Lady for her numerous contributions to the D.C. community. The Rosalynn Carter Appreciation Resolution noted the range of community activities undertaken by the First Lady, marking her distinctiveness among First Ladies in her commitment to the District of Columbia. The First Lady's community participation was a continuation of her involvement in the Carters' hometown of Plains, Georgia and her activities as First Lady of Georgia. Extensive as they are, Rosalynn's activities in Georgia and as First Lady are only a fraction of the contributions she has made in the years since leaving the White House. This brief biography sketches the life of First Lady Rosalynn Carter from her childhood in Plains, through her years in the White House and beyond.

Upbringing

Eleanor Rosalynn Smith was born in Plains, Georgia on August 18, 1927. Rosalynn was the first of four children born to Frances Allethea Murray Smith and Wilburn Edgar Smith. Wilburn Smith owned an auto repair shop, drove the school bus, worked in a mercantile store on the weekends, and ran a small farm. Before her own marriage, Rosalynn's mother Allethea graduated from college with a teacher's diploma. As Rosalynn describes in her autobiography, "our family didn't have much money, but neither did anyone else, so as far as we knew, we were well off."

When Rosalynn was 13, her father died of leukemia, and her mother went to work as a seamstress. Rosalynn helped out with her three younger siblings and began working herself. A dedicated student, she graduated high school as class valedictorian. Following high school,

Rosalynn attended Georgia Southwestern, a junior college close enough to Plains that she could live at home.

MRS. CARTER

Rosalynn had known James Earl Carter, Jr. all her life. She was a close friend of his sister, Ruth, but she and Jimmy did not become close until they began dating. Jimmy was three years older than Rosalynn, and following high school, he attended Georgia Southwestern, the Georgia Institute of Technology, and the U.S. Naval Academy in Annapolis. On one of Jimmy's trips home from college during the summer of 1945, he and Rosalynn became romantically involved. On July 7, 1946, Rosalynn and Jimmy married, and together they left Plains for Norfolk, Virginia, where Jimmy was stationed. Over the next seven years, Jimmy's naval career took them to Connecticut, Hawaii, San Diego, and Schenectady, N.Y., and the couple's three sons, John William, James Earl III, and Donnel Jeffrey were born.

In 1953, following the death of Jimmy's father, Rosalynn and Jimmy returned to Plains. Jimmy resigned from a promising career in the Navy and took over his family's business. Rosalynn was unhappy with her husband's decision to leave the Navy and return to Plains. She valued the independence she had gained as a Navy wife, and she did not want to give up the new life that she and Jimmy shared. Back in Plains, however, Rosalynn began to help Jimmy with the business, and they both became actively involved in the community.

Jimmy was appointed to the county school board in 1955, a year after the *Brown* v. *Board of Education* decision. Jimmy and Rosalynn supported efforts to consolidate local schools and improve the quality of education, but they faced opposition from those who saw consolidation as a prelude to integration. The Carters failed to gain local support for changes in education, but Jimmy successfully ran for the Georgia senate in 1962 and was reelected in 1964. Rosalynn found that she enjoyed being the wife of an elected official. She stayed in Plains and took care of the family and their business while Jimmy was away in Atlanta for the legislative session. As she describes in her autobiography, Rosalynn saw herself more as a political partner to Jimmy than as a political wife, and she felt she was making an important contribution by making it possible for Jimmy to pursue a career in politics.

In 1966, Jimmy ran for governor of Georgia, and Rosalynn became involved as a full-time campaigner. Jimmy did not win his first gubernatorial campaign, but he did not give up his effort to gain the office. In 1967, as they were preparing for his second run for governor, Rosalynn and Jimmy had their fourth and final child, daughter Amy Lynn. Three years later, Jimmy was successful in his gubernatorial bid. As First Lady of Georgia, Rosalynn found herself in a position with the potential for great influence. She began to make choices about the kinds of concerns that she would support and pursue, and her top priority became mental health. Jimmy appointed her to the Georgia Governor's Commission to Improve Services for the Mentally and Emotionally Handicapped, and many of the recommendations made by the Commission were enacted into state law. When Jimmy became president in 1976, Rosalynn continued her work on mental health issues and extended her influence and activities as First Lady of the nation.

FIRST LADY

In the White House, the partnership that Rosalynn and Jimmy had come to share in their years together continued. Rosalynn was an important adviser to her husband, and although President Carter did not always follow the advice of the First Lady, he frequently sought her counsel. Rosalynn played a central role in both the 1976 and 1980 presidential campaigns: planning strategy; raising campaign funds; giving interviews; making innumerable speeches; and holding press conferences. President Carter discussed his most important concerns with her, and other than highly secret matters of national security, the First Lady was well informed about these concerns. In the second year of his Presidency, Jimmy invited Rosalynn to attend cabinet meetings. The President wanted the First Lady to be aware of what the Carter Administration was doing and why.

Envoy to Latin America

In his first year of office, President Carter took on a range of domestic and international initiatives. The President had emphasized the need for the United States to reach out to the international community during his campaign, and he thought it was important to demonstrate his administration's commitment to human rights and democracy in the Western Hemisphere. To show the importance he attached to U.S. relations with Latin America, the President chose the First Lady to lead a delegation representing the United States to seven Latin American countries, including Jamaica, Costa Rica, Ecuador, Peru, Brazil, Columbia, and Venezuela. Rosalynn and Jimmy had traveled in Central and South America a number of times, and they had studied Spanish for many years. Rosalynn was not fluent, but she began taking Spanish lessons three times a week to prepare for her trip.

The First Lady spent the two months before her visit studying the history of U.S. relations with the countries she would visit and the current issues facing these countries and their relationships with the United States. Latin American scholars and officials from the State Department, the Treasury Department, the National Security Council, and the Organization of American States briefed the First Lady. She read extensively about Latin America, including poetry and novels.

The First Lady faced concerns by some who questioned President Carter's choice of her as envoy to Latin America. In one of Rosalynn's briefings, Florida Congressman Dante Fascell expressed reservations with the statement "The Latins are macho and they hate gringos and women. What else do you want to know?" Similarly, others questioned whether the First Lady would be taken seriously by Latin American leaders. The President, however, had complete confidence in the First Lady. In Latin America, some leaders were surprised by her command of the information, but they quickly learned that the First Lady was prepared to discuss important concerns of the United States and their countries. In spite of some criticism, the trip was somewhat successful, and the First Lady maintained contacts with leaders in a number of the countries after the visit.

The nations Rosalynn visited were chosen because they were either democracies or leaning toward democracy, and she particularly emphasized the importance of human rights and democracy in her meetings with the leaders of these nations. In Ecuador, the First Lady commented to Admiral Alfredo Poveda, the leader of the nation's military junta, that he would be a national hero if he spent the nation's money on education rather than arms. In Peru, the First Lady promised General Francisco Morales Bermudez, the leader of the military government, that she would return when the nation inaugurated a democratically elected leader. In 1979 in Peru and 1980 in Ecuador, the First Lady attended inaugurations of democratically elected presidents in each country.

Mental Health

During the 1976 campaign, the First Lady's sole campaign promise was to study the mental health needs of the nation. After winning the election, President Carter signed an Executive Order to create the President's Commission on Mental Health and appointed the First Lady honorary chairperson of the Commission. The Commission held public hearings across the nation and sought comprehensive statements to assess the status of research, prevention, and needs in the area of mental healthcare. Based on the results of a year of study, the Commission prepared a set of recommendations for President Carter. The President directed executive departments affected by the recommendations to set up timetables and make plans to implement recommendations that did not require congressional action, and in May of 1979 he submitted the Mental Health Systems Act to Congress. In September of 1980, Congress passed the legislation and allocated funding. This was the first major reform of federally funded mental health programs since 1963. Among the many honors for her work on mental healthcare, the First Lady received the Volunteer of the Decade Award from the National Mental Health Association in 1980. This was followed in 1982 by a Presidential Citation from the American Psychological Association and in 1984 by the Nathan S. Kline Medal of Merit from the International Committee against Mental Illness.

Women, Children, and Community Involvement

In addition to mental health and other issues, First Lady Rosalynn Carter worked on behalf of concerns for women, children, and the elderly. As an advocate for the Equal Rights Amendment, she lobbied state legislators, supported fund-raisers, made speeches, and sponsored meetings and events in support of the ERA. In 1976, the National Organization of Women honored Rosalynn with an Award of Merit in recognition of her advocacy for the ERA.

The First Lady helped to develop and maintain an up-to-date list of women qualified for positions in the federal government, and President Carter appointed record numbers of women to a variety of positions: cabinet secretaries, undersecretaries, and assistant secretaries; federal judges; ambassadors; members of federal boards and commissions; and members of delegations representing the United States at international conferences. The First Lady also worked to ensure that representatives from women's groups were included in White House activities and government consultations and briefings on issues such as arms agreements, Middle East peace, inflation, energy, education, and progress for women.

As First Lady, Rosalynn was able to gain attention and support for a variety of causes. Betty Bumpers came to the First Lady for help on a childhood immunization plan to eradicate measles, and by October 1979, 90 percent of the nation's children had been immunized for measles. Moreover, the program had the effect of decreasing the incidence of other serious childhood diseases, as children received additional immunizations when they received their measles vaccination.

At the start of the Carter Presidency, Washington did not have a strong community foundation to encourage private contributions in support of local needs. The chairman of the Community Foundation of Greater Washington solicited the First Lady's assistance in encouraging major philanthropic organizations to assist efforts to improve the D.C. community. By the end of the Carter administration, the Foundation had received grants in the areas of family aid, mental health, youth, and the elderly. The First Lady regularly traveled the country in support of community programs such as those she supported in Washington, D.C., working to point out ways that additional efforts could improve local conditions in a variety of areas.

LIFE AFTER THE WHITE HOUSE

Following defeat in the 1980 election, the Carters began to plan what they would do with their lives after leaving the White House. They wanted to use the influence that Jimmy had gained as President and continue to work in support of the ideals that had motivated the Carter administration. In 1982, Jimmy and Rosalynn founded the Carter Center in Atlanta. The Carter Center is guided by a fundamental commitment to human rights and is dedicated to promoting peace and health. The Center monitors elections in developing democracies and promotes economic development and healthcare in Africa, Asia, and Latin America. Rosalynn is a full partner in the activities of the Carter Center, and she serves as Vice Chair of the Center's Board of Trustees. She is the founder and chair of the Center's Mental Health Task Force, and she hosts the annual Rosalynn Carter Symposium on Mental Health Policy, which brings mental health experts together to address critical concerns. Through her work at the Carter Center, Rosalynn also promotes early childhood immunization, human rights, conflict resolution, and the empowerment of urban communities.

In 1987, the Rosalynn Carter Institute was founded in honor of the former First Lady at Georgia Southwestern State University. The Institute works to help family and professional care-givers and is dedicated to research and education in the areas of mental health, chronic illnesses, developmental disabilities, and the health of the elderly. Rosalynn serves as president of the Institute's board of directors. The former First Lady has written an autobiography and co-authored (with President Carter) a book about life after the White House, and she has written two books (with Susan K. Golant) for care-givers. Rosalynn also works with Habitat for Humanity, Project Interconnections, and the Friendship Force.

The former First Lady has received many honors and awards, including the Notre Dame Award for International Humanitarian Service; the Eleanor Roosevelt Living World Award from Peace Links; the Kiwanis World Service Medal from Kiwanis International Foundation; the Jefferson Award from the American Institute for Public Service; and the Georgia Woman of the Year Award from the Georgia Commission on Women. In 1999, Rosalynn and Jimmy Carter were awarded the Presidential Medal of Freedom, the highest civilian honor of the United States. In his presentation of the award, President Clinton acknowledged the former

President and First Lady as having "done more good things for more people than any other couple on the face of the earth."

Chapter 28

NANCY REAGAN

Mary Linehan

UPBRINGING

Anne Frances "Nancy" Robbins was born July 6, 1921, the only child of actress Edith Luckett and Kenneth Robbins, a car salesman. Shortly after the birth, her parents divorced. After that, Nancy rarely saw her father. Edith Luckett continued to work as a stage actress and Nancy spent her early years as a "backstage baby." Her mother remarried in 1929 and they moved to Chicago. Nancy's stepfather, Loyal Davis, was a prominent neurosurgeon and chair of the Department of Surgery at Northwestern University. His ultraconservative political views may well have shaped Nancy's thinking, but as a girl she disliked politics. She did come to love her stepfather, and at fourteen she initiated adoption proceedings and became Nancy Davis.

Through her teens and twenties, Nancy's first love was theater. Only an average student at the exclusive Girls' Latin School, she acted in all the school plays. In her senior year, she played the lead in *First Lady* by George S. Kauffman. In 1939, Nancy had her debut and entered Smith College where she majored in English and Drama. Nancy acted in several college plays, but her real experience in theater came during vacations when she worked as an apprentice in the summer stock companies of New England.

Nancy's first professional role came in 1943 when a friend of her mother's offered her a three-line part in the traveling company of a play called *Ramshackle Inn*. The show eventually made it to New York and when the run was over, Nancy decided to stay. For several years, she acted on the "subway circuit" in the outer boroughs. A Metro Goldwyn Mayer scout saw her in a production and arranged for a movie contract.

Nancy Davis had a short film career. In most of her eleven films she was cast as a young mother or a pregnant woman. This corresponded with her personal ambition, "to have a successful marriage." She always knew she would give up her career, "when the right man came along." In 1949, Nancy asked a producer to introduce her to Ronald Reagan. She had seen the actor in movies and "liked what I saw." When they met, Nancy claimed it was very nearly "love at first sight." The courtship proceeded slowly however, as Reagan was still on the rebound after his divorce from actress Jane Wyman.

MRS. REAGAN

Nancy Davis and Ronald Reagan finally married in a private ceremony on March 4, 1952. Their first child, Patti, was born on October 22, 1952. She had two half-siblings – Maureen and Michael – from Ronald Reagan's first marriage. A fourth child, Ron, was born on May 20, 1958. Nancy was described as an affectionate, but demanding and over-protective, mother. She wanted her children to be as neat and orderly as she was, but they were caught up in the counterculture of the 1960s.

In the 1950s and early 1960s, Ronald Reagan was a traveling spokesperson for General Electric. During that time, the couple communicated with letters from "Daddie Poo Pants" to "Mommie Poo Pants." These letters, which continued throughout the marriage, reflect a deeply emotional love affair. As he wrote in 1955, "I love you and miss you... I've always loved and missed you but never has it been such an actual ache... The clock is standing still and....I find myself hating these people for keeping us apart. Please be real careful because you carry my life with you every second."

In 1966, conservative Californians persuaded Ronald Reagan to run for Governor. Nancy supported her husband's decision but wanted no part of campaigning. She was shy, uncomfortable in crowds, and terrified of making speeches. As the campaign progressed, however, Reagan's staff convinced her that in order to cover the large state and win the election she would have to take a larger role. She accepted this as the legitimate function of a woman who loved a man who happened to be a politician. Nancy learned to enjoy the give and take with voters. She was proud to return home every evening and share their concerns with the candidate. Ronald Reagan won the election by a landslide.

As First Lady of California, Nancy was subjected to intense criticism. She was called a racist for refusing to live in the inner-city Governor's Mansion. The speaker of the state legislature charged that she solicited donations of antique furniture for her own personal use. Others criticized her for "the gaze," the rapturous way she stared at her husband while he was making speeches. One reporter described it as "a kind of transfixed adoration more appropriate to a witness of the Virgin Birth." Less attention was paid to Nancy's accomplishments. She was an enthusiastic supporter of the Foster Grandparent Program, which paired older people with special needs children. Nancy was also deeply concerned with the plight of American soldiers in Vietnam. She visited veteran's hospitals, donated the profits from her newspaper column to a program for prisoners of war, and invited returning POWs to her home for dinner.

Although she was an active Governor's wife, Nancy insisted her first priority was providing her husband with a warm and loving home, "a source of comfort and strength." Nonetheless, by the end of Reagan's second term as Governor, the press and prominent Republicans were suggesting that Nancy had too much power over her husband and his policy decisions. She responded that her "sole joy" was being Mrs. Ronald Reagan. When asked if she would like to be First Lady of the United States, Nancy coyly replied: "I just want to be Ronald Reagan's wife."

First Lady

After failed campaigns in 1968 and 1976, Ronald Reagan was elected president in 1980. Nancy considered 1981 the worst year of her life. It began with published reports that she had asked the Carters to move out of the White House three weeks early so she could redecorate. Her wardrobe was fodder for malicious gossip. Nancy's inaugural ensemble included a $25,000 gown, a $10,000 mink coat, and a $1,500 alligator purse. This apparent excess was hotly criticized at a time when national unemployment neared ten percent. Even before she had a chance to prove herself as First Lady, Nancy Reagan was accused of being obsessed with wealth and status.

She did not help herself by immediately beginning a massive restoration of the private quarters of the White House. This included new china valued at $1,400 per place setting. The donation of the china was unfortunately announced the same day the Reagan administration proposed a $41 billion tax cut in welfare programs and the Department of Agriculture declared ketchup an acceptable vegetable for school lunch programs. This was followed by charges that Nancy violated the 1977 Ethics in Government Act by not reporting gifts from fashion designers. In a country ensnared in recession, Nancy Reagan appeared insensitive to the problems of ordinary Americans.

People sympathized with Nancy, after the attempted assassination of the President, but once he recovered, the censure of the First Lady resumed. In the summer she attended the London wedding of Prince Charles and Diana Spencer. Nancy took along 18 attendants including her personal hairdresser, nurse, and photographer. She presented the couple with a $75,000 bowl and wore $250,000 worth of diamonds and rubies. The British mocked Nancy's excess, dubbing her "Queen Nancy." This satire soon made it back to the United States where a caricature of the First Lady in a crown and ermine robes appeared on postcards and posters.

By the end of 1981, Nancy Reagan had a higher disapproval rating than any modern First Lady ... and possibly since Mary Lincoln, had polls been conducted. The President's advisors considered her a liability and encouraged her to take up a socially useful project. At first, Nancy resisted. Her first concern was always the welfare of her husband. She insisted that he was her "project." When the advisers explained to Nancy that her shallow and supercilious image was hurting the President, she understood that taking up a cause was a way of serving her husband. With this inspiration she immediately and whole-heartedly took up the issue of drug abuse.

In 1982, Nancy Reagan entered this reform as a mother trying to help other parents deal with their children. She was empathetic in her approach and admitted that her children also used drugs. Facing criticism because her husband had cut 25 percent from the budget for drug education and treatment programs, Nancy claimed parents were "the answer to it all," and emphasized non-profit efforts, volunteerism, and the value of testimonies from young people who had overcome their own addictions. She denied that government action was necessary in the war against drugs and cited Alcoholics Anonymous as a successful, free program.

Over the next few years, Nancy Reagan used her position as First Lady to publicize the problem of drug abuse. She hosted a meeting of Governor's wives and told them there was a secret war in the United States that was capturing and killing millions of children. She told these young people to "Just Say No" to drugs, an expression that became a national battle cry. Nancy visited more than 100 small towns across America warning that no area was safe from drugs. Wherever she went, Nancy inspected drug treatment centers. She appeared in music videos and on television programs to publicize her crusade. By the end of 1984, her popularity reached 71 percent and the image of "Queen Nancy" was largely forgotten.

In 1985, Nancy hosted an unprecedented session on drug abuse for "First Ladies" from thirty nations. It was the first time an incumbent First Lady addressed the United Nations and the first time so many wives of international leaders had met for any purpose. Nancy's presentation led to new laws and programs in several countries. The following year, in the first joint address by a presidential couple, the Reagans called for a national crusade against the "cancer" of drugs. Together, they promised to push for increased federal spending on drug programs. No longer simply a sympathetic motherly figure, Nancy Reagan had become a powerful political force. This was especially evident in 1988 when she became the first First Lady to address a full body of official United Nation's representatives.

The sense of power and mission Nancy experienced as an anti-drug crusader led her to take an increasingly active role in her husband's second term. More than one journalist called this new Nancy "Associate President." She successfully pushed for historic summits and treaties with the Soviet Union. In 1985, the President was diagnosed with cancer and scheduled for immediate surgery. While shielding the public – and her husband – from the truth of his condition, Nancy moved to establish her own authority. She exercised "veto power" over any appointments, rearranged the President's schedule for the coming weeks, and controlled all access to her husband. Nancy, rather than the Vice President, filled in for Reagan at official functions.

In 1987, the Iran-Contra scandal broke and Ronald Reagan was accused of selling arms to America's enemies. The President's approval rating plummeted. Nancy responded by taking charge and demanding that her husband remove three aides including his Chief of Staff, Donald Regan. The President acceded to his wife's wishes. The press once again became critical of the strong First Lady. *The New York Times* called her "power hungry" and likened her to Edith Wilson, unelected and unaccountable, but controlling the actions of the executive branch. Regan, the disposed former chief of staff, compared Nancy to the "ruthless" Livia who ruled the Roman Empire by manipulating her hapless husband, the emperor.

Nancy Reagan, who had timidly retreated from media censure in 1981, now stood up to her critics. In a speech to news editors she defended her actions as consistent with the requirements of her position. She insisted it was legitimate for a First Lady to look after a President's welfare. If that meant advocating the removal of aides who failed to serve the President, she was only doing her job. As for asserting her opinion on policy matters, Nancy claimed, "it's silly to suggest that my opinion should not carry some weight with a man I've been married to for 35 years. I'm a woman who loves her husband and I make no apologies for looking out for his personal and political welfare." Surveys showed that the American public agreed and Nancy left office in 1989 with soaring approval ratings.

LIFE AFTER THE WHITE HOUSE

The Reagans retired to California. Nancy wrote two books and took control of her husband's care after the former President was diagnosed with Alzheimer's disease. No one could question her devotion to the President, but her legacy as First Lady has been difficult to categorize. In eight controversial years, she evolved from a political liability to a position of almost unlimited power. She succeeded in filling many roles as a conservative wife and mother; as an advocate for social change; and as a woman who enjoyed the exercise of political power. She resolved these seemingly contradictory roles by interpreting her efforts as the legitimate functions of a woman who loved a man who happened to be President.

BARBARA BUSH

Jean Becker

INTRODUCTION

When Barbara Pierce fell in love with a young Navy pilot named George Bush during the summer of 1943, it was difficult, if not impossible, to imagine the future that might lay ahead for the two of them. Just teenagers (she was 17, he was 18), their world was consumed by only two things: The love they had for each other; and the World War that would soon separate them.

Ironically, both George and Barbara Bush now remember that their dreams for the future then were very simple: To be able to get married, raise and support a family, and just be together. In fact, soon after their secret engagement, Barbara dropped out of Smith College to prepare for the only two jobs she really wanted: wife and mother. All of which makes the life story of Barbara Pierce Bush even more remarkable. Nearly 56 years after marrying George Herbert Walker Bush, she still says that being a wife and mother have been her life's mission. Never mind that she was the wife of the 41st President of the United States and the mother of the 43rd. Never mind that she became a leading advocate for literacy, a best-selling author, and a popular public speaker known for her quick humor and uncommon frankness.

Together, George and Barbara Bush have lived a life that has taken them from their protected, East Coast childhoods to the dusty oilfields of West Texas, to Congress, to the United Nations, to China, to the CIA, to the White House, and finally back home to Texas. Along the way they lost a child to leukemia and found a lifelong passion that continues today in their fight against cancer.

The Bushes had six children and 14 grandchildren while living in 30 different houses in 17 different cities in two different countries. They have known the great joy of victory and depression of public defeat. Through it all, when asked recently about her life, Barbara Bush said simply, "I am the luckiest woman in the world."

UPBRINGING

To fully understand the plain-spoken woman who would become First Lady, it is probably best to go back to the beginning. Barbara Pierce was born on June 8, 1925 in suburban New York City to Marvin and Pauline Pierce, the third of four children. She was very close to her father, who worked for the McCall's Corporation and became its president in 1946. She would later write in her memoirs, published in 1994, that Marvin Pierce was the "fairest man I knew, until I met George Bush."

Barbara was not as close to her mother, whom she described as a beautiful, talented woman who really did not appreciate the life she had. "My mother often talked about 'when her ship would come,'" Barbara wrote. "She had a husband who worshipped the ground she walked on, four loving children, and a world of friends. Her ship had come in – she just didn't know it." Her mother had inadvertently taught her a valuable lesson. As Barbara wrote: "You have two choices in life: You can like what you do, or you can dislike it. I have chosen to like it." Despite disagreements with her mother, Barbara Bush considered her childhood a happy one, filled with love, friends, security, and lots of books. She first developed a love of reading and books from many long evenings spent in the living room when everyone in the family would be reading a favorite book or magazine.

During her 16th year, while home from boarding school, Barbara Pierce met George Bush at a Christmas dance. Pearl Harbor had just been bombed a few weeks earlier, but Barbara remembers being oblivious to almost everything except her new beau. "I married the first man I kissed," she once told an audience. "It makes my children sick when they hear that, but it's true."

In the midst of the romance and resulting engagement, George Bush – then the youngest pilot in the Navy at age 18 – shipped out with his squadron for the South Pacific. Despite their separation, his almost daily love letters left no doubt in her mind that he would come back to her, as shown in a note that he wrote her shortly after they became engaged: "I love you, precious, with all my heart and to know that you love me means my life. How often I have thought about the immeasurable joy that will be ours some day. How lucky our children will be to have a mother like you."

The romance nearly ended in disaster when, on September 2, 1944, George's plane was shot down while he was on bombing mission near the island of Chichi Jima. Although his two crewmates were killed, George parachuted out of the plane and was eventually picked up by an American submarine. A number of days – "all of them a complete blur" – would pass between Barbara's learning that George had been shot down and that he had been rescued.

They finally married January 6, 1945. After the war ended George went to Yale and Barbara had their first child, George Walker. When George graduated in 1948, the young family made what would become one of many bold moves in their life to come: They left the protected environment of their families and friends on the East Coast and moved to the dusty oilfields of West Texas.

MRS. BUSH

It did not take long for the young Bush family to realize how different their new life was to be. Their first home, in wind-swept Odessa, Texas, was a tiny duplex, which they shared with a mother and her daughter who seemed to have questionable occupations. The two families shared a single bathroom, which became quite a problem at night when the two women neighbors entertained their gentlemen callers! The "visitors" often forgot that when they left the bathroom from their side, they had to unlock the bathroom door that led to the Bush family side of the duplex. Nevertheless, the Bushes thrived in Texas. After starting as a supply salesman, George quickly moved up the corporate ladder and eventually ventured out on his own into the oil business. There were plenty of dry wells along the way, but enough successful ones to enable George and his partners to become true pioneers in the off-shore drilling business.

And they continued to have babies. By 1953 the family included not only George W., but a daughter Robin, and the new baby, nicknamed "Jeb." As Barbara wrote in her memoirs, "life seemed almost too good to be true." However, a short time after Jeb was born, 3-year-old Robin was diagnosed with leukemia. She died six months later, leaving the family heartbroken; George W., who was 6 at the time, was bewildered. The story of how Barbara finally pulled herself out of her deep mourning has often been told: She overhead little George tell his friends one day that he would not be able to come out and play, as he had to play with his mother to cheer her up. She realized then that it was time she put aside her grief and "come back" to her family who needed her. Barbara has said, "George and I love and value every person more because of Robin. She lives on in our hearts, memories, and actions." Today, George and Barbara Bush are co-chairs of a national movement – the National Dialogue on Cancer – which is seeking to reduce the risk of the dreaded disease.

Three more children followed: Neil, Marvin, and Dorothy, whom they would call Doro. The family eventually moved from West Texas to Houston where George Bush's off-shore oil business continued to thrive but his growing interest in politics and public service would soon chart a whole new course for the entire family.

After losing a bid for the U.S. Senate in 1964, George Bush was elected to the House of Representatives in 1966. The family packed up and moved to Washington, not realizing it would be more than 25 years before they would move back to Texas for good. Bush's career would include service as ambassador to the United Nations, chairman of the Republican National Committee during the Watergate years, the American envoy to China, director of the CIA, and Vice President of the United States. It was an incredible journey during which Barbara Bush, a former car pool mom and Cub Scout den mother, learned the tools of diplomacy, entertaining, media relations, public speaking, and living a very public life.

But she never lost sight of what she considered her most important job – making a home for her husband children. From Houston to Washington to New York to China and back, she lugged family photos, furniture, dogs, keepsakes so they would feel at home. She wrote in her memoirs that the very first thing she did after her husband became President on January 20, 1989, was "to unpack some of our personal pictures to set around on the tables so this great big house would feel more like home."

FIRST LADY

By the time Barbara Bush entered the White House, her plan to simply be a wife and mother were no longer feasible. As the wife of the Vice President, she had very quietly devoted herself to the cause of literacy and had spent a great deal of time traveling around the country to visit and encourage literacy programs. As First Lady, she was faced with the prospect of assuming a position that came with no job description and no salary, but with enormous potential to do good. Mrs. Bush decided to balance her approach – on one hand she was determined to stay out of her husband's Presidency ("They elected George, not me," she said), yet she took her cue from one of her predecessors and role models, Lady Bird Johnson, who had described the position as First Lady as the best bully pulpit in the world. In her very first staff meeting, Barbara told her East Wing team that she wanted to do something every single day to help others. That would be her approach to the office.

In her four years as First Lady, Barbara Bush used that bully pulpit in many ways and often simply followed her heart. When she read in the newspaper that Washington area malls were banning Salvation Army bellringers because they disturbed Christmas shoppers, she immediately went to the closest mall (taking the press with her), found a bellringer, and made a point of making a donation while talking about the importance of this Christmas tradition. (The malls changed their policy.)

As she learned more about the AIDS virus and how frightened of the disease the American people were, she visited a place in Washington called "Grandma's Place," to make the point that all AIDS victims – children and adults – needed love and care. When a young man told her in front of the media that his own mother was too afraid and too ashamed to hug him, she immediately got up and gave the young man a huge hug. The First Lady also traveled across the country visiting homeless shelters, food banks, abused women's shelters, Boys and Girls Clubs, schools, hospitals, and orphanages.

Despite these varied concerns and causes, Barbara devoted most of her energies to literacy, which she had adopted as her main cause while wife of the Vice President. However, with the increased visibility that comes with the White House, she became the true champion of a growing movement to make America a more literate nation. For four years, she was tireless in visiting literacy programs in almost every state in the nation, encouraging students, the tutors, and the professional staff to continue their work and talking to nearly anyone who would listen to her arguments about the importance of literacy to the nation's future. Mrs. Bush stood proudly by her husband as he signed the 1991 National Literacy Act, the first piece of legislation ever enacted specifically for literacy. She also established the Barbara Bush Foundation for Family Literacy, which continues to thrive and has, at the time of this writing, given nearly $8 million to 262 literacy programs around the country. When asked recently in a speech why she devoted so much time to family literacy, Barbara Bush said:

> Like the experts, I truly feel that if more people could read, write, and comprehend, so many of our social problems could be solved. If you can read and write, you can learn. If you can learn, you can get a job and support yourself and your family. You will be less tempted to turn to drugs, alcohol, or crime; to drop out of school or get pregnant before you are ready. You will have pride and dignity, and will be able to enjoy the best things in life, including a good book, or bedtime stories with your child.

The public was treated to one of Mrs. Bush's passions when her dog, Millie, gave birth to six puppies in March 1989. As Millie's "ghost author," Barbara wrote about the puppies and life at the White House in her tongue-in-cheek best seller, Millie's Book. The book, published in 1990, earned more than $1 million for the Barbara Bush Foundation for Family Literacy. The puppies, presence of grandchildren in the White House, and Barbara's sense of humor further endeared her to the nation.

Barbara Bush received very high approval ratings in opinion poll as First Lady. When asked about her popularity, the First Lady typically shrugged off the question, crediting her white hair and less-than-perfect figure. But others knew that it was more about her sharp wit, outspoken but down-to-earth nature, and reputation as a gracious hostess.

Despite her popularity, Mrs. Bush at times found herself in hot water, usually because of an inadvertent quote she gave a reporter. But the only controversy still remembered today occurred in 1991, when Wellesley College invited her to be their commencement speaker. A handful of the graduates protested the selection, circulating a petition saying "Barbara Bush has gained recognition only through the achievements of her husband." Before long, the protests became a leading story in the media and the First Lady was forced to defend the life she had chosen for herself – that of wife and mother. The flap ended the day she finally gave her speech, during which she tried to bridge the distance between the two generations of women, bringing Russian First Lady Raisa Gorbachev with her to the ceremony and stating:

> Cherish your human connection: your relationships with friends and family. For several years, you've had impressed upon you the importance to your career of dedication and hard work. This is true, but as important as your obligations as a doctor, lawyer or business leader will be, you are a human being first and those human connections – with spouses, with children, with friends – Bare the most important investments you will ever make. At the end of your life, you will never regret not having passed one more test, not winning one more verdict or not closing one more deal. You will regret time not spent with a husband, a friend, a child or a parent.

She closed her speech with the now-famous quote: "And who knows? Somewhere out in this audience may even be someone who will one day follow my footsteps, and preside over the White House as the President's spouse. I wish *him* well!"

LIFE AFTER THE WHITE HOUSE

Devastated by her husband's reelection defeat in 1992, Barbara Bush nonetheless left the White House very much ready to return to private life. She told friends that she and George moved back to Houston prepared to stay out of sight. She went back to cooking (admittedly with little success) and to driving a car for the first time in 12 years. She wrote her memoirs (another best-seller) and planned to devote more time to her children and grandchildren.

But retiring from public life was not to be. She was in great demand as a public speaker and continued her involvement with her literacy foundation. The decisions by two of her sons to pursue public office kept the family in the spotlight. Following their father into the political arena, George W. ran for Governor of Texas and Jeb pursued the same office in Florida, despite their mother's advice against pursuing elected office (she later explained that she "did not want them to get hurt in case they lost."). Both were elected, Jeb on his second attempt.

Barbara Bush holds the distinction held by only one other woman in U. S. history: to be both the wife and mother of a President.

Chapter 30

HILLARY RODHAM CLINTON

Myra G. Gutin

UPBRINGING

Hillary Diane Rodham was born in Chicago on October 26, 1947. The oldest child and only daughter of Dorothy and Hugh Rodham, Hillary was an intelligent, serious child. While a student a Maine East High School, she became acquainted with Don Jones, a young minister hired to work with the youth group at Hillary's church. Jones influenced Hillary to read Reinhold Niebuhr and Paul Tillich; later he arranged for Hillary and other students in the group to hear a speech by Dr. Martin Luther King, Jr. After the presentation, the group had the opportunity to meet Dr. King. Her readings in philosophy and the meeting with Dr. King greatly influenced Hillary's emerging world view and interest in social reform.

Hillary entered Wellesley College in the fall of 1965. She established a reputation as a vocal, opinionated, campus leader. During her junior year, she was elected student government President. Ever the reformer, she advocated change, but from within, rather than outside the college. This idea would serve as the underpinning for her later endeavors.

Hillary was chosen as the first-ever Wellesley College student commencement speaker. Senator Edward Brooke of Massachusetts, the principal commencement speaker, told the graduates that America was strong and the world awaited them. Upon hearing Brooke's remarks, Hillary discarded her carefully written speech and in comments that would alternately be labeled shocking, audacious, and bold, told the senator and the audience that her generation was looking for a new vision for America, they were tired of promises for change. She said, "the challenge now is to practice politics as the art of making what appears to be impossible, possible." The response earned Hillary her first national publicity as her speech was mentioned in an article in *Life* magazine.

Hillary had been raised in a strongly Republican family. In 1964 she had been a "Goldwater Girl" and had worked for the House Republican Conference. However, the winds of political change were blowing, and her college years saw her ideology drifting to the left. In 1968 she worked for Democrat Eugene McCarthy. Later, she said that she would have voted for Hubert Humphrey for President if she had been old enough to vote in that year's presidential election.

After graduation, Hillary continued her education at Yale University Law School. Influenced by activist Marian Wright Edelman, Hillary developed a life-long interest in protecting the rights of children. Serious and focused, she served on the Board of Editors of the *Yale Review of Law and Social Activism*.

An important consequence of Hillary's years at Yale was meeting a fellow law student, Bill Clinton. The duo became inseparable, and Hillary delayed her graduation to spend time with Clinton and study for an extra year in a law school program devoted to children's rights.

Bill Clinton had already made clear his intention upon graduation to return to his home state of Arkansas and run for public office. Bill and Hillary were both political activists and during the summer of 1972 worked for Senator George McGovern's presidential campaign in Texas. Though McGovern lost the election, the couple were developing a national network of supporters and friends in the Democratic party. Clinton and Rodham graduated from Yale Law School in 1973.

When Clinton returned, as promised, to Arkansas, to teach law at the University of Arkansas Law School and plan his first campaign, Hillary took a position with Edelman's Children Defense Fund in Cambridge, Massachusetts. In early 1974, Hillary was hired as a staff attorney for the House Judiciary Committee that was considering impeachment proceedings against President Richard Nixon. Her employment ended when Nixon resigned the Presidency in August 1974.

MRS. CLINTON

Hillary joined Bill in Arkansas and also taught at the law school. They were married in October 1975. The next year, Bill Clinton was elected Attorney General of Arkansas. Shortly after the election, Hillary was offered a job at the Rose law firm, the most prestigious law firm in the state. Concurrently, Hillary was appointed to the board of the Legal Services Corporation, eventually becoming chair of the board.

In 1978, Bill Clinton was elected Governor of Arkansas, the youngest governor in the country. The new First Lady of Arkansas worked tirelessly for children, families, and education. She founded the Arkansas Advocates for Children and Families and served as chair of the Arkansas Education Standards Committee. Hillary became a partner at Rose Law Firm in 1979 and became the first to take advantage of its new maternity policy when Chelsea Victoria Clinton was born in February 1980.

With the exception of one two-year period, Clinton was reelected Governor several times. His sights set on the Presidency, Clinton was in the thick of the race when Gennifer Flowers charged that she and Clinton had conducted a 12-year affair. The candidate denied Flowers' allegations and he and Hillary appeared on CBS' *60 Minutes* where Hillary made her now famous statement: "I'm not sitting here because I'm some little woman standing by her man... I'm sitting here because I love him and respect him and I honor what he's been through and... if that's not good enough, then heck, don't vote for him." People admired Hillary's tough style. Moreover, they responded to both Bill and Hillary and the candidacy was saved.

Telling American that they would get "two for the price of one," the Clinton juggernaut, portending the possibility of a co-presidency, chugged on. More than any other prospective First Lady, Hillary was quizzed about her own views and her possible role in her husband's administration. While many voters were wary of the duo, Clinton soundly defeated George Bush in the 1992 election.

FIRST LADY

Shortly after taking office, Mrs. Clinton was named to head the President's Task Force on National Health Care Reform. Clinton had campaigned on this theme and had intimated that Hillary would lead reform efforts. There was some precedent for the appointment: Eleanor Roosevelt had served as Assistant Director of Civilian Defense, and Rosalynn Carter had been named Honorary Chair of the President's Commission on Mental Health. However, neither Mrs. Roosevelt nor Mrs. Carter had the staff, funds, or clout of Mrs. Clinton.

Unfortunately, the whole health care reform enterprise almost immediately became a nightmare. There were nearly 600 people working in sub-groups and task forces. To achieve her goals, the First Lady closed meetings to the media and the public causing frustration and anger. The Association of American Physicians and Surgeons brought suit in federal court to open the meetings. A federal judge ruled that the task force was guilty of misconduct in withholding documents; later, however, the United States Court of Appeals for the District of Columbia held that Mrs. Clinton was a "de facto officer or employee" of the government, and that the Task Force was not obligated to open its hearings.

The ruling was a victory for Mrs. Clinton, but the victory tarnished when the Task Force unveiled its sweeping, controversial reform plan. There seemed to be something to offend everyone, and the bureaucracy, regulations, and rules made the viability of the new plan questionable. Compromises were offered that might have won support of both Democrats and Republicans, but Mrs. Clinton remained unyielding, particularly on the provision of universal coverage. The First Lady gambled and lost: the health care plan collapsed completely in August 1994. Reverberations were felt during the 1994 midterm elections when the Democrats lost control of Congress. Though it was not the most compelling reason for widespread Democratic losses, the health care debacle was certainly one of the factors.

Mrs. Clinton seemed to take a step back and retrench. For a time, she embraced a more traditional First Lady stance, addressing groups and conferences, and touring Asia with Chelsea. She initiated a weekly syndicated newspaper column, reminiscent of Eleanor Roosevelt's *My Day*; Mrs. Clinton's column was titled *Talking It Over*.

Most presidential couples are afforded a short "honeymoon" with the press when they arrive at the White House. For a short period of time, the President and First Lady are assured of little if any criticism of their actions of initiatives; the Clintons never enjoyed this brief respite. During the health care reform project, the couple had to deal with questions about and criticism of firings in the White House Travel Office (later known as Travelgate), the disappearance and reappearance of Hillary's billing records at the Rose Law Office, the suicide of Hillary's former partner at Rose, Deputy White House Counsel Vincent Foster, Hillary's commodities trading; and, perhaps the most damaging of all scandals, (which continues to dog the Clintons to the present) Whitewater. At times, it seemed that the Clintons moved from scandal to scandal, from one emotional precipice to another.

Mrs. Clinton emerged in another incarnation in September 1995, when she attended the United Nations Fourth World Conference of Women in Beijing. There had been a question as to whether Mrs. Clinton would attend the conference at all due to U.S.-China tensions exacerbated by the United States' continued protests over China's poor human rights record. She was granted permission to attend the conference a few days before the opening session. Once in China, she wasted little time castigating the governments of that country, India, Bosnia, and a number of Middle Eastern countries for practices that she considered abhorrent. In a memorable speech she said "If there is one message that echoes forth from this conference, let it be that human rights are women's rights. And women's rights are human rights, once and for all."

Both Democratic and Republican delegates to the conference applauded Mrs. Clinton's remarks. Some observers believe that the First Lady's comments complicated relations with China; others found her speech to be both bold and long overdue. After the health care retreat, her four speeches in China were seen as victories for Hillary Clinton.

Another victory, of a more gentle sort, occurred in January 1996 when Mrs. Clinton published *It Takes a Village*. Drawing on her lifelong interest in children, and her experiences as a mother, Mrs. Clinton wrote about the ways in which children develop and their relationships with their parents and society. The Grammy was awarded to her for the oral performance of the book.

By the time that she appeared at the 1996 Democratic convention to discuss the importance of family, Mrs. Clinton seemed to have regained considerable political momentum. This was underscored by protests from Republicans who did not want Mrs. Clinton to become actively involved in the on-going national debate about welfare reform. For the next year and a half, the First Lady traveled throughout the country calling attention to the plight of children, highlighting various historical sites and continuing to cement political relationships by speaking on behalf of numerous Democratic candidates for office.

Perhaps most jarring to the Clintons were allegations in January 1998 that the President had conducted a sexual affair with a White House intern, Monica Lewinsky. The President angrily and repeatedly denied the charges and Mrs. Clinton continued the offensive with an appearance on *The Today Show*. In the course of an interview, Mrs. Clinton decried a "right-wing conspiracy" that had been attempting to discredit her husband for a decade.

After evidence emerged that the affair was real and impeachment proceedings moved forward against the President, Mrs. Clinton continued to "stand by her man." Americans told pollsters that they admired the First Lady's steadfast support of the President and her public approval rating was high. Perhaps it was the unsavory experience of the impeachment and the enthusiastic support that she received that made the First Lady seriously consider a run for the New York Senate.

During the summer of 1999 she announced that she would undertake a "listening tour" of New York state to test the waters for a candidacy. The results were positive and she became a part-time First Lady and a full-time campaigner on New Year's Day 2000. She formally entered the Senate race on February 6, 2000. Her long, hard-fought campaigned proved successful and she became the first First Lady to be elected to a public office.

LIFE AFTER THE WHITE HOUSE

One scholar noted that Hillary Clinton was the most controversial and arguably one of the most politically powerful women of the latter twentieth century. Her White House tenure was fraught with controversy and scandal, but also marked by achievement. Mrs. Clinton seemed to deal with each setback, learn from each misstep, and always moved forward.

Her legacy is two-fold. First, there are few limits remaining on what the First Lady can do in terms of precedent. Mrs. Clinton moved the Office of the First Lady from one that champions only innocuous and safe issues to one involved in all issues. Mrs. Clinton evolved from personal advisor to public spokesperson to point person on public policy issues. Her stature as a presidential advisor was such that she assumed an office in the West Wing of the White House, near the President's office. Future First Ladies may elect to take less public roles, but the opportunity to be actively and publicly involved in discussion of the national agenda is now a possibility.

Second, Mrs. Clinton further pushed the boundaries of the role of First Lady by running for public office prior to the conclusion of her husband's term as President. No sitting First Lady had ever done this. As a full partner in the Clinton Presidency, Hillary Rodham Clinton participated in many of the initiatives of the administration. She truly lived the challenge set forth in her Wellesley commencement address: to practice politics as the art of making what appears impossible, possible. And there is more to come, as the former First Lady embarks on a new political career, one of her own.

Chapter 31

LAURA BUSH

Molly Meijer Wertheimer

UPBRINGING

Laura Lane Welch was born on November 4, 1946, in Midland, an oil boom town in West Texas. The only child of Harold Bruce Welch, a successful contractor, and wife, Jenna Hawkins Welch, a homemaker who kept the books for her husband's business, Laura had a secure family life where she felt loved and protected. Her childhood was filled with activities such as sleepovers with friends, Brownie and Girl Scout meetings, playing the piano, and singing in the church choir. What she like to do most was read. From the time she was a baby, Laura's mother read to her and when she was old enough, her mother took her to the local library. Today, Laura praises her mother for giving her "a most precious gift — a lifelong passion for reading."

While growing up, Laura was popular as well as studious. The only low point during her high school years was a car accident that resulted in the death of a close friend. In time, she was able to extract a valuable lesson from the trauma: how precarious life is and how much a gift. She credits both of her parents with instilling in her a deep faith as well as an appetite for learning and a desire to do her best.

From the time she was seven years old, Laura wanted to be a teacher. She would line up her dolls and teach them lessons. Years later, she followed her childhood passion, majoring in education at Southern Methodist University. After graduating in 1968, she taught third graders for a year in Dallas, before moving to Houston to teach second-graders at a predominantly African American school. In 1972, she enrolled in a Master of Library Science Degree program at the University of Texas in Austin, completing the degree a year later. She returned to Houston to become a children's librarian and in 1974, she returned to Austin to become a librarian in an elementary school attended largely by Hispanic students. She remained in that position until 1977.

Laura Lane Welch and George W. Bush attended the same junior high school in Midland; however, according to Barbara Bush, "they had not been aware of each other." Laura's official meeting with George was at a barbecue given by their mutual friends, Joey and Jan

O'Neill. The first time they invited her to meet him, she turned them down, saying she had little interest in politics. Eventually, she accepted their invitation. When Laura met George, she thought he was "really cute" and a lot of fun. She told her mother: "The thing I like[d] about him was that he made me laugh." George also liked her; he wrote in his autobiography: "If it wasn't love at first sight, it happened shortly thereafter.... My wife is gorgeous, good-humored, quick to laugh, down-to-earth, and very smart. I recognized those attributes right away in roughly that order....We both, very quickly, fell in love with one another." They were married three months later, on November 5, 1977. After a short honeymoon in Mexico, Laura moved into George's home in Midland.

MRS. BUSH

The Bushes campaigned all across West Texas to help George get elected to a seat in the United States House of Representatives. Although Laura had always considered herself a Democrat, she became a Republican through marriage. Before they were married, George had promised Laura she would never have to give a political speech. Three months after they were married, however, he was scheduled to be in two places at one time. Although she was not comfortable in the role of campaigner, Laura acted as George's surrogate in Muleshoe, Texas. As she stood on the courthouse steps in front of a small audience, she uttered her prepared remarks, but too soon ran out of things to say. Later, during an interview with television's Matt Lauer, she said, "I had a really great start to my speech, but I hadn't gotten far enough to have a very good ending. So I stood up and gave my few — what I thought were really pretty good — lines at the start, and then I had to mumble and sit down." She was embarrassed, but also angry with herself for not preparing better. Underestimating what it takes to speak to an audience would not be a mistake she would make again.

On November 25, 1981, Laura gave birth to twin daughters, Barbara and Jenna, named after their two grandmothers. George was in the delivery room when they were born. Afterwards, he helped Laura take care of the children: "There was never any question that I would help take care of them," he said, "I was a modern dad." For the next several years, Laura devoted herself to raising the children as her husband worked to build his energy company. They were both active members of the First United Methodist Church and were engaged in community service — Laura, the Junior League and George, the United Way. Their lives were settled — happy, peaceful.

In late 1986, Vice President George Herbert Walker Bush assembled the family at Camp David to announce his plans to run for the U.S. presidency. To help with the campaign, George and Laura moved their family to Washington, D.C. for eighteen months. When Laura's father-in-law was elected the 41st president of the United States, she and her husband returned to Texas. Both had learned a great deal about political campaigns from this experience, which they used when George W. challenged incumbent Ann Richards during the 1994 race for governor of Texas.

Laura was an unproved political asset at this time. She still had knots in her stomach when she spoke to the media or to a civic group. Her husband didn't push her because he knew she was not yet comfortable in the role campaigner. However, she did speak to Republican women's groups across the state; they were supportive and non-confrontational.

When the race ended, she had visited 30 of Texas's 254 counties. On November 8, George won the race for Governor of Texas, and the Bushes headed for Austin.

As the First Lady of Texas, Mrs. Bush quickly realized she could actually do something about the issues she cared about most such as early childhood education. Her husband said that she grew increasingly confident when she realized "people listened to her." She set up an office in the Texas Governor's mansion, the first First Lady ever to do so, and she used the office to make a difference in people's lives.

One of the first events Mrs. Bush planned was a literary celebration. She invited seven Texas writers to read from their works as part of her husband's inaugural festivities. She was nervous about speaking at the event. Some of the authors had neither supported her husband, nor voted for him. However, their inclusion early set a bipartisan tone to her husband's administration. One writer, Sarah Bird, told her audience how impressed she was to have been invited to read because she considered herself a "raging liberal." The fact that she was invited, she said, boded well for the Bush administration. It also boded well for the kind of political partnership the Bushes would develop. During her time as First Lady of Texas, Mrs. Bush promoted many bipartisan initiatives to support the visual and literary arts, education, libraries, and other issues including women's health.

Mrs. Bush's signature issue was early childhood education and literacy, as it would continue to be when she became first lady of the United States in 2001. This was consistent with her husband's agenda, especially during his reelection campaign of 1996, when he emphasized reading and literacy. Politically, these were important issues that appealed to women and minority voters. They were also issues to which Laura Bush, as a former teacher and librarian, felt strongly committed. In the two terms she served as First Lady of Texas, she either supported or launched many programs aimed at improving education. She worked with legislators, social service personnel, and literacy experts on an "Early Childhood Development Initiative," consisting of four components: a Family Literacy Initiative, Reach Out and Read, Texas Ready to Read, and *Take Time for Kids* (a parenting magazine).

Laura Bush's crowning achievement as First Lady of Texas was the Texas Book Festival, which she would later elevate to a national level when she became First Lady of the United States. In 1996, she joined together with the Texas Library Association, the Austin Writers League, and the Texas State Library and Archives Commission to inaugurate a celebration of writers and readers. The only one of its kind in the country, the Texas Book Festival was a combination of literary event and fundraiser. From 1996 to 2000, almost 400 Texas libraries shared the nearly $1 million dollars raised. The Bushes also gained political capital because many of the authors celebrated were liberals.

When Laura Bush left the position of First Lady of Texas, both Republicans and Democrats judged her to be one of the best, if not the best, ever to have served. As an advocate for education, she achieved major policy success when she helped write and secure passage of legislation to teach preschool children in Texas to read. Liz Carpenter, a Texas Democrat who worked for Lady Bird Johnson, praised Mrs. Bush's projects and personality, saying Laura was loved and appreciated across the state.

When George W. launched his campaign for election to the presidency in 2000, Laura was hesitant about stepping into the national spotlight. However, she had been a political apprentice for years, campaigning in state and national contests run by her husband and father-in-law. She had become part of the Bush "family business" of politics. Setting aside her reluctance, she proved to be a valuable asset during the approximately 100 days she spent on the campaign trail, traveling solo about 75 percent of the time. During the primary season, she spoke mainly to Republican women's groups and read to children in elementary schools. After her daughters left for college in the fall, she stood by her husband's side, a microphone in hand, introducing him to audiences and even taking her own questions after the speeches. Mrs. Bush helped to persuade voters — especially women and minorities — that education would be a Bush administration priority

Laura Bush spoke at the Republican National Convention, July 31, 2000. This speech was the first major event of the convention, delivered prime time. Together with Colin Powell, who spoke immediately after her, she was given the responsibility of kicking off the four-day celebration. Newspaper articles appeared before her speech, introducing her to the public as a woman who gives her husband a steadiness, evenness, who reins him in. Journalists also contrasted her role as her husband's helpmate with Hillary Clinton's personal ambition.

In an interview before her speech, Laura Bush admitted to getting butterflies in her stomach just thinking about it. And when she began her speech, she said she felt "a little overwhelmed" to be playing such a major role at the convention. She used humor to say that she and her husband were about to become empty nesters, and running for president seemed an extreme way to handle the situation. To promote credibility and foster identification with teachers, she talked about her early love of teaching and her experience teaching second and third graders to read. She promoted her husband's record on education in Texas, and pledged to continue this work on a national scale and to focus on children younger than school age. After the speech, her husband commented on her performance, saying he realized "how at ease" his wife had become in her public role as he "watched her deliver flawless remarks before a national television audience."

During the fall, Laura continued to help her husband's campaign. She traveled with her mother-in-law and other Republican women on a "W is for women" bus trip. They visited several venues in the highly contested states of Michigan, Pennsylvania, and Wisconsin, all rich in electoral votes. Barbara Bush, recovering from back surgery and still enormously popular, introduced her daughter-in-law to audiences; Laura was the featured speaker, and she handled the press conferences after the speeches.

The election between George W. Bush and Al Gore was the closest in American history. Voting day was November 7, 2000, but the outcome of the race was debated for days because of confusion with the voting process in Florida. On December 12, George W. Bush was announced the winner; on January 20, 2001, he was sworn in as the forty-third President of the United States. Laura Bush became the First Lady.

FIRST LADY

When Laura Bush became First Lady of the United States, she was well positioned to play the roles expected of her. She was keenly aware of the opportunity she would have to effect change. When she moved the First Lady's office back to the East Wing, she indicated symbolically that her methods for achieving change would be different from her immediate predecessor's, Hillary Clinton. She also hired a staff and was ready to serve as an active first lady on projects she knew and cared about. "I know about education," she said, "I know about things that I've worked on... . Most other issues I don't know that much about." With some degree of trepidation natural for a woman described as "private," she was determined to make a difference. In her first week as first lady, she acknowledged: "I have a forum... . I won't always have it. The time is now."

Mrs. Bush worked on several fronts in her role as first lady, including education, literacy, libraries, literature, American authors, museums, historic places, and women's health. She also grew into the role of international diplomat, speaking out in support of the rights of women and children in Afghanistan, Peru, and Iraq. She also functioned as a Bush administration ambassador, for example, on a fence-mending mission to France in fall 2003. To promote many of the initiatives, she sponsored special events at the White House, testified before Senate and House committees, issued press releases, and delivered public speeches as she traveled widely at home and abroad.

Mrs. Bush's approach to education was multifaceted. She worked on early cognitive development and prereading skills, and on teacher recruitment and training. In a letter posted on the White House website, she explained: "Our challenge is to reach all children early so that every child starts school with the skills needed to learn. Once in the classroom, our children deserve excellent teachers and a high-quality education." To provide children with skills, she spotlighted successful programs such as Reach Out and Read, a Boston based initiative, where parents are given "prescriptions" by their pediatricians to read to their infants and young children. She also promoted the Ready to Read, Ready to Learn initiative, which showcased successful prereading programs.

To recruit and train new teachers, Mrs. Bush traveled across the country, speaking on behalf of groups such as Troops to Teachers, the New Teacher Project, and Teach for America. Information found on the White House website indicates how successful these programs have been: "Troops to Teachers has placed 5,000 former military personnel in teaching positions, the New Teacher Project has implemented 39 programs in 19 states and prepared more than 6,500 new teachers, and Teach for America's 9,000 corps members have taught more than 1.25 million children." Certainly the first lady's celebrity and speaking ability helped achieve these significant results.

Laura Bush promoted American literature — its authors, books, and libraries. Together with Librarian James H. Billington of the Library of Congress, she helped arrange National Book Festivals, held yearly since 2001. In a speech given at the first festival, Mrs. Bush called the Library of Congress an "American Treasure," home of "many of our country's great written treasures." She described the purpose of the festival in an interview: "This event gives us an opportunity to inspire parents and caregivers to read to their children as early as possible and to encourage reading as a lifelong activity."

Mrs. Bush also sponsored a series of literary events at the White House. They were designed to celebrate significant American authors and to encourage the public — especially children — to read classic works. Contemporary writers and an assortment of readers were invited to spend a day discussing the distinctively American voices of such authors as Mark Twain, the subject of the first symposium held in November 2001. A second symposium, held in March 2002, celebrated diverse authors of the Harlem Renaissance such as Langston Hughes, Countee Cullen, and Zora Neale Huston. A third symposium, held in September 2002, on Women of the American West featured Willa Cather, Edna Ferber, and Laura Ingalls Wilder. A fourth symposium, devoted to American poets, Emily Dickinson, Walt Whitman, and Langston Hughes, was scheduled for February 2003. Unfortunately, Mrs. Bush had to cancel the event, once she discovered that one of the invited poets was planning to turn the symposium into a political protest by collecting anti-war poetry to present to her as a reaction to the impending war in Iraq. When the event was cancelled, however, ancillary anti-war poetry readings were held at different venues across the United States.

As a former librarian, Laura Bush sponsored events to improve American libraries and to encourage the public to use them. On June 4, 2002, she held a White House Conference on School Libraries which focused on the role libraries play in student achievement. During her closing remarks, she thanked many of the donors who had given gifts to the Laura Bush Foundation for America's Libraries, calling the new resources "the fulfillment of a dream." Four months later, she held a Colloquium on Libraries, Museums, and Lifelong Learning. In a statement published on the White House website, she praised books found in libraries, works of art and pieces of history found in museums, and historical sites found in communities as vehicles for lifelong learning. She associated herself with the Institute of Museum and Library Services (IMLS), a federal agency that supports those institutions, and she visited libraries both at home and abroad. She helped her husband carry out an executive order to "Preserve America," by visiting museums and other historic institutions. She worked with the History Channel to produce a manual to show how teachers, students, and other volunteers might help preserve historical sites in their communities.

Women's health was another area important to Mrs. Bush during her husband's presidency. She championed two causes especially — breast cancer and heart disease. She spoke about breast cancer on several occasions, especially early in her term as first lady. She took a personal interest in the disease because her mother was one of its victims. Her interest in women's heart health grew as she discovered that more women in the United States die from heart disease than from all forms of cancer combined. This was one of the findings of the White House Conference on Women's Health, held in 2001. Seventy doctors met to design an action plan to deal with this leading killer of the nation's women. To promote heart health, Mrs. Bush spoke at events and encouraged journalists at press conferences to "get the word out to women," since most heart disease is preventable through a healthy diet, exercise, and regular check-ups. In February 2004, she helped launch the Red Dress Project, an initiative which uses a red dress as the national symbol of women's heart disease. Nineteen of America's most prestigious designers contributed red dresses to this widely covered event. According to information on Laura Bush's website, in the future these dresses will travel across the country to events that are designed to raise women's awareness of heart disease.

Lastly, Mrs. Bush has been active as a diplomat, both at home entertaining foreign leaders and their spouses, and through international travel. She has planned state dinners and other events at the White House, Camp David, and Prairie Chapel, the Bush's ranch in Crawford, Texas. As her mother-in-law, Barbara Bush, writes in her memoirs, much diplomacy is carried out during social occasions where protocol may be minimized and warm personal relationships developed. Internationally, Laura Bush has traveled abroad solo on behalf of the Bush administration. Her commitment to education extends to children and women all over the world, and she has often spoken as an advocate for these constituencies. She believes education should teach children basic skills as well as general knowledge about the world around them. When students have an education, in her view, especially the ability to read and write, they grow up with hope; they see the possibility of changing their lives, their communities, and their countries for the better. Mrs. Bush also represented the Bush administration at a rededication ceremony in France, when the United States rejoined the

United Nation Educational, Scientific, and Cultural Organization (UNESCO) after nearly two decades of absence. In a speech given at this ceremony, she presented startling statistics, for example, that two-thirds of the world's nearly 900 million illiterate adults are women.

Although committed to education for all the world's inhabitants, Laura Bush has spoken on different occasions specifically about the plight of women and children in Afghanistan and later in Iraq. During her Radio Address in November 2001, and her speech to the United Nations in honor of International Women's Day in March 2002, she advocated passionately for the right of Afghani women and children to an education and to full participation in society. She spoke similarly in speeches given in New York and France, yet she went further on those occasions to include the education and health of the women of Iraq, a country where three out of four women are illiterate.

Mrs. Bush has grown tremendously as a public figure, especially since her first appearance as her husband's surrogate in Muleshoe, Texas. Laura has continued to develop her skills as a spokeswoman and advocate from the early days when she would speak only from a prepared manuscript to supportive Republican women's groups to the present where she travels solo on diplomatic missions as an ambassador of the Bush administration. Marveling at her accomplishments, her husband told reporters before he was elected president: "If I'd have said, 'Honey, you'll be the kickoff speaker at the Republican Convention in the year 2000,' she would have said, 'You've totally lost your mind and I'm not marrying you.'" What would she have said if her husband had told her: "You'll be speaking to an audience of 700 on a solo diplomatic trip to Europe in 2002, and visiting the French President Jacque Chirac on a fence-mending mission in 2003?"

APPENDIX

THE PRESIDENTS' WIVES

Name	Years	First Lady
Martha Dandridge Custis Washington	1731-1802	1789-1797
Abigail Smith Adams	1744-1818	1797-1801
Martha Wayles Skelton Jefferson	1748-1782	
Dolley Payne Todd Madison	1768-1849	1809-1817
Elizabeth Kortright Monroe	1768-1830	1817-1825
Louisa Catherine Johnson Adams	1775-1852	1825-1829
Rachel Donelson Jackson	1767-1828	
Hannah Hoes Van Buren	1783-1819	
Anna Tuthill Symmes Harrison	1775-1864	1841
Letitia Christian Tyler	1790-1842	1841-1842
Julia Gardiner Tyler	1820-1889	1844-1845
Sarah Childress Polk	1803-1891	1845-1849
Margaret Mackall Smith Taylor	1788-1852	1849-1850
Abigail Powers Fillmore	1798-1853	1850-1853
Jane Means Appleton Pierce	1806-1863	1853-1857
Mary Ann Todd Lincoln	1818-1882	1861-1865
Eliza McCardle Johnson	1810-1876	1865-1869
Julie Dent Grant	1826-1902	1869-1877
Lucy Ware Webb Hayes	1831-1889	1877-1881
Lucretia Rudolph Garfield	1832-1918	1881
Ellen Lewis Herndon Arthur	1837-1880	
Frances Clara Folsom Cleveland [Preston]	1864-1947	1886-1889, 1893-1897
Caroline Lavinia Scott Harrison	1832-1892	1889-1892
Ida Saxton McKinley	1847-1907	1897-1901
Edith Kermit Carow Roosevelt	1861-1948	1901-1909
Helen Herron Taft	1861-1943	1909-1913
Ellen Louise Axson Wilson	1860-1914	1913-1914
Edith Bolling Galt Wilson	1872-1961	1915-1921

Florence Mabel Kling Harding	1860-1924	1921-1923
Grace Goodhue Coolidge	1879-1957	1923-1929
Lou Henry Hoover	1874-1944	1929-1933
Anna Eleanor Roosevelt Roosevelt	1884-1962	1933-1945
Elizabeth "Bess" Virginia Wallace Truman	1885-1982	1945-1953
Mamie Geneva Doud Eisenhower	1896-1979	1953-1961
Jacqueline Lee Bouvier Kennedy [Onassis]	1929-1994	1961-1963
Claudia "Lady Bird" Alta Taylor Johnson	1912-2007	1963-1969
Thelma "Pat" Catherine Ryan Nixon	1912-1993	1969-1974
Elizabeth "Betty" Ann Bloomer Ford	1918-	1974-1977
Eleanor Rosalynn Smith Carter	1927-	1977-1981
Anne "Nancy" Frances Robbins Davis Reagan	1921-	1981-1989
Barbara Pierce Bush	1925-	1989-1993
Hillary Diane Rodham Clinton	1947-	1993-2001
Laura Welch Bush	1946-	2001-2009

ABOUT THE CONTRIBUTORS

Catherine Allgor is Professor of History at the University of California at Riverside, where she teaches classes on early America, politics, and the history of women. She also taught at Simmons College, a college for women in Boston, and previously enjoyed a career in the theater. Allgor attended Mount Holyoke College as a Frances Perkins Scholar and graduated summa cum laude in History. She received her Ph.D. with distinction from Yale University, where she also won the Yale Teaching Award. Her dissertation on women and politics in early Washington garnered the George Washington Egleston Prize for the best dissertation in American History at Yale and the Lerner-Scott Prize for the best dissertation in U.S. Women's History in the country. Allgor is the author of *Parlor Politics: In Which the Ladies of Washington Help Build a City and a Government*, which won the James H. Broussard First Book Prize from the Society for Historians of the Early American Republic. From 2002 to 2004, Professor Allgor was a Fellow at the Radcliffe Institute for Advanced Study and a Visiting Professor of History at Harvard University. Her latest book, *A Perfect Union: Dolley Madison and the Creation of the American Nation*, was a finalist for the George Washington Prize and the 2007-2008 selection for the UCR First Book.

Claudia Wilson Anderson served as Senior Archivist at the Lyndon B. Johnson Library and was on the staff since 1969. Her work included processing and reference, specializing in domestic policy, legislative liaison between the White House and Congress, President Johnson's recorded telephone conversations, President Johnson's pre-presidential career, and Mrs. Johnson. Ms. Anderson often writes and speaks on Mrs. Johnson's life and career.

Carl Sferrazza Anthony is an independent scholar, former speechwriter for First Lady Nancy Reagan, former contributor to *George* magazine, and frequent media commentator on the First Ladies. He is the author of *First Ladies: The Saga of the Presidents' Wives and their Power*; *Florence Harding: The First Lady, the Jazz Age, and the Death of America's Most Scandalous President*; and *America's First Families: An Inside View of 200 Years of Private Life in the White House*.

Jeffrey S. Ashley, Ph.D. is Associate Professor of Political Science at Eastern Illinois University. His research interests include natural resources policy, American Indian politics, public administration, the Presidency, and First Ladies. He is the co-author or co-editor of two books and is completing a biography of Betty Ford.

Jean Becker served as the Chief of Staff for former President George Bush and was First Lady Barbara Bush's Deputy Press Secretary at the White House. She assisted Mrs. Bush with her memoirs, *Barbara Bush: A Memoir*, published in 1994, and was editor of President Bush's book of letters, *All the Best*, published in 1999. Before joining the Bush administration in 1989, she was a newspaper reporter for 10 years, including four years at *USA Today*.

Patricia Brady served as the Director of Publications at the Historic New Orleans Collection. The author of dozens of essays on southern history, she has written on Martha Washington and her family, including "Martha Washington" in *American First Ladies: Their Lives and Legacy*, "Martha Washington: Founding First Lady" in *The Presidential Companion: Readings on the First Ladies*, and she is the editor of *George Washington's Beautiful Nelly: The Letters of Eleanor Parke Custis Lewis to Elizabeth Bordley Gibson* and *Nelly Custis Lewis' Housekeeping Book*. Dr. Brady received her Ph.D. in history from Tulane University and is presently working on a biography of Martha Washington.

Susan Roth Breitzer completed her Ph.D. in History at the University of Iowa. Her research and writing interests include civil rights, Jewish women, Jewish history, and the First Ladies. She is currently completing a biography of Eleanor Roosevelt and has written essays on both Eleanor and Edith Roosevelt.

Barbara C. Burrell, Ph.D. is Professor of Political Science and Director of Graduate Studies in the Department of Political Science at Northern Illinois University. She formerly served as the Associate Director of NIU's Public Opinion Laboratory. She is the author of *A Woman's Place is in the House: Campaigning for Congress in the Feminist Era* and *Public Opinion, the First Ladyship and Hillary Rodham Clinton*. Burrell was the President of the Women's Caucus (2007-2008) of the American Political Science Association and earned her Ph.D. from the University of Michigan.

Virginia A. Chanley, Ph.D. is a research analyst with the U.S. Government Accountability Office in Washington, D.C. Prior to going to work for GAO, Dr. Chanley worked as a research associate with Abacus Associates and taught at Florida International University and the University of Minnesota. Her research focuses on public policy, public opinion, political behavior, and the presidency and first ladyship, and has been published in journals such as *Public Opinion Quarterly, American Politics Quarterly, Political Psychology, White House Studies,* and *Political Behavior*, and she is currently writing a biography of former First Lady Rosalynn Carter.

Robert E. Dewhirst, Ph.D. is Professor of Political Science at Northwest Missouri State University. His teaching and research have focused on American national and state politics and political institutions. He is the author of *Rights of Passage: Congress Makes Laws*, the *Almanac of Missouri Politics 2000*, and *Dutiful Service: The Life of Mamie Eisenhower*. His edited books include four co-edited with Sunil Ahuja: *Government at Work, The Roads to Congress 1998, The Roads to Congress 2000,* and *The Roads to Congress 2002*. He is co-editing *The Encyclopedia of the United States Congress* with David Rausch. Dewhirst is currently writing a biography of Dwight Eisenhower and co-editing the next book in the

"Roads to Congress" series. He also has contributed chapters to numerous reference books and edited collections.

Anthony J. Eksterowicz, Ph.D. is Professor of Political Science at James Madison University, where he teaches courses on the presidency, Congress, American government, first ladies, health care, and political reform. He has published over forty articles and five books on various subjects such as foreign policy and the presidency, first ladies, politics and pain care, political parties, stem cell research, the presidential pardoning power, and citizen participation. His books include *The Post Cold War Presidency*, *Public Journalism and Political Knowledge*, *The President and Foreign Policy: Chief Architect or General Contractor*, and *The Presidential Companion: Readings on the First Ladies*.

Raymond Frey, Ph.D. is Professor of History, formerly the Dean of the Faculty, and Executive Director of the Center for the Study and Teaching of New Jersey History at Centenary College, where he has taught since 1990. Dr. Frey is the recipient of the Lindback Foundation Award for Distinguished Teaching, Centenary's highest teaching honor. In 2006, he was the Gates-Ferry Foundation Distinguished Lecturer at Centenary. He has published widely in the areas of American history and culture, has written several essays on Bess Truman, and is completing a biography of Mrs. Truman. In 2002, he was the keynote speaker at the Truman Presidential Library, commemorating Bess Truman's birthday and he has participated in several Truman Legacy Symposium programs at the Harry S. Truman Little White House. Frey holds graduate degrees in history and philosophy from Fordham University and Drew University.

Frances Hughes Glendening was the First Lady of Maryland and a chief legal and policy advisor with the Federal Election Commission. A champion of and leader in numerous community causes, Ms. Glendening served on the boards of several organizations including the Hospice of Prince George's County, Prince George's Suicide Prevention Center and Hotline, and Prince George's Community Foundation. She also spearheaded projects chronicling the achievements of women from Prince George's County, Maryland and the state of Maryland, which resulted in books, and was responsible for assembling the collection of portraits of the First Ladies of Maryland which is on display at the governor's official residence. Ms. Glendening is currently the head of Jobs for America's Graduates, a private, not-for-profit organization, an adjunct professor at the University of Maryland, College Park, and the President of the Board of Directors of the Maryland Women's Heritage Center. She holds a B.A. in Government and Politics as well as English, an MPA from the University of Maryland, and her J.D. from Catholic University School of Law, where she was Associate Editor of the *Law Review*.

Myra G. Gutin received her Ph.D. in Communication from the University of Michigan and is Professor of Communication at Rider University in New Jersey. She is the author of *The President's Partner: The First Lady in the Twentieth Century* and *Gerald R. Ford: Restoring the Presidency*, as well as several articles, chapters, and essays on the First Ladies. Gutin is at work on a new book on Barbra Bush. She has been interviewed many times by CNN, Fox, ABC Online, *The New York Times*, *USA Today*, and other leading news organizations, and teaches a course titled "The American First Lady."

Lori Cox Han, Ph.D. is Professor of Political Science at Chapman University in Orange, California. Her major area of emphasis is American government, with research and teaching interests in the presidency, women and politics, media and politics, and political leadership. She is the author of *Governing From Center Stage: White House Communication Strategies During the Television Age of Politics*, and *Women and American Politics: The Challenges of Political Leadership*. She is also co-editor of *Rethinking Madam Presidency: Are We Ready for a Woman in the White House?*, *In the Public Domain: Presidents and the Challenge of Public Leadership*, and *The Presidency and the Challenge of Democracy*. In addition, Dr. Han served as President of the Presidency Research Group, an organized section of the American Political Science Association devoted to the study of the presidency, in 2006-2007, and is currently a member of the Executive Council for Pi Sigma Alpha, the national political science honor society. She received her Ph.D. in Political Science from the University of Southern California.

Sindee Kerker received her undergraduate degree in Criminal Justice from the University of Florida and a J.D. from Whittier Law School. Kerker is an Assistant Professor of Criminal Justice at Lynn University, teaching courses on criminal justice, criminal law and procedures, judicial administration, civil rights, and trial advocacy. She also studied comparative criminal procedure and civil liberties at Oxford University and has been admitted to the State Bar in California and Florida, as well as to the Supreme Court of the United States. Kerker served as a prosecutor in the Los Angeles County District Attorney's office for seven years and was an instructor for the Los Angeles County Sheriff's department teaching advanced courses in sexual assault investigation, courtroom testimony, and trial tactics.

Pat Krider is head librarian at the National First Ladies' Library in Canton, Ohio.

Mary Linehan earned her Ph.D. in U.S. History from Notre Dame and is Assistant Professor of History at the College of Wooster. She taught previously at Spalding University in Louisville, Kentucky. Her research and publications focus on women's history and the First Ladies.

Edith P. Mayo is Curator Emeritus in Political History at the National Museum of American History, with over 25 years of experience as a curator and historian at the Smithsonian Institution. She has organized several major conferences on women's history and curated several major exhibitions on political and women's history including the permanent exhibition "From Parlor to Politics: Women and Reform in America" and the famous "First Ladies: Political Role and Public Image." She is the editor of *American Material Culture*, *First Ladies: Political Role and Public Image*, and *The Smithsonian's Book of the First Ladies*. Mayo graduated Phi Beta Kappa from George Washington University.

Nancy Kegan Smith graduated cum laude and Phi Beta Kappa from the University of Texas with a degree in History and Government and is the Director of the Presidential Materials Staff of the National Archives and Records Administration. She first joined NARA in 1973 as an archivist with the Lyndon B. Johnson Library, then worked as Senior Archivist in the Office of Presidential Libraries and Access Officer for Presidential Holdings in

NARA's Office of General Council. She is the author or *Women and the White House: A Look at the Women's Papers in the Lyndon B. Johnson Library* and *A Journey of the Heart: The Papers of Lady Bird Johnson*, and co-editor of *Modern First Ladies: Their Documentary Legacy*.

Elizabeth Lorelei Thacker-Estrada is a Branch Library Manager at the San Francisco Public Library. She received her Master of Library and Information Studies degree at the University of California at Berkeley. Her work has appeared in the books *The Presidential Companion* (2003, 2006), *American First Ladies* (2001, 2006), *Life in the White House* (2004), and the journal *White House Studies* (2001). Thacker-Estrada serves on the Editorial Board of the First White House library Catalogue, a project of the National First Ladies' Library and the Bibliographical Society of America. She is preparing her book *Abigail Powers Fillmore: The Light of the White House*, for publication, and is completing her book, *Jane Means Appleton Pierce: The Shadow in the White House*.

Gil Troy, Ph.D. is Professor of History at McGill University in Montreal. A native of Queens, New York, he received his bachelor's, master's, and doctoral degrees from Harvard University. He is the author of *See How They Ran: The Changing Role of the Presidential Candidate* and *Mr. and Mrs. President: From the Trumans to the Clintons*, an updated version of *Affairs of State: The Rise and Rejection of the Presidential Couple*. He comments frequently about presidential politics on television and in print, with recently published articles and reviews in, among others, *The New York Times*, *The Wall Street Journal*, *The Washington Post*, *The Wilson Quarterly*, and *The Journal of American History*.

T. Alissa Warters, Ph.D. is Assistant Professor of Political Science and Co-Director of the Robert McNair Center for Government and History at Francis Marion University in South Carolina. She is the author of several articles on the political roles of First Ladies and presidential children. The most recent is "The Relationship between Presidential Approval and Media Coverage of First Families: A Content Analysis, 1960-2004," co-authored with Mandi Bailey in *The American Review of Politics* (2007). Warters holds a B.A. and M.A. in Political Science from Virginia Tech and a Ph.D. in Political Science from the University of Tennessee in Knoxville. Her research areas include the American presidency, First Ladies, and first families.

Robert P. Watson, Ph.D. directs the American Studies Program at Lynn University in Florida. Watson is the author or editor of 27 books and has published hundreds of scholarly articles, book chapters, reference essays, and newspaper columns on topics in American politics and history. His works on the First Ladies include: *The Presidents' Wives: Reassessing the Office of First Lady* (2001); *First Ladies of the United States: A Biographical Dictionary* (2002); and *The Presidential Companion: Readings on the First Ladies* (2006; 2003). Watson also edited the encyclopedia *American First Ladies* (2006; 2002) and is the series editor of "The Presidential Wives Series," a collection of 20 books on the First Ladies published by Nova. A frequent media commentator, he has been interviewed by CNN, MSNBC, NBC, the BBC, *USA Today*, *The New York Times*, *Time*, and many other media outlets, and has made several appearances on C-SPAN's *Book TV* program. He has convened or co-convened a half-dozen national conferences on the presidency, sits on the boards of numerous scholarly journals and presidential foundations, has served as a visiting scholar/fellow at many universities and historic presidential sites, and has won numerous awards for his scholarship, community service, and teaching, such as Florida Atlantic University's Distinguished Professor of the Year and Faculty Service Award.

Molly Meijer Wertheimer, Ph.D. is Professor of Communication Arts and Sciences and Affiliate Professor of Women's Studies at The Pennsylvania State University Hazelton campus. She teaches courses on public speaking and on women, the humanities, and the arts, and is editor of *Listening to Their Voices: The Rhetorical Activities of Historical Women* and Inventing a Voice: The Rhetoric of American First Ladies of the Twentieth Century. She is also co-author of *Speaking from the Heart: A Rhetorical Biography of Elizabeth Hanford Dole* and *Public Speaking as a Liberal Art*, 6th ed. Her research and reviews have been appeared in journals such as *Philosophy and Rhetoric*, the *Quarterly Journal of Speech*, and *Rhetorica*.

Betty Houchin Winfield, Ph.D. has served as the University of Missouri Curators' Professor at the Columbia campus where as a media scholar she specializes in political communication. She has received the Cathy Covert AEJMC Award for the best 2007 publication in journalism history for "The Continuous Past: Historical Referents in Nineteenth Century Journalism," the Thomas Jefferson Fellowship Award for a career reflecting the ideals of Thomas Jefferson, the Frank Luther Mott finalist for best scholarly book in journalism for FDR and the News Media (1994, 1990), and teaching honors from Washington State University (1994, 1990) and the University of Missouri Alumni (2000). She has also received NEH grants and post-doctoral fellowships at Columbia University and the John F. Kennedy School of Government at Harvard. She is the author of four books, including the upcoming *Journalism: 1908: Birth of a Profession*, and more than 90 other publications including refereed journal articles and review essays. Her publications have appeared in such journals as *Journalism and Mass Communication Quarterly*, *Political Communication, Journalism History, American Journalism, Journal of American History, Journalism Studies, Missouri Law Review, Presidential Studies Quarterly*, and others. Frequently, Winfield is a commentator on White House media coverage for regional and national broadcast and print media and a reviewer in scholarly journals. She completed her B.S. from the University of Arkansas, her M.A. from the University of Michigan, and her Ph.D. from the University of Washington.